# THE
# SEVEN
# DEADLY SINS OF
## SMALL GROUP
## MINISTRY

Other Books by Bill Donahue and Russ Robinson
*Building a Church of Small Groups*
*Leading Life-Changing Small Groups*

# THE
# SEVEN DEADLY SINS OF
## SMALL GROUP MINISTRY

A **TROUBLESHOOTING GUIDE** FOR CHURCH LEADERS

# BILL**DONAHUE**     RUSS**ROBINSON**

ZONDERVAN™

GRAND RAPIDS, MICHIGAN 49530 USA

WILLOW
Willow Creek Resources

**Z̶ONDERVAN™**

*The Seven Deadly Sins of Small Group Ministry*
Copyright © 2002 by Willow Creek Association

Requests for information should be addressed to:
Zondervan, *Grand Rapids, Michigan 49530*

**Library of Congress Cataloging-in-Publication Data**

Donahue, Bill.
　　　The seven deadly sins of small group ministry : a troubleshooting guide for church
leaders / Bill Donahue and Russ Robinson.
　　　　　p. cm.
　　　Includes bibliographical references.
　　　ISBN-10: 0-310-26711-0
　　　ISBN-13: 978-0-310-26711-9
　　　1. Church group work. 2. Small groups — Religious aspects — Christianity.
　　　I. Robinson, Russ. II. Title.
BV652.2.D657 2002
253'.7 — dc21

2002009645
CIP

*Interior design by Susan Ambs*

*Printed in the United States of America*

05  06  07  08  09  10  /❖ DCI/ 10  9  8  7  6  5  4  3  2  1

# Contents

# Introduction

## Does Your Church
## Need a Troubleshooting Guide?

If your church has a small group ministry, you can probably relate to the following story of one church that has hit the wall.

Four years ago, First Community Church launched three ministry initiatives, including the revival of a dormant small group ministry. They asked their Christian education director—who was already overseeing adult and children's Sunday school, AWANA, a handful of discipleship small groups, and a women's ministry—to tackle the small group initiative. The effort yielded eleven new small groups that year, but none the next.

Nobody was particularly bothered. As the church has grown, it's become more departmentalized. As long as each ministry, including the small groups department, keeps its audience happy and avoids trouble, it has been allowed to develop. Small groups are seen as positive. The church believes the small groups are on track theologically, because each uses one of two curricula, both written by the associate pastor.

Last year the church finished its new facility, doubling both sanctuary and ministry space, and attendance grew 60 percent in six months. More newcomers, however, complain that they can't assimilate into the church. The existing small groups now average seventeen people each, and there are no new leaders in sight. The Christian education director complains of burnout from trying to keep up with sixteen leaders as well as all the other ministries—including a new singles' ministry.

First Community's elders are tired of complaints. They've asked the senior pastor to work with the staff and recommend solutions. The elders are divided on the small groups initiative. Some know of churches where small groups meet the needs of rapid growth while deepening attendees' discipleship. One elder, who has seen small groups initiatives come and go, doubts such strategies will ever work at First Community. (After all, small groups are not for everyone.) And the

**8**

senior pastor and two other staff members aren't really "into" small group ministry, mostly because they've always led traditional, program-based ministries.

Where should First Community begin as they strategize a new future for their small group ministry? Perhaps they should analyze their current tactics. Or they could study small groups throughout Scripture and church history. What should they assess first? How should they prioritize key problems, given the church's limited time, money, and people? And who knows whether new strategies will work?

If you can answer these questions clearly, then turn this book in for a refund. If not, you're in good company.

## A Troubleshooting Guide

The First Community account is fictional, but it is typical of churches we've worked with, including Willow Creek Community Church. Remember, misery loves company, so it's good to have you with us. In other words, we feel your pain!

We are gadget guys. We love figuring out how gadgets work. So when we open the box and find those indispensable manufacturer's instructions, we grab pencil, paper, and coffee and begin noting every written detail. Sure. If you believe that, you are not a gadget guy! Real men—especially gadget men—don't ask for directions and never read instructions. That's the point. It's the adventure, the mystery, the challenge! You get to figure it out.

But even gadget guys read the end of the instructions, because something always goes wrong, so they need the troubleshooting guide. Fortunately, though instructions may cover dozens of pages, troubleshooting guides are short. Most summarize gadget complications into two columns. The left column lists problems, and the right column suggests things to check. Even the most complex gadgets have relatively few "most likely to go wrong" categories.

You already know that small group ministry is more complex than the average gadget. Don't you wish your small group ministry came with both an owner's manual and a troubleshooting guide, one designed especially for your church? By now, the "owner's manuals" on small groups probably total tens of thousands of pages. What we've longed for is a troubleshooting guide to simplify diagnosis and recommend solutions that work.

Through working with Willow Creek and consulting with other churches, we've identified common causes—we call them "the seven deadly sins"—of small group ministry breakdown. During years of helping Willow Creek and others untangle similar problems, we've navigated great frustration, quick fixes, "worst decisions," and "best practices" to discover basic solutions that work. This book is our best shot at providing you with a troubleshooting guide for small group ministry.

It would grieve God's heart to see Jesus' dream for community (as expressed in John 17) unravel because you think you're facing unforeseen, unsolvable obstacles. The truth is these issues are predictable. Chances are, if you're having trouble building a small group ministry, your problems can be traced to one of these seven deadly sins. Figure out how to work these seven areas—like discovering the inner workings of a complex gadget—and usually your small group ministry will work just fine. This book will help you discern problems and implement solutions.

While developing this troubleshooting method, however, we discovered it's a good news–bad news deal. The bad news is you cannot cheat the small group system. You really can't. Ignoring even one of the seven key issues will wreak havoc on your small group ministry. Now the good news: you can't cheat the small group system. (Didn't we just say that? Reminds you of Yogi Berra: "It's déjà vu all over again!") So why do we call the bad news the good news? Despite not being able to cheat this system, it's a really great system. It is a great way to do ministry. The fact that you cannot cheat actually works to your advantage.

## An Overview of the Seven Deadly Sins

This book devotes two chapters to each of the seven deadly sins of small group ministry. The first helps you diagnose the problem, and the second provides solutions, or the "fix." There is a logical order to the seven sins, but feel free to read out of sequence. You can read this overview, then turn immediately to the help you need most right now.

THE SEVEN DEADLY SINS OF SMALL GROUP MINISTRY

This overview also gives you a ready reference for future troubleshooting. Like us, you may find you have committed most, or even all, of the seven sins. That's okay. Penance will be prescribed. (However, no indulgences can be purchased.)

### Sin One: Unclear Ministry Objectives

Chapter 1 will help you diagnose whether you suffer from unclear ministry objectives. The fundamental question is whether you've decided on how you want small groups to fit into your overall church mission—what small groups will be when you "grow up"—and whether you've chosen a structure to achieve your clear objectives. We will help you think through the choice between being a church *with* small groups or a church *of* small groups, focusing particularly on the importance of making a clear decision. When you finish this chapter, we guarantee you'll be able to judge your current level of clarity.

Chapter 2 offers strategies and tools for developing clear ministry objectives, on a whole-church and ministry-specific basis. We examine alternative strategies, including span of care, leadership requirements, group purpose and meeting components, assimilation, and group multiplication. This will involve whole-church ministry planning and ministry-to-ministry connection, through communication, coordination, and collaboration.

### Sin Two: Lack of Point Leadership

Chapter 3 will help you diagnose point leadership problems. "Point leader" is Willow Creek's term for the person who champions small group ministry in a church. We focus on the key fork-in-the-road decisions that a point leader will face and how to choose a point leader and create their job description. Getting this right sets you up for long-term growth and sustainability.

Chapter 4's strategies and tools for effectively deploying point leadership will resolve problems. We reveal essential point leader qualities and explain what point leaders must focus on. We help point leaders determine vision and strategy, select people, work in teams, and monitor progress.

### Sin Three: Poor Coaching Structures

Every church we've worked with wrestles with the issue covered in chapter 5—identifying symptoms and causes of poor coaching for small group leaders. We define healthy spans of care, analyze a shepherding strategy coaches can use with leaders, and tell how to support and develop great coaches.

Chapter 6 provides strategies and tools for effective coaching structures. It includes traits required for effective coaching and practical models for training coaches. We also discuss the best ways for church staffs to oversee coaching huddles.

### Sin Four: Neglect of Ongoing Leadership Development

Chapter 7 spotlights the dangers and results of the failure to develop leaders. We describe an effective leadership development culture so you can compare it to a church without one. We explain why it's critical to personally model leadership development in your ministry. *Warning:* If you do not employ a strategy of apprenticeship to develop leaders, including maintaining the distinction between assistant and apprentice leaders, your sin will find you out!

The good news is that chapter 8 gives strategies and tools for developing leaders. We detail "turbo groups," a significant solution for increasing the number of leaders. We also explain how to create a climate for leadership development so that it becomes embedded in the small group system.

### Sin Five: Closed Group Mind-Set

Chapter 9 takes a look at the problem and root causes of closed groups—groups without an open chair. Having too many closed groups inhibits small group ministry effectiveness. Root causes of closed groups include lack of vision, failure to track and respond to group size, poor modeling of the open chair, and misunderstanding of how people build relational integrity with seekers.

Chapter 10 tells how to open closed groups. We have seen groups actually fill open chairs with unconnected believers and seekers. We'll explain how to do this in your church by casting a courageous vision as you empower a grassroots movement for your congregation to build community, one group and one life at a time.

### Sin Six: Narrow Definition of a Small Group

Chapter 11 will help you diagnose whether you have too narrow a definition of small groups. We examine popular small group definitions and describe the breadth of small group possibilities. You need leaders who understand their small group's purpose. We show how to use the "small group continuum" concept so you can pinpoint dynamics that limit your ministry.

Chapter 12 explores how to broaden the range of small groups you offer. Many churches are discovering countless types of small groups that connect people and help them develop spiritually. We describe development patterns so you can creatively expand your definition of small groups and infuse more group life into your congregation.

### Sin Seven: Neglect of the Assimilation Process

Chapter 13 covers a major lesson we had to learn while making a greater commitment to small group ministry. When developing assimilation strategies, ignorance is not bliss. Don't underestimate the potential of larger gatherings to "feed" small groups. Medium-sized gatherings, such as Sunday schools, adult Bible fellowship, and special programs, can help groups assimilate into the larger body of the church. Discover whether you're neglecting assimilation possibilities in your current structure.

Chapter 14 shows how to connect people through well-designed assimilation events. We reveal a churchwide strategy for helping people move between ministries or small groups so they build community in ever-increasing networks. We show you how to gather and track data to make this happen.

## Before You Enter the Confessional

Throughout this book you'll find stories from churches at various stages of small groups transition. Our transition tips and leadership tips focus on a specific leadership decision or insight—to reassure you that the light at the end of the tunnel is not a train.

We expect you'll find the appendices very useful. They include tools that we or other churches have used to implement the strategies described in this book. Even if these tools don't exactly fit your situation, they'll likely seed your thoughts as you develop strategies appropriate to your own church.

You may have committed to small group ministry after reading our book *Building a Church of Small Groups*. Nevertheless, it's inevitable that you'll hit plateaus and barriers—just as First Community Church did. Life never works according to plan, and small group ministry never follows the model exactly.

Remember *Apollo 13* Commander Jim Lovell's now-famous understatement? "Houston, we've had a problem," he said, after an oxygen tank exploded. The explosion damaged the other oxygen tank, as well as power, water, and navigational systems in the command module. Forced to take refuge in the lunar module, the astronauts realized that carbon dioxide filters were faltering. The square filter canisters they'd salvaged from the command module weren't compatible with the lunar module's round canister openings. They needed to solve this problem—or die.

We love the scene that takes place in both the movie and the book when Houston ground controllers grasp the problem's magnitude. Engineers assemble around a table covered with what appear to be garage sale leftovers—plastic bags, gloves, cardboard, tape, and string. Their leader says, "This is all they have to work with. It's your job to design a way to attach the filter canisters using only these materials, and then teach them how to do it. We only have a few hours before the air becomes deadly."

The stakes were high. Time, resources, and people were scarce. (Sounds like the local church, doesn't it?) Thankfully, the team produced a lifesaving device that cleared the air for three desperate astronauts. The successful rescue is now history.

Your situation is not much different. You face the overwhelming challenge of building a small group infrastructure that will infuse the church with community life, providing support and spiritual transformation to the many entrusted to your care. But no corps of engineers stands by, ready to help you assemble available resources into a fix for your small group system. Until now, most churches— including ours—have been on their own in troubleshooting. We hope this book will function as your ground control team.

# Chapter 1

# Sin One:
# Unclear Ministry Objectives

*Symptoms of Unclear Ministry Objectives*

> *Leaders don't agree on the purpose for small groups*
> *The church's road to ministry progress is blocked*
> *Relationships are breaking down among those most committed to community*
> *Church members expect too much attention from the staff*
> *Small groups have a myopic vision and don't know their role in the overall church strategy*

It was the meeting to end all meetings. I (Bill) still get a shudder when I think of it. My son was in the Cub Scouts, and a meeting had been called for boys and their parents to attend. We arrived on time and took our place among the eleven boys and fifteen parents who were able to attend.

"Okay, so let's get started," began Kevin, the forty-five-year-old scoutmaster. "It is that time again when we should be thinking about the annual Cub Scout campout. Does anyone have any thoughts?"

"We will need some trucks to carry the garbage out after the boys leave," said one father.

"Why don't we have a different menu than last year?" asked Maria. "I think the boys are getting tired of peanut butter!"

About thirty seconds of silence reigned among us as we gathered in the cluttered church basement where these dreadful meetings were endured. Then seven-year-old Bobby broke the silence.

"What if it rains again? I hate it when it rains."

"You're a wimp!" said Mark, an eight-year-old veteran of camping life, whose speech was often laced with such encouraging words for his fellow Scouts. Others chimed in with their cracks and jokes.

"Okay, calm down. Let's just stay with the program we did last year," the scoutmaster suggested. "It seems like that worked fine."

16 Unless, that is, like our family, you were not involved last year. We had no idea what to expect this year or what had taken place last year as hundreds of young boys invaded the forests of Illinois.

"Last year was great . . ." started young Mike, pausing long enough for Kevin and the parents to think this whole camping experience might actually have some impact, ". . . if you like mosquitoes and mud!" The room erupted in laughter. Little Mike pleaded, "Please don't make us go to the same campground! That place was a swamp!" By now the boys were roaring hysterically and parents were needed to help restore order.

"That's enough boys—settle down. Parents, we need your help with this event. Who would like to volunteer to help this year?" asked Kevin. "We'll need about ten people. Our troop is responsible for organizing the sports equipment and games."

The response was unanimous: fifteen parents sat motionless as they pondered why they had chosen scouting instead of swimming lessons. *I could be lounging by the pool, getting a tan, watching my kids frolic in the warm summer sun. Instead I will probably be trudging through a sweltering forest, fending off insect attacks, and struggling to get three hours of sleep in a tent with a group of second graders whose life ambition is to do exactly the opposite of everything I say.*

"What about skills? Will the boys learn any skills?" asked Harold. At a Scout camp in 1967 Harold had learned to tie an assortment of knots. "I want my boy to learn something while he's there. Won't they learn to set up a tent, or carve something, or maybe build a fire?"

Harold's plea caught Kevin off guard. He was thinking logistics, not skills. He had parents to recruit, not kids to train.

Harold's comment forced me to think. *Isn't that what scouting is for? Isn't scouting supposed to train young men in the fine art of frontier survival—to impart skills for fending off wild animals without a weapon, catching fish with their bare hands, and building a log home without an axe? Scout camps should be raising up the next generation of Daniel Boones and Davy Crockets!*

"I don't want *my* son playing with fire," said Linda, who thinks the Cub Scouts are a babysitting service with uniforms. "The last thing I need is to spend all day in the emergency room! Oh, and my son Jimmy has a question. He wants to know if the kids will be allowed to bring video games along."

*Sure. And why not a portable refrigerator, a mobile phone, and a laptop computer so he and the boys can keep up with the latest trends in the stock market? So much for developing the next King of the Wild Frontier.*

"There will be plenty of safe things for the boys to do," assured a frustrated scoutmaster. "But no video games are allowed. Now, as I was saying, we will need people to plan the activities and supervise the boys at each of the sporting events. Does anyone have a bow and arrow and know how to shoot it?"

At this point in the meeting I wished I had brought one along. This misery had to end, one way or another. Others seemed to share this sentiment. (A few parents in the back of the room were contemplating a game of Russian roulette, several mothers were angry that their husbands were home watching baseball, and the boys—who had crossed the boredom threshold long ago—were beginning to plot the abduction of the scoutmaster one evening at camp.)

Mrs. Peters and her son Jeffrey, late arrivals to the meeting, suggested that all the parents attend the camp and share a tent so they could all "experience scouting firsthand." She was never seen again. Authorities are still looking for her. Well, actually that's not true, but it got pretty close.

"Why don't we just skip this year? Nobody has time to take three days off work in the middle of the week to help." A few others nodded.

"But then there would be no archery, BB guns, rope swings, or late-night campfire stories" lamented the boys.

*And no mosquitoes, no portable toilets, and no muscle cramps,* thought the parents.

By this point even our beloved scoutmaster had had about all he could take, so he raised his voice to get everyone's attention. "Look, we have to do this camp—all the other troops will be there, and it will be just fine! Now, who can help?"

Reluctantly parents began to volunteer, the boys agreed to quiet down long enough for some order to be maintained, and another summer scouting camp was on the calendar.

As I reflect on the experience, I realize it had all the makings of disaster from the start. In some general sense everyone knows that scouting is good for these boys and that camp is fun for them. But there was no clear vision for the event, no understanding of how it fit into the overall plan for developing these young kids, and no structure or process for getting to the desired outcomes. Every parent has a different definition of success for scouting and for the camp, so no consensus can be reached. People were frustrated and angry with the leader and with one another. Other than that, everything was just fine!

Small group ministries often suffer the same fate. There is a general sense that building community in the church is the right thing to do and that somehow small groups will help. But few understand or even agree on what must be done to get there. The leadership has failed to provide clarity—about God's call, the vision for their church, the purpose of groups, and the role each member plays in achieving the God-given vision. Other than that, every thing is just fine!

Why does this happen?

Because too many churches plunge into small group ministry without an end in mind. They're like the college kid who happily studies art and German poetry, works as a lifeguard each summer, then decides at graduation that he really wants to be a rocket scientist when he grows up. In church after church (Willow Creek included!), otherwise savvy adults begin building small groups without deciding what they want small group ministry to be "when it grows up."

In the excitement of starting groups, these churches might have great discussions about ministry models, group types, and spiritual formation objectives. But they never actually decide on the purpose of small groups or define how small groups will fit into church life. Inevitably these small group efforts reach an impasse. Church leaders who influence the congregation's strategic direction say the road to ministry progress seems blocked. Small group members, leaders, and coaches feel confused, angry, or indifferent about their groups' role in the church.

## Lost in the Soup?

If the following case study sounds familiar, then your church probably suffers from unclear ministry objectives. We've changed the **19** names, but here's what happened in a real meeting at a real church—a church that hasn't yet decided what it wants to be when it grows up. This church never really chose a small group ministry structure or analyzed the underlying values of different small group models.

Ten years ago this church started some groups, eventually assimilating about 30 percent of its adults into the groups. The board wants to grow the small groups ministry, so three months ago it unanimously approved a new small group model presented by Jennifer, the small groups pastor.

Jennifer now gives the board an enthusiastic update: "Things are going well. We have thirty-five groups, and I'm training coaches to oversee small group leaders. This will free me to develop and train more new leaders."

Suddenly Doug, a seasoned elder and board chairman, asks, "Bob, how's your class going? I see more people each Sunday. Does it use groups?" Jennifer pauses for Bob's response. Bob says the class doesn't use groups, but he loves teaching, and more members join each week. Doug says, "Classes are a great way to connect people that groups can't reach. We've had groups here for ten years, but many people haven't joined. We should beef up the classes."

Before Jennifer can jump in, Hank speaks. "What if we really promoted the classes? We have gifted teachers. Our service attendance is skyrocketing and we're bursting at the seams. If we don't get these people into a class or something soon, we'll lose them."

"Let's put that on the next agenda," Doug says. "Thanks, Jennifer, for spending a few minutes with us. You're doing fine work with small groups. Keep it up." Jennifer doesn't bow out yet, because she wants clarity. She says, "It was my understanding that our limited classroom facilities made small groups an imperative. We said that if we promote classes too much, we'll frustrate people." A few board members agree.

But then Mike says, "That's why we have to move even faster on the facilities options. Sarah, did you get that report on prospective sites?"

(Not privy to these discussions, Jennifer is surprised to learn that two weeks ago the board stepped up its land search.) Sarah, the building committee chairperson, says, "We've got some viable options. If people respond well, we could be in a new building in eighteen months!"

"Then we can really take a run at our space problem," Hank says. "Let's be sure to include six to ten new adult classrooms. That should accommodate the jump in attendance and help everyone find a place in the church. Let's take a look at possible locations right now."

Doug gracefully dismisses Jennifer. "Sorry, Jennifer, but we'll have to continue this discussion at another meeting. Now we need to jump on those potential properties, and it's confidential financial business. Thanks, again, for your input."

Jennifer leaves dejected. *Why build a group model,* she wonders, *that won't be supported or promoted? Why was the board so excited about groups three months ago but now appears ambivalent? Don't they see how groups and classes can work together to build community?*

When churches fail to choose a small group ministry model and define its underlying values, staff members become disillusioned, people remain unconnected, and the cause of Christ limps along instead of running at full throttle.

## Small Group Models

Visionary leaders such as Ralph Neighbour, Carl George, Lyman Coleman, Roberta Hestenes, and Gareth Icenogle have provided great ideas for building transformational community through small groups. Together, their ideas comprise a continuum of small group models. Though each small group model is different, most fall into one of three categories along the continuum. We admit these categories risk over-simplification but believe they'll help you determine a direction and purpose for small groups in your church.

At one end of the continuum is the "church *with* small groups" category. In this model, small groups form a department, one of many in the church. At the continuum's other end is the "church *is* small groups" category. This model views each cell group as a little church. The "church *of* small groups" category views each group as a little community within the larger church. This church's staff and ministries are all built on a small groups skeleton, so that every member is connected through community to the church.

As we say repeatedly in public settings, Willow Creek Community Church has elected to be a church *of* small groups. But that model might not be best for your church. The deadly sin here isn't choosing a different model than we did. The sin is failing to wrestle this issue to the ground and make a clear statement of intent so that everyone in your church understands where small groups fit in your overall vision and strategy.

The telltale symptom of unclear ministry objectives is relationship breakdown among those people most committed to community. In the beginning everything is rosy. People discover a powerful vision for community—rooted in God's very nature. They see God using small groups to change lives. Leaders hone their leadership skills, shepherd people with intention, and develop the next generation of rising leaders. More people ask to get connected to groups.

But soon tough questions mount. "How do small groups work in the church? What happens to Sunday school? What are the implications for staff, volunteers, and current ministry initiatives?" As the church struggles to manage the tension, conflict rises. People ask why the senior pastor and board won't "get on board." Staff members wonder about their roles and job security and have trouble sustaining leaders and support systems. Meanwhile, senior leaders wonder why small groups won't get with the existing program. Some fear that renegade groups, flush with success, may spin off to form a new church.

It's ironic how much trouble could be avoided if churches first analyzed, then chose, from among the small group ministry models described in the following chart. We suggest you immerse yourself in the current literature about small groups. Remember, it's fine to pick and choose the values and strategies that best fit your ministry philosophy. You can use the chart to avoid mixing and matching incompatible components.

## Small Group Models

|  | **CHURCH WITH GROUPS** | **CHURCH OF GROUPS** | **CHURCH IS GROUPS** |
|---|---|---|---|
| **Purpose** | Help People find a Place in the Church | A Means of Building the Church as Community | The Primary Expression of the Church |
| **Organizing Principle** | Someone Wants to Start a Group | Strategy using Affinity with Geography considered | Strategy using Geography with Affinity considered |
| **Getting in a Group** | Placement System (Centralized) | Group Invitation or Assimilation Event (Decentralized) | Assigned by Geography (Group responsible) |
| **Group Membership** | Optional for Growth<br><br>Not Required for Church Membership | Essential for Growth<br><br>Required for Church Membership | Essential for Growth<br><br>Required for Church Membership |
| **Role of Group Leaders** | Mostly Reactive Leader | Proactive Shepherd-Leader | Pastoral Shepherd-Authority |
| **Use of Curriculum** | Chosen by Leader | Recommended by Staff or Chosen by Leader | Designated by Staff |
| **Group Meeting Format** | Designed by Leader or Curriculum | Designed by Leader + Ministry Strategy | Designed by Leader + Designated Pattern |
| **Church Authority over Group** | Low | Low | High |
| **Church Monitoring of Groups** | Low | High | High |
| **Group-based Evangelistic Activity** | Possible | Encouraged | Expected |

### *Church* with *Small Groups*

In the church *with* small groups model, everyone sees the purpose of small groups as one way for an interested person to connect with **23** others. Other ministries are seen as equally valid ways to connect. Typical comments in such a church would be: "Hey, it's great you're in a group. Oh, you're in a class and not in a group? That's great too. Oh, you're on a committee, but you're not in a group or a class? That's great too." In other words, it's a choice, a way to connect. As long as you are connected somewhere, you're "in."

Turf wars are an inherent risk in churches *with* small groups, because the small group ministry competes with all other departments for leaders, financial support, meeting space, and visibility. Turf wars can get nasty every year at budget time: "How can you drop my guest speaker funding before you cut the brochure budget?" "Who needs a new church sign anyway?" "Let the youth bring their own furniture and food!"

### *Church* of *Small Groups*

As you examine the chart of small group models, you could draw a heavy vertical line between the *church with* and *church of* models. Everything to the right of *church with* assumes that the whole church will be involved in groups. Crossing that line requires a total shift in church philosophy, the gravity of which must be weighed seriously.

The purpose of small groups in the *church of* model is to build the church as community. This model sees the larger community as a network of smaller communities that develop people in Christ. Therefore, the small groups concept penetrates every area of the church. Ministry leaders and congregation members become accustomed to designing and building ministry around a small group infrastructure. Small groups are not limited to any one department or subministry. But neither do they become the full expression of local church community life. In this philosophy you will hear neither "we have a small groups department" nor "the group is our church."

### *Church* Is *Small Groups*

You will, however, hear "the group is our church" in the *church is* model. This model is obviously on the same continuum as *church of.*

But the *church is* model often differs in its theology of the nature and expression of church and in its intensity of small group emphasis.

The purpose for small groups in the *church is* paradigm is to be the church in its smallest form. This model sees small groups as the centerpiece of congregational life. Some advocates teach that "the church is the cell; the cell is the church." They emphasize that evangelism, worship, communion, and Bible study all take place in the group.

Let's face it. Regardless of the model you choose—*church with, of,* or *is*—your theology of the church will influence your decision. Some theologians believe a small group represents all the fullness of the bride of Christ. Others, however, would argue that small groups must be tied to a larger congregation for effective and accountable pastoral leadership, appropriate administration of the sacraments (even when observed at the small group level), sound biblical teaching, and church discipline.

### Are Your Underlying Values Clear?

Churches that never commit to a ministry model lose the opportunity to define the underlying values of their small group ministry. Without defining your underlying values, how can you know what your small groups should accomplish or how they will change people?

At Willow Creek Community Church, we want to become a church *of* small groups. It is not a right or wrong decision. It is a clear decision. We all—from Senior Pastor Bill Hybels to elders, board, staff, and key volunteers—agreed on a dream to give every person that calls Willow Creek their church home a place in community. Small groups are central to our practice of community life and are our primary method for accomplishing ministry.

Beyond simply saying we want to give everyone a place in community, we decided to adopt—and adapt—the metachurch model developed by Carl George. The biblical theme underlying this model is its focus on enfolding the individual into community life, so each person is cared for and the community remains intact.

This theme surfaces in Exodus 18, when Jethro, Moses' father-in-law, observes that Israel, a complex nation, is not properly organized to adjudicate conflict among its members. Jethro prescribes guidelines for structuring the nation so all its people will be cared for but leaders won't burn out. (Don't you wish your father-in-law would do the same for your church?) Through his teaching ministry and writing, Carl George became a Jethro for us. He explained how Scripture—from Exodus 18 to Ezekiel 34 to Acts 6—shows God's concern that the individual never be overlooked within the larger community. God acts to ensure that people develop spiritually, resolve conflicts, have basic needs met, and are shepherded well by competent leaders.

Once we understood how these underlying biblical principles could be embodied in a ministry model, we shaped the way we organized small groups and modified the results we expect from them. Drawing on the examples of Jethro and Jesus, Carl George coined the term "span of care," which refers to the ability of one person to effectively respond to the needs of those they shepherd. Everyone should be cared for, but no one should be responsible for the care of too many. A reasonable span of care is that leaders should have no more than ten people in a group, and coaches should oversee only four or five leaders. Our coaches gather leaders in "huddles" to connect them for mutual learning and support. Coaches visit small groups to encourage leaders and groups as they build community together. And coaches meet one-on-one with small group leaders to develop and care for them. While these activities are never rigidly prescribed, they are practiced to ensure care for the flock.

### Straining Gnats and Swallowing Camels

Over the last several months I (Russ) have visited several huddles and "superhuddles" (which include leaders, coaches, and staff leaders.) After numerous conversations with coaches, leaders, and apprentice leaders, a common theme emerged—too many people are not clear about our strategy. I thought, *This can't be! Didn't we already decide this?* After reflecting further, I realized that attaining clear ministry objectives requires more than a decision; it demands vigilance. We committed sin numero uno—again!

Two glaring symptoms led to our diagnosis that although our congregation has clearly embraced the goal of getting every member into a group, we've lost clarity about how groups fit into local church community life. One symptom is that many people are disappointed about not getting staff attention. They want Willow Creek Community Church to function like a traditional church, where they would call on the staff to address their needs. In turn, too many of us are being unduly responsive to those calls, so we lose the opportunity to have people cared for by their group or their small group leader. We are not honoring the strategy and structure we have put in place.

The second symptom of this ugly sin is that more and more people say, "I do groups, so I'm exempt from all other church activities, particularly evangelism." People have focused so intently on one part of our vision—groups—that they have missed the overall purpose of our church: to turn irreligious people into fully devoted followers of Christ. This comes dangerously close to pharisaic patterns of church life. And we cannot tolerate it.

The Pharisees became so focused on the system that they lost the big idea. They cleaned cups instead of hearts and followed the letter of the law but killed the spirit. As Jesus put it in Matthew 23:24, they strained gnats but swallowed camels. Our people have embraced group life, and have embraced it well. And we are thrilled. But some of them have contracted myopia and now see only the community, not those who stand outside it, far from God. If uncorrected, this nearsighted vision will result in "seeker blindness," the inability to see the plight of lost people. You likely have comparable issues to overcome as you dovetail small groups with other core objectives, whether evangelism, worship, or global ministry efforts.

At Willow Creek Community Church we're not just pursuing a metachurch model, we are also pursuing a seeker-targeted model. Jon Wallace, who led our small groups ministry from 1993 to 1995, once stated that Willow Creek was trying to do something unprecedented in church history. Willow Creek was pursuing a seeker-targeted, aggressively evangelistic weekend service model, while simultaneously pursuing the metachurch small group strategy, an aggressively community-oriented model. That combination has required intense effort and committed leadership every step of the way. (Which makes it clear why we have hit a few potholes on the implementation highway!)

Don't miss this issue. Whenever people grouse about your public services, evangelistic strategy, or any other central ministry philosophy, you have a clarity challenge. When you add small group issues to the mix, whether the metachurch model or another, you need even more ministry-level clarity on how small groups fit into the church. The two root causes of this confusion are fuzzy churchwide goals and ministry nonalignment.

### Fuzzy Churchwide Goals

I (Bill) recently flew to Europe to teach on behalf of the Willow Creek Association, a worldwide network of over seven thousand local churches with similar values. While I waited for a plane from Frankfurt to Geneva, the loudspeaker said: "Mr. Sagamoto, please report to gate B24 immediately. Flight 1135 is waiting. Mr. Sagamoto, please report to the gate." Ten minutes later the message came again. Then again.

My guess is that flight 1135 had 238 passengers on the list and 237 of them were getting angry. I pictured Mr. Sagamoto sitting in an airport lounge, sound asleep from the jet lag after a fifteen-hour flight. "Your flight is waiting. Please report to the gate!" Even the announcer sounded peeved. By then, if I were Mr. Sagamoto, I might have decided to take another flight, if only to avoid 237 angry passengers. I'd imagine my picture and story on the news: "Transatlantic flight delayed by sleeping passenger. Passengers miss connecting flights all over Europe. Economy suffers setback. Sagamoto beaten with pillows and blankets while boarding. Remains in critical condition."

Some churches are stuck at the small group departure gate because someone is not on board and refuses to fly. It may be the pastor, a key elder, or a staff member. Or it may be that everyone agrees flying is the right thing to do; they just all want different planes and schedules. A stuck church have worked through the *church with-of-is* issue to gain consensus on how they want to live out community. They've selected a model and adapted it to their context, creating a "when our small groups grow up" goal. Yet they can't get the plane off the ground, because it's not enough to create conceptual clarity about direction and design. You must also translate these concepts for every ministry setting where you expect small groups to take root. All the ministries must get on board for this flight to take off. Simply agreeing to the process (flying) and objective (Paris) is not enough. We must fly the same plane together and arrive as a community.

At Willow Creek we've agreed on a churchwide set of terms to clearly embed goals in every ministry setting. We've expressed our small group goals through both quantitative and qualitative statements.

### The Five Gs: Our Term for Individual and Organizational Goals

We use "the five Gs" as a framework for individual spiritual development. For example, when a person becomes an official member, we ask them questions in each area.

- *Grace.* How does someone become a Christian in the true sense of the word? How did that happen for you?

- *Growth.* How are you presently nurturing your spiritual growth through spiritual disciplines on your own?

- *Group.* Are you connected to a small group of believers here at Willow Creek for the purpose of growth, loving support, and accountability?

- *Gifts.* Are you responsibly using your spiritual gifts in a place of service within the church?

- *Good Stewardship.* In light of the tithe as a biblical precedent for giving, do you regularly support this body, using 10 percent as a goal to reach (or surpass as God prospers)?

This common terminology for goals helps individuals affirm their commitment to Christ and this church, as well as assess their next steps for spiritual growth. We form our small group curricula around the five Gs, so small group leaders use the same ideas and language in their groups as we do in the church. We also apply the five Gs to organizational goals. Regarding our goal to grow in grace, we talk about individuals experiencing and extending grace, and we also describe how we think God wants to build Willow Creek as a grace-filled community.

*Qualitative and Quantitative Goals*

At Willow Creek we get a lot more specific than simply saying we want to become a church *of* small groups. We clarify our churchwide **29** and ministry-level objectives by making *qualitative* and *quantitative* statements about small groups. Setting and reaching such goals is a challenge. For example, in 1995 we set a goal to "give everyone who calls Willow Creek their church home a place in community." Try that in a church where weekend attendance exceeds 17,000.

We qualitatively defined "a place in community." It meant that every person needed to be connected to a group with an identified, qualified leader. We wanted every person in every group (beginning at age three in Promiseland, our children's ministry) to view their group as their primary community. This implied that every group needed to become a community of care for each individual. And it required quality leaders who would do their best to nurture each person along spiritually.

Regarding quantity, we wanted it to become abnormal for a person not to be in a group. When a person showed up at Willow Creek and was asked, "What small group are you in?" and they answered, "I'm not in one," there would be shock and dismay, because it would be viewed as abnormal to be disconnected from the community.

We went so far as to put a number and timeline to this goal. For example, in 1995 we had approximately 8,000 people in small groups, so we thought we could connect 20,000 people in small groups by the end of the year 2000.

Clear whole-church objectives, fleshed out in the form of goals, forced us to draw a line in the sand. It was a declaration that Willow Creek Community Church would become a different kind of church in five years, as God worked among us. It would become our expression of the body of Christ, working together for his purposes, in South Barrington, Illinois, for the next five years.

We still needed to give each leader a part to play in achieving the dream. Having declared what the future might look like if God so blessed, we broke the churchwide goal into pieces so that those in each ministry—couples, singles, men, women, students, children, seekers, the hurting, and volunteers—could share in the objective. It made our dream tangible. Every ministry had a commitment to a clear ministry objective.

*Ministries out of Alignment*

Besides setting clear churchwide goals, we also needed to align our ministries, both vertically (with the church's mission) and horizontally (with one another). Churches with ministry-level nonalignment will not bridge the gap between clear objectives and the realization of their dream for community.

Setting goals and then breaking them down to a departmental level leads to interesting conversations, because people have to start pursuing the church's agenda and not simply their own. These conversations have brought out the best from our leaders. From musicians to women's leaders, from care-based ministries and men's ministry to single adults and students, we have come together to try to build a church *together*. It forces alignment.

Vertical alignment means matching leadership objectives with leadership practice. It declares, "Our church knows our direction. We prayed it through, listened to wise counsel, and have come to consensus among our senior leaders. We've specified it, described it, and diagrammed it. We have paid attention to quality and quantity outputs for each ministry and the church as a whole. Now, everybody, let's get together and work toward that goal."

Horizontal alignment gets everyone in sync as they move toward the vertical, or overall, churchwide goal. Horizontal alignment requires moving ministry leaders beyond simply communicating with each other, toward coordinating and collaborating with each other. At first, ministries moving toward vertical goals are like a marching band with great music but no sense of formation or cadence. They step on each other's toes and bungle opportunities. Later they learn to address opportunities together.

For example, our Promiseland ministry presents wonderful opportunities for horizontal ministry alignment, because so many children visit our campus each year. Their parents may not want to attend church yet and may simply drop off their older kids or send their children with another family. They may think, *Church is good for my kids, but not for me yet.*

Remember the pharisaical problem we described in groups that have tunnel vision and are losing sight of seekers? They've embraced the Group G goal for individuals within their small groups, but they've forgotten that Willow Creek promotes community for a cause. If, however, we encourage key groups to realign horizontally, imagine the possibilities. They can capitalize on the Promiseland opportunity. Our couples' ministry, men's ministry, and women's ministry can probably work through those Promiseland children to reach their not-yet-attending parents. We just need to sit down together and dream.

How clear have you been with each ministry about your objectives as a church? Have you created qualitative and quantitative goals for becoming a church of small groups, having people realize the Group G in their daily experience as Christ followers? Is everyone clear about his or her part of the mission? Does everyone understand how their small group aligns with other groups in fulfilling the whole-church mission?

## Graduate-Level Clarity

Forming a clear purpose for your church and its small group direction and carrying it out throughout the church requires a graduate school work ethic. Once the sin of unclear ministry objectives is exposed and confessed, the real labor begins. But here's the good news. When you determine your small groups direction, express that in a well-formulated model, and then align yourselves around specific goals, you'll feel remarkable energy. While we at Willow Creek still commit our fair share of sin in this area, our hard work has paid off. We now have several thousand leaders moving us in the same direction.

The next chapter will describe strategies and tools that helped us along the way. We hope that as you use them or adapt them, you will gain clarity about where you are headed and how to get there with integrity and focus.

We might wonder what would have happened in Jennifer's life had the meeting described earlier in this chapter taken a different turn. What if the church had really known what it was called to become, had worked to clarify a strategy and model, had adapted the core components of that model to its setting and culture, and had then aligned the ministries around achieving that aim? She would have finished her presentation and the board would have had increased confidence in her leadership.

Jennifer would probably be back in her office taking the next step in the small group process. She'd be putting together strategies and tools so leaders could implement what the elders, board, and staff had so wholeheartedly committed to. And her task, despite its challenges and occasional heartbreaks, would allow her to travel to challenging ministry destinations instead of staying stuck, idling at the gate. *Please stand by while we try to get you an update on the delayed departure of flight 1135.* No thanks. We're changing airlines.

# Chapter 2

# Strategies and Tools for Developing Clear Ministry Objectives

Now that we have all confessed our lack of clarity (and repented with sackcloth and ashes), let's take action to remedy any shortcoming you may have discovered in the last chapter. As your church decides on the purpose and underlying values of its small groups, remember this: you want to develop clear ministry objectives appropriate to *your* church's unique design. The small group model you choose will likely include features you feel comfortable with. But in the end, you must do what *you* want to do, unambiguously. We always remind ourselves that the structure serves the people; the people do not serve the structure.

Once you have defined a strategy and structure and have applied it to your setting, you face an implementation challenge. In other words, how will you infuse your small group model into the entire church— so that everyone understands how small groups fit into the church's overall mission and so that groups and ministries work together? After all, if you merely gain clarity on a conceptual level, you've only won half of the game. The real victory occurs when you formulate practical next steps and make your model live and breathe.

## Choosing Small Group Design Features

I (Bill) just moved my family to a new home. In 1992 we came to work for Willow Creek and bought a home that met our needs. It was a typical pastor's home—forty-six acres of prime real estate, an Olympic indoor pool, nine bedrooms, and four fireplaces, if you count the one in the servants' quarters. Seriously, we found a wonderful house where the three of us could build a foundation for life and ministry in the Chicagoland area.

Since then we have had another child (actually, my wife did the having while I watched), my travel increased as my ministry expanded globally, and explosive housing growth quadrupled local traffic. Our growing and more mobile family needed to move to a more convenient location.

As we contemplated a different house, we focused on questions that had seemed irrelevant during our first house search. How many bedrooms do we need? What kitchen layout do we want? Will Gail have a place from which to expand her ministry at the church? Is there space—with natural light and a view—for me to write? (In our first Chicagoland house, I had a desk in the basement, close enough for me reach out and hug the hot water unit. You might say our relationship was usually warm and bubbly, but occasionally hot-tempered.)

We answered these and other questions but, after an arduous search, hadn't found the right house. Then God provided one that fit the bill (and Gail, Ryan, and Kinsley!). How did we recognize his blessing? We started with our *design criteria*. We knew we needed a house that was close to school and church, included space for our work, and was consistent with family goals that honor God and how he has made us. And we're happy we waited until we found such a place.

Having specific design criteria is like having a floor plan in your head while searching for a home. You know the feeling—you walk into a hundred homes that have 80 percent of what you are looking for, trying to make them fit the picture in your mind. "This one might work if we could add on a study, knock out two walls, and add counter space in the kitchen." When you have to work that hard to shoehorn the home into your mental model, it's either the wrong home or you have a latent and repressed desire to star in *The Home Show*. What a difference it makes to walk into a house and realize, "This is it!" You still have adjustments to make and work to do, but the floor plan meets your criteria.

Clarifying ministry objectives in your church requires a floor plan, one that will help you build a structure to match your needs. After all, if you have sought God in the process and trusted him with the decision, you'll *know* when you've reached the destination.

The following criteria will help you design your church's small group ministry. They are based on what we've learned watching Willow Creek and other churches choose, design, and implement their small group ministry structures.

### Affinity

We built our small group infrastructure around affinity. Groups are formed around likenesses (common age, interest, or need), common tasks, or whatever will draw people together. Affinity is a point of contact, a means of helping people enter group life. Whatever reason people can find to pull a group together serves as a starting point. That has meant having the typical gatherings for families, couples, singles, men, and women, as well as for students and children. Our care and support groups have grown dramatically, as seeker small groups capitalize on the common search for answers to spiritual questions.

Even sports teams have transitioned to add a group experience to their games as they encourage believers and enfold seekers into the church. Missions, what we call "Extension Ministries," happen locally, nationally, and internationally through teams formed around passion-based affinity. Serving teams have become serving communities. Here's the bottom line: wherever people gather, we build groups.

Not long ago, we learned of a church that started a small group around teams who love playing bridge, the card game. Let's face it, the idea of a bridge group did not immediately conjure up images of the disciples sitting around the fire. "Hey, Nathaniel, did you bid three hearts or three spades?" But an older woman in a retirement community approached her church leaders with an idea. "Every Tuesday I play bridge with forty women. Most of them don't know God. I wonder if we could start a small group or two after the games, and invite the women to stay. We could reach out to them where they are!" The church loved the idea.

Small group opportunities lie just past every curve on the road to building a church of groups. Almost any affinity can be leveraged for building groups, provided you have an appropriately trained leader who is connected to your church structure and employs the right community values and practices. (We describe these values and practices in depth in *Building a Church of Small Groups* and *Leading Life-Changing Small Groups.*) So experiment and explore!

### Geography

Churches like New Hope in Portland, Oregon, have typically used geography to connect people. Everyone, including church members, fills out an information card each week and places it in the offering basket. Group leaders contact newcomers from their neighborhood (organized by postal code) and invite them to a small group. Other churches provide newcomers with a list of small groups in their geographic area and suggest they call the appropriate leader for more information.

It is not unusual to design small groups based on geography. For decades cell group models have been designed within districts or zones. In *The Connecting Church*, Randy Frazee describes why and how the Dallas-area Pantego Bible Church chose this approach.

At Willow Creek Community Church, we have used geographic breakdowns in selected ministries, combining affinity with geography. For some people, driving across town for the sake of affinity is more compelling than being close to home. Once again we have tried to meet people where they sense *they* have need. Offering both options—affinity and geography—helps us connect more people. Families usually want to be in the same geographic location because of potential school and neighborhood relationships. Groups that focus on a task, however, may draw from both genders and from many locations, ages, and ethnic backgrounds, because the affinity is the common mission, not geography.

### Getting into a Group

Some churches use a placement system, where the church plays a centralized role in putting people in small groups. Others use an invitation system, decentralizing the job of connecting people to individual small groups. It's especially easy for churches to play a centralized role when they place people into groups by geography. Other churches do a combination of centralized placing and decentralized inviting, so there is an initial possibility of several group opportunities based on geography, often combined with an invitation extended by those groups in their geographical area.

We have had positive and negative experiences with both **37** approaches—centralized and decentralized. For many years, groups at Willow Creek were created in a quite centralized manner, but today the system is more decentralized. Either approach can work; what matters is that you clearly decide.

If you decide to use a centralized system to connect people into affinity groups, avoid letting people state too many preferences. In one church I (Bill) was the small groups pastor and placement guru. Don't do it the way I did, unless you want your ministry to produce the same feelings oral surgery does—without anesthesia. Each week I prayed that God's Spirit would rush into the room like a mighty wind, sending the stack of small group membership applications to the four corners of the earth. Reluctantly I'd pick up one and read, "I'd like a small group for single women that meets outside the city on Tuesday nights and studies Romans." Next I'd find a request from married folks who'd been Christians for thirty years: "We'd like to be in a couples' group with committed, seasoned Christians, who meet weekly, pray for all our missionaries by name, and study Revelation—verse by verse."

I did the best I could to play matchmaker, but sometimes it was months before I got to all the requests. Then, after placing someone, I'd inevitably receive phone calls from the group or the person. "What are you doing? This isn't what I asked for. That women's singles' group just added three men, meets Thursdays now, and is studying the prayer lives of celibate monks!" Here was the harsh reality. I could not keep up with the demographics of all of the small groups (meeting time, location, topics, membership), and people often lost interest by the time I made a match.

Also, to be candid, there were a few groups I didn't want to send anybody to because of poor leadership or a bizarre constituency. I sent people there and they never returned to our church (a kind of a small group black hole). On the other hand, I discovered that groups with good leaders and healthy dynamics often invited people naturally through relational connections. That decentralized invitational system made more sense to me.

### Belonging to a Small Group

In a church *with* groups, small group membership is usually optional. But in the *church of* or *church is* models, belonging to a small group is either essential to the ministry or an almost mandatory component of church participation. In some churches, if you want to be a member, you must be in a group.

We put a high value on group participation at Willow Creek, but we allow a person to become a "participating member" of the church even if the person isn't yet in a group. We monitor those who are not in a group as they connect with various ministries in the church and then envision and prompt them to move toward formal group life. We want them to sense that we regard it as normal to be in a group, but it is just short of a hard and fast line. You definitely feel unconnected if you are not in a group.

### Group Leaders

The design feature here is plain and simple. At Willow Creek there is no such thing as a leaderless group. That does not mean we are right and the leaderless group approach is wrong. It simply means we are clear. We like to have a point person who will take responsibility for a group, agree to create an environment of care, keep members envisioned regarding church mission and strategy, and prompt people to take next steps in spiritual growth.

Some churches have adopted a model employing groups with shared leadership approaches. While some may experience pockets of effectiveness, we have seen few churchwide small group initiatives take root and bear fruit apart from a commitment to developing good leaders.

### Structure of Meetings

Risking oversimplification once again, the structure of meetings seems to lean one of two ways. On the one hand, the church or department to which a group is attached creates a pattern for meetings. On the other hand, many churches invest the leader with an overall strategy on how to build a meeting but also give them the freedom to choose the pattern for their group's meeting.

We've visited cell group churches that typically define the pattern for groups. Every group in the church follows a similar pattern. An example of this is Welcome, Worship, Word, and Works (or Witness). (See Joel Comiskey's work *How to Lead a Great Cell Group Meeting* for more on this.) The pattern is important because the group *is* the church in many cases, and patterns ensure that appropriate attention is given to all desired components of group process. Just think of your weekend services and note the importance of pattern.

In contrast, we at Willow Creek, with few exceptions, allow the leader to design the pattern, with some coaching about how they might structure a meeting. Again, this is not an issue of good or bad, because in some places people need or desire more structure. Early in the life cycle of a group it is important to provide more structure, so leaders can create a sense of safety and familiarity, making it easier for members to feel the group is safe. But the degree of meeting structure is up to you.

### Curriculum

Will the use of small group curriculum be optional, recommended, or prescribed? We have made curriculum selection optional, to be determined by the group as part of its covenant. Our staff designs group format and curriculum for ministries set up to meet a specific need, such as divorce recovery. With any new group, it often works well to start with a curriculum that focuses on the topic of becoming a group. One good example is Bill Hybels' *Interactions Series,* a six-week study on community.

Typically our coaches help leaders make the wisest selection for the group's benefit. The risk in this approach is that the leader or group may be prone to false teaching, as we experienced during our transition from prescribed to optional curriculum. Good coaching can intercept the problem, however, and the longer we've used an optional approach, the fewer such issues we have encountered. It's a leadership training issue. If you are concerned about false teaching but want to give leaders some leeway, consider offering a recommended list of approved materials from which they may choose.

Willow Creek has developed and published a wide variety of studies, which leaders use and appreciate. Our bookstore screens materials for quality and features the best series available from Christian publishers. Our internal curriculum and bookstore offerings make it easy for us to recommend specific resources to our groups. As a result, an increasing percentage of our groups are progressing through similar material.

Some churches, especially cell model churches, use their pastor's message as a basis for group curriculum. They begin with a message delivered at a service, convert it into a group study, distribute it to all their groups, and have the groups use that study for the week. Consequently, the curriculum is basically prescribed, and the church gains the benefit of everybody moving in the same direction, on the same issues, doctrine, or themes. The advantage of this approach is that members are not exposed to a multiplicity of messages and themes each week, so you avoid message overload. The disadvantage is that groups have less ability to focus on needs and topics important to them that are not within the realm of the current preaching series. Again, we have taken a "both/and" approach. We offer groups outlines from our midweek messages as one option but allow them to choose the curriculum that meets group needs.

You want your small group structure to meet clear ministry objectives. That's why you should define how curriculum choices will be made, or modify your decision from time to time as it fits your church's circumstances. Be sure to tell group leaders and participants how you handle curriculum selection and why you have elected to do so.

### Monitoring Groups

In monitoring our small groups, we have adopted a low-control, high-monitor model. That means we provide only nominal guidelines (control) for group membership, study materials, and meeting length and location. Instead we monitor groups by emphasizing leader training and spiritual formation outcomes and by gathering lots of information. Coaches and staff ask questions about groups, conduct surveys and focus groups, and interact regularly with group leaders about what is transpiring in their little communities. We make small group visits, in which staff or coaches attend group meetings to affirm leaders and experience groups in action. We listen and discover.

Your choice about the level of group monitoring will determine which leadership structures and systems you'll need. Coaching, reporting, databases, and more, all covered elsewhere in this book, flow from your decisions about monitoring group activity.

### Evangelism

In most *church with* situations, evangelism is possible through group efforts, but it is up to the leader or a group member. There's no churchwide strategy to reinforce evangelism. At the other end of the spectrum, we admire how the *church is* or cell model approach encourages evangelism, often mandating evangelism as part of the leader's job description. Groups simply assume that their group experience will include evangelism. Some churches instruct each cell group that their core mission is to find two people who don't know Christ, work at building relationships with them for a year, get them into the group, and lead them to Christ. If you want to build small groups that are very active evangelistically, study cell group churches such as Bethany World Prayer Center in Baton Rouge, Louisiana, where evangelism in every cell is an integral part of the strategy.

More and more, we encourage a practice called "the open chair." The open chair encourages a group to invite someone who may or may not be a Christian but isn't yet experiencing community. We've learned that moving nonevangelistic groups to increasing levels of evangelism is a long, slow push. Also, as is true with most Christians, groups usually move away from evangelism over time.

If you want your groups to reach out to lost people, then start by clearly stating—and frequently reinforcing—this mission. Groups generally fall short of your desired intensity unless leaders continually emphasize and personally model evangelism.

## Working for Consensus

Whether you choose a *church with*, *of*, or *is* structure, you'll need to make clear choices about the design criteria described above. Each small group model and design element has strengths and weaknesses. There is no *right* choice—other than that you must clarify your ministry objectives. Only then can you determine where your church is today and where it is going.

42 We have been personally involved in churches where lack of clarity produced painful frustration and ineffective stewardship of kingdom resources—people, time, and money. They thought we were building a *church of* model, while everyone else was operating with a *church with* mind-set. Some churches use *church of* language but remain stuck in *church with* practices. This is evident when staff and leaders are not actively building groups in their ministry areas, money is not being allocated for training leaders, community life through small groups is not taught from the pulpit as an integral part of discipleship, and a common group structure is not being implemented throughout the church. Everyone's job is easier when the church clearly decides, understands, and commits to specific goals.

For the past decade our Willow Creek experience, and our work with other churches, has given us a front-row look at churches with clear direction and design. Ministry grows much more effectively and quickly in an environment of certainty and consensus. Once you've defined the purpose and design of small groups in your church, you can tackle the challenge of aligning each group strategically and relationally.

### Vertical Alignment: Linking with the Church's Mission

Vertical alignment is a strategic challenge, a whole-church ministry planning process. It means helping each church ministry and small group move toward a common set of church objectives.

Under the leadership of Greg Hawkins, executive pastor, Willow Creek began a process of strategic and ministry planning so that all our ministries would move in a common direction. After formulating a whole-church strategic plan with a handful of common objectives, we began in January 1996 with a semiannual planning cycle.

Over the past few years, every June and December our ministries set specific goals and outline key activities representing their contribution to the overall plan. Because we really believe God has called us toward certain opportunities and responsibilities as a church, it is absolutely essential that we work together to align with God's direction. While the planning experiment created some internal controversy and questions, it has matured into a framework and process that yields high energy, shared learning, and progress. (Appendix 1 includes sample ministry plans).

For example, in the area of evangelism (the Grace G), we created **43** a *qualitative* objective to leverage our campus to reach as many people for Christ as we could from 1995 through 2000. Our facilities are God-given tools placed at our disposal as stewards for kingdom impact. Our evangelistic activity includes not only members' personal and group efforts but also the strategic use of our facility for events and services. We set a *quantitative* goal of 20,000 people weekly attending our week-end services by the end of the year 2000.

We could have sat back and watched attendance records, but we learned that certain activities could enhance our evangelistic effective-ness. By offering *Contagious Christian* training to improve our congre-gation's personal evangelism, we increased the likelihood that people would evangelize in their neighborhoods, schools, workplaces, and families. We asked each ministry to strategize how they could get more ministry participants to take our *Contagious Christian* course. Some ministries set goals to have 100 percent of staff, 70 percent of coaches, and 50 percent of leaders receive the training. We monitored ministry progress over six months, learned what did or didn't work, and saw God work through these equipped people to bear evangelistic fruit.

Because we vertically aligned our ministries and their associated small groups, we met our goal of inspiring many more people to work toward our church's redemptive potential. As departments experi-mented with new ideas for evangelism, spiritual formation, group life, and serving, we increased our ability to serve people and other churches. It was so much fun watching clear ministry objectives move from paper strategy to people reality!

### *Horizontal Alignment: Building the Church Together*

Whereas vertical alignment calls for a strategic solution, horizontal alignment demands a relational solution. Horizontal alignment means that the whole church functions as a team to achieve the church's overall objectives. This is extraordinarily hard. It's day-in, day-out work to over-come old patterns of isolated agendas and embrace a new "let's do it together" mind-set.

You can imagine how important horizontal alignment is in a church as large as ours. But it's just as important in smaller churches. In a church of 150 members, not every ministry is staffed, but each is led. Committees, teams, boards, and groups all have the potential for confusion and contradiction without alignment.

We've tried many approaches, but our best horizontal alignment resulted from placing the heads of Willow Creek's various ministries on one team. Most recently, that has meant gathering twelve people each week to work on ministry challenges together. Each ministry head had plans for vertically aligning his or her ministry with the church. But we needed them to align with each other as they carried out their activities.

When I (Russ) was leading this team, I often said, "Friends, when you walk in that door, you take off your ministry hat—your men's ministry or women's ministry hat, your extension or evangelism hat. You take off that hat because, here, we are the 'ministries board' of Willow Creek Community Church. We have to figure out *together* how to get the ministry done."

It took time. It was hard work. But over time, even under my flawed leadership, the team increasingly worked together. They became more sensitive to each other's needs. They even started to connect on their own on relevant issues or when crossed wires disrupted outcomes. Over time we adopted the language of Ron Nobles, a key volunteer. Ron is an independent consultant, formerly with Amoco Oil Corporation. His work helping to align and organize a vast and complex corporation was invaluable to us as we sought to make a large church function cohesively. He described our horizontal alignment goals as communication, coordination, and collaboration.

### Communication

The starting point for ministry-to-ministry alignment was simple communication between ministries. Ministry heads described what they were going to do and when they would do it. Knowing more about one another's activities reduced our potential for interference and conflict, especially in timing ministry events.

Communication helped us avoid timing conflicts that might compromise a ministry's facilities or require a Willow Creek family to deliver family members to several locations at once. You might predict that large churches would have such problems. But as we dig into smaller churches' ministry-to-ministry stresses, we see that lack of communication causes the same troubles for them as well.

### Coordination

Once ministries or departments improved communication, we began to experiment with coordination. Coordination means that two or more ministries sequence and leverage individual activities for collective gains.

Our Promiseland children's ministry sometimes has an event called "the Mega-Sleepover." Mega, as we call it, gives older kids an opportunity to bring their nonchurched friends to a safe, entry-level church event. It has provided great gains for Promiseland, gathering over 800 fourth and fifth graders. Coordination provided even greater gains, though, when our evangelism area worked *with* Promiseland to offer a parenting seminar the evening Mega began.

We were thrilled that Mega introduced 800 children to our ministry. We were even more thrilled that over 1,600 adults attended our parenting seminar, thus starting their journey to connecting with our church and a small group. This coordination took horizontal alignment to a new level. We were pleasantly overwhelmed. Parents were already coming to drop kids off, so why not build something together that could serve them? It takes about two brain cells to figure that deal out. (Thankfully, Bill and I have at least three each.)

The opportunities for coordination in most churches are more plentiful than can be imagined. While communication depends on a forum for describing ministry activity, coordination requires creativity to see the opportunities presented by currently disparate ministry activities.

### Collaboration

The ultimate in horizontal ministry alignment is collaboration, which happens when leaders of individual departments find win-win ministry approaches. We're seeing more collaboration at Willow Creek.

Our ministry heads discovered that several ministries were creating marketplace small groups. Our evangelism department started seeker small groups in local businesses, as did our executive men's ministry and executive women's ministry. Other niches started similar groups, each without much connection to another ministry area. Over time, however, with increased communication and with coordination experiments, these varied ministries began to collaborate. The result is (1) shared learning about how marketplace groups work best and (2) growing fruitfulness as several ministries work together to connect businesspeople to Willow Creek.

If communication needs a forum, and coordination demands creativity, then collaboration requires mutual servanthood. Leaders have to share the agenda and determine how to make the most of everyone's best practices to meet the common ministry objective. Our recent "blanket the city" effort allowed several ministries to work together with our inner-city partners in dozens of needy areas, mobilizing small groups and resources in a churchwide effort to serve the poor and help the underresourced. Without such coordination, groups may have actually competed with one another for people and projects as they sought to accomplish the mission. Instead, each ministry brought its best to the table.

### The Wisdom of Clarity

Imagine a group of friends opening a restaurant. They build a facility, move in tables and chairs, set plates, glasses, and silverware, then open the doors. As guests arrive, one owner welcomes a guest to the new German restaurant. Another stunned owner interrupts, saying, "I thought we were opening an Italian café." "No," says another, "this is a French bistro." The final owner hides his embarrassment by remaining speechless; he thought it was going to be a sushi bar. Only then do the embarrassed friends realize they had never really decided what the restaurant would be, and in the rush to open the restaurant, they had neglected to create a menu.

As silly as the story sounds, too many churches have opened a "small groups restaurant" without deciding what kind of establishment it will be. The guests are arriving and no menus are in hand. When those partaking in the fare offered begin to complain, the response is surprise. The conclusion? Restaurants don't work. The conclusion is erroneous, of course. The real issue is much different—the lack of clarity about elementary decisions that demand resolution before the **47** doors are opened.

So far as it depends on you, correct whatever has been missed in the commission of sin 1, unclear ministry objectives. Gaining clarity is challenging but can be achieved when the right people persist in the right conversations. Clear ministry objectives will unleash energy and direction. They'll help leaders champion the small groups movement in your church with joy and determination. Until you commit sin 2. (Oh well, it is a fallen world.)

# Chapter 3

# Sin Two: Lack of Point Leadership

*Symptoms of the Lack of Point Leadership*

> *The small group ministry does not have a designated, passionate leader*
> *An already busy staff member has been placed in charge of the small group ministry.*
> *Trying to have everyone do a little, instead of having a leader*
> *The point leader lacks a clear job description and clear ministry objectives*

The first two sins presented in this book are a chicken and egg conundrum. Which comes first—the leader or the mission? When starting a small groups initiative, some churches start with the leader—a point leader—a person who can embody the vision of the initiative and help answer the kinds of questions discussed in the previous two chapters. A point leader will help churches figure out where their small group ministry is going. Other churches must first set clear ministry objectives before deciding which person should be given responsibility for championing the cause of community throughout the congregation.

The important question is not, Which is first? but rather, Do we have a match? Mission and leader must work together. Clarifying the mission and choosing the leadership to take you there can be a messy process. The good news is that once you have successfully worked through these first two sins, you can be confident you will have a leader who can guide the church using a clear set of objectives.

Without forsightful leadership, disaster awaits. As quoted from *The Sacred Romance* by Brent Curtis and John Eldredge,[1]

> In her essay *An Expedition to the Pole*, Annie Dillard describes the provision carried along by nineteenth-century explorers in their search for the North Pole:

Each sailing vessel carried an auxiliary steam engine and a twelve-day supply of coal for the entire projected two or three years' voyage. Instead of additional coal ... each ship made room for a 1,200-volume library, "a hand-organ playing fifty tunes," china place settings for officers and men, cut-glass wine goblets, and sterling silver flatware. ... The expedition carried no special clothing for the Artic, only the uniforms of Her Majesty's Navy.

Years later, Inuit Eskimos came across frozen remains of the expedition, men dressed in their finery and pulling a lifeboat laden with place settings of sterling silver and some chocolate. Their naïveté is almost beyond comprehension, but perhaps it will motivate us to be better outfitted for our own journey.

The small groups journey is similarly arduous, crying out for an insightful point leader to assure proper outfitting. A point leader is someone who carries the responsibility for embedding small groups in the church. Most churches recognize they need an identified person to own the children's ministry, run the youth department, or inspire the music program, whether this person is paid staff or a volunteer. Each segment or department of the church is given the leadership it needs to function as God directs. But things work a little differently in the small groups arena.

At Willow Creek Community Church, Bill Hybels, our senior pastor, has made sure we don't commit the sin of lack of point leadership. He says:

The lack of a designated point leader over small groups will doom a ministry before it even gets off the ground. When you look at the kind of individual you want to oversee this organization in terms of small groups, what are some of the qualities and characteristics and experiences that you want that person to have? It all rises and falls on leadership. For churches thinking of starting a small group ministry, the most critical decision to make is whom has God anointed for this mission. Who will be the man or the woman who will embody and cast the vision, organize and implement the small group ministry? The selection of that individual sets the dominos in motion for everything that follows.

We've had several different people lead our small group min-  **51**
istries over the years at Willow, but I always made sure that they have the spiritual gift of leadership. This is a leadership-intensive position around a church. This is not just an administrative function, not just a shepherding function, even if that's what small groups are about. This person has to catalyze the entire church for the cause of small groups. And their leadership must have "range," so they can reach into every department of the church and envision them for small groups.

As Bill Hybels points out, rather than supervising a defined segment of the church's ministry, the point leader of small groups has responsibility for a defined *objective*, potentially for the whole church. Whenever a ministry function (like community, evangelism, or spiritual formation) spans multiple ministry arenas where others have established authority, the leadership dynamics get tricky. As in a corporation's human resources or finance departments, which support the company's performance with people and money, leadership functions designed to serve the whole church are only as good as the leaders who champion them. Ineffective point leaders can become gadflies buzzing around leaders focused on their individual mission. Point leaders who serve effectively can make the difference in a church becoming all it can be.

Identifying and positioning such a leader will determine the effectiveness of the small group initiative in any church. It's easy to sin in this arena, either by failing to properly designate a point leader or by neglecting to set performance criteria.

## The One Sin We Didn't Commit

The year 1992 marked the beginning of Willow Creek Community Church's transition from a church *with* small groups to a church *of* small groups. Once our elders, board, and management team (the church's three leadership groups) gained clarity on our small group ministry direction, we designated a leader. We seemingly got the point leadership challenge right as Jim Dethmer led the charge. He did a terrific job with this new effort, no small challenge when over 15,000 people needed a small group. He started building the teams, managing the chaos of change, envisioning the church body, and riding the wave of initial success.

But Jim left our staff two years into the transition process. We scrambled to deal with this blow, then drafted Jon Wallace as point leader. Jon was "on loan" to Willow Creek from Azusa Pacific University (APU) for eighteen months. We knew he had the leadership horsepower (a Harvard Ph.D. in organizational management), but we wondered how we might persuade him to stay beyond two years. Would he and his family trade smog-infested Los Angeles for our balmy Chicago winters? Fat chance. Jon chose warm smog over cold snow. Actually, he has a great passion for college students and was eager to return to his primary calling. He has since become president of APU.

So, in February 1995, we were fully vested in making small groups happen, with 8,000 people connected. A leadership corps was building, and momentum was swinging our way. But we had to transition a third point leader in three years. Not the ideal design for any emerging ministry effort.

Most observers would term our situation a leadership disaster. Especially when the next leader we selected had no small group organization experience and, worst of all, had to make one of the most challenging career transformations imaginable—the metamorphosis from lawyer to minister. When Russ Robinson's name was mentioned, more than a few people were scratching their heads.

Looking back on the multiple point leader experience today, it seems that somehow—purely by the grace of God—we beat the odds. But changing leaders three times in three years should have destroyed the effort before it got off the ground. We knew God was in this—in a big way. We had a dedicated staff and volunteer team who worked even harder when leadership changed. And our senior leadership persisted to see the change through.

So why did it work in spite of our problems? Although we changed point leaders faster than George Steinbrenner fires New York Yankees managers, we never worked without a point leader. During the entire transition, there was always a designated champion of the small groups movement within Willow Creek Community Church. As we review each of the seven sins outlined in this book, this is the one we did not **53** commit. A point leader was always waving the banner of community.

If you want great worship and music, designate a worship leader. If you want great preaching and teaching, get someone who excels in those areas and devotes prime energy toward it. And if you expect the community value to be firmly embedded in your congregation through small groups, you'd better get a point leader. Such a champion will need focus, authority, resources, and spiritual support. He or she will have to be selected with care, then assessed and developed in performance. Perhaps there are a few shortcuts in building a great church. If there are, then rest assured: selecting and deploying a small group champion will never be one of them.

## Playing Point-Leader Roulette

We have consulted with many churches that clearly chose their small groups ministry objectives but failed to properly designate a point leader. The symptoms are easy to see. The person or people supposedly in charge of small groups ministry lack enthusiasm for the task. Volunteers feel frustrated; small group coaches and leaders feel neglected. In some churches, competing models of small groups emerge. In other churches, everyone seems clear on small group purpose and how these groups fit into the church's overall structure, yet there seems to be no progress.

These symptoms suggest a simple diagnosis, usually traceable to one of two bad decisions. As we described in *Building a Church of Small Groups,* some churches simply add the small group point leadership to some staff member's or volunteer's existing responsibilities. Other churches try to spread the responsibility around and expect everyone to help carry the load. Following the publication of our previous book, we've seen even more flaws in these decisions.

### Overwhelming the Overcommitted

If your church is guilty of this sin, you probably have a ready explanation. Perhaps you feel your church can't afford to hire more staff or you already have too few lay leaders doing too much work. There is a strong temptation to add the community-building mission to an existing player's ministry, and there might be short-term effectiveness with this approach, but the probability of sustained momentum in building groups is slim. The reasons become evident upon actually playing out the strategy.

Lack of passion will be the first signal. In most situations, the new small groups champion already had a full dance card, based on what they were originally asked to do. For example, you might put small groups on the youth pastor's plate, then find he or she can't escape students' demands and defaults to the original mission. Christian education directors will typically favor supervising the classes or events they are most comfortable creating. Or the discipleship committee will have small groups tagged onto their responsibility and will probably elect a small group subcommittee. Such efforts do not make these people bad or "uncommitted" to your vision. It is simply natural for them to focus on their primary passion. On the rare occasion when small groups passion wins out, the loss is merely shifted, because that leader then begins to neglect their original duties.

If your church has currently tackled the small group point leader challenge by adding the responsibility to those of a paid or unpaid leader involved in another area of ministry, check the leader's passion factor. If you see passion for one area waning while another thrives, it is only a matter of time before the ministry will suffer.

Another problem with the add-on approach is also inevitable: divided loyalty will result in increasingly misallocated resources. The person begins to make ministry decisions that align with the needs of their primary ministry rather than with the needs of the whole church. Rather than implementing the right strategy based on clear objectives and senior leadership consensus, the leader's view will become clouded by personal ministry biases. The associate pastor with a counseling background will tend to spend more time healing the wounded and less time developing leaders.

With the add-on approach, not only will resources be mismanaged, but people will become increasingly frustrated as well. Ministry volunteers will receive less attention as the leader tries to allocate time and energy to the small group effort. The volunteers will suspect that if the ministry leader wasn't burdened by less important demands, they would get what they need. And the ministry leader will feel guilty for not being able to respond to the needs of people as well as before. **55**

Finally, the disappointments of small group coaches and leaders will become most evident. The small groups champion will get caught between responding to people and administrating a new ministry effort. His or her capacity to sustain existing relationships and build a new structure will be diminished. Leaders and coaches will feel neglected, lose hope, and potentially throw in the leadership towel. Losing coaches and leaders will be the beginning of the end. The dream of community, once clear and compelling, will fade.

### Divide and Flounder

With the "divide and conquer" strategy, nobody in particular is put in charge of carrying the small groups ball. Everyone assumes that getting clear on strategy (building a church *of* small groups) is enough to carry the effort forward. It becomes the job of all staff and volunteers to infuse their ministries with small groups, because the future has been declared.

Like Israel under poor leadership, everyone does "what is right in his own eyes." Each department follows its own approach to group life, leadership selection and training, and spiritual development. When volunteers move from one ministry to another, they start all over, learning a new system. Whole-church momentum becomes a pipe dream. No one is waving the small groups banner, casting a unifying vision, or monitoring levels of commitment and training. Soon a variety of small group models emerges, each reflecting the biases of individual ministry leaders. Church *with*, *of*, or *is* becomes irrelevant as any unifying strategy is scattered to the wind.

And you can just forget ministry alignment. When departments communicate, it is as if they are speaking different languages. Coordination becomes competition, further reinforcing independent strategies. Collaboration is eclipsed by too many staff and lay leaders whose identities become more important than what the church is becoming in service of its community.

If we sound alarmist, you're hearing us just fine. There really are extreme consequences for adding small group point leadership to someone's existing responsibilities or divvying up the job among many. The real experiences we have faced in consulting situations serve as painful precedents for making this diagnosis urgent. In severe cases churches have simply given up on the idea that lasting, rich community can be experienced in their congregation. After all, in many churches you only get one shot at the small group initiative. Some congregations have very long memories. A second try is often five to ten years away.

In any areas where you conclude we have overstated the case, examine your situation carefully for early indications of trouble. Bill Hybels often exhorts, "The job of the leader is to intercept entropy." The purpose of early diagnosis is to avoid letting bad situations get worse.

You may wonder, Does a smaller church really need a small groups point leader? The answer is yes! But how you go about it is a matter of degree. We have seen smaller congregations of 250 with just two staff members hand one of them the church's small group responsibility as their sole focus. The small groups in these churches are flourishing, because they are building the ministry through a small groups strategy owned and monitored by a focused champion. And the dedicated leader provides the vision, administration, discernment, strategy, and problem solving to deal with the other ministry issues that would otherwise arise if a non–small group strategy were being used.

In other situations a gifted and called layperson can have mammoth impact, especially when protected from other ministry involvement. (You know how tempting it is to use a high-impact leader in multiple settings.) Unpaid staff make a unique contribution by modeling the influence others can have when they lead or coach small groups.

In recent years we have seen the impact of such unpaid staff in churches that have settled the point leader issue. A dentist in New Jersey provided leadership for his church in the area of small groups before a small group staff member was ultimately hired. Doug scaled back his dental practice so that he could lead the small group ministry, developing leaders and integrating group life into the broader framework of the church.

Brenda, a businesswoman, helped build the small group ministry at the Wesleyan church she attended, devoting much of her energy to the cause. When the existing small group pastor left the staff, she was asked to cover the role in a part-time capacity while the church looked for a replacement. It was not long before they realized Brenda was the person for the role. She now spends relatively little time in her former business, and provides point leadership on the staff for small groups.

And a veterinarian who came to Christ through his local church began devoting one day per week to its ministry. Because small groups at his church had so dramatically changed his personal life, he began to serve as a group leader. Soon this church of eighty had grown to three hundred members, with over a dozen groups, and he was asked by his pastor to become the small group champion. He balances time equally between his veterinarian practice and leading the small group effort as a volunteer. Such people have had remarkable impact—as unpaid and as paid servants.

We have had to make firm statements to church leadership teams who have set clear small group objectives yet don't progress. More than once our answer has been very direct and, perhaps, crass: "You have a point leadership problem. You keep calling us for help, because you won't make the tough call (or don't have the courage) to take a person out of some other ministry. You need to fully deploy one person in the small group effort. Until you're willing to make that decision for the cause of community, you'll have to live with the same results."

## Tackling the Point Leader Job

In my (Bill) junior year of college football, a preseason injury diminished my chances for making first string. With sixty guys on a team and twenty-two starters, I struggled to regain a regular role. I worked hard in practice but saw no real action in the games except on the kickoff team. I thought little of it and lamented not being able to play the outside linebacker spot I wanted. Then one week, we kicked off, and I ran downfield to see if I could make the tackle. There was a gap in the wall of blockers who were shielding the runner, so I decided to blast through the gap at full speed and try to cause a pileup. Just

**58**

then the runner turned and headed through the same gap. We hit head-on at full speed and both of us ricocheted backward.

When I got off the ground I couldn't hear anything but saw two of everything—two coaches, two teams on our sideline, and two goal-posts at each end of the field—true double vision. As I hobbled to the sidelines, people were cheering and my teammates were screaming, but I heard nothing until my head stopped ringing and my eyes cleared up. Coaches slapped me on the shoulder saying, "Great hit! Nice play!" The next week I was back in action. I wish I had known earlier that a play like that would get me noticed more than a good practice session. But no one gave me any "performance criteria." I had to figure out on my own how to please the coaches and get back on the field.

Having a point leader is one thing; having the right point leader doing the right things is another. As the small group movement reaches churches worldwide, many churches have selected a small groups champion. We are thrilled with their initiative and focus. But how do you assess the point leader's performance? Everyone involved needs to understand the point leader's job description, so he or she can do it well.

A point leader's job description or ministry profile should provide a basis for assessment. We'll discuss point leader qualities more specif-ically in the next chapter. But what follows will help you diagnose whether you've failed to set performance criteria for your small groups champion. The point leader's performance criteria should, at minimum, include the following tasks.

### Champion the Small Groups Movement

As champion of community within the congregation, the point leader must be viewed as the alter ego of group life in the church. Point leaders motivate the congregation to set a high priority on building loving relationships, whether from the platform or in a personal con-versation. We call this the banner-waving aspect of the role.

But being point leader involves more than casting vision and rais-ing the value of small group participation. The point leader is the chief strategist, connecting the congregation to the mission and handling issues that threaten to derail the church. He or she should have some natural aptitude for organizational dynamics, a sixth sense about what might be missing in the current small groups picture. Point leaders need a reservoir of knowledge about small group models, so they can easily grasp and discuss ministry objectives.

Point leaders must oversee the change process. They champion small group vision by creating urgency, coalescing opinion, building consensus, and celebrating successes. They know the difference between change for wise reasons and change for its own sake. Patience and tenacity will press consistent strategy into the fabric of the church. Prayer, listening, and wise counsel will help the point leader gauge the timing and pace of change.

The point leader must champion the cause with multiple audiences, such as elders, deacons, and church boards so that the vision stays clear and resources are allocated. Depending on church size, the small groups champion must influence staff members and opinion leaders toward the dream of community. The small groups champion will be the face of connection among core members, newcomers, and even the socially awkward people who have trouble finding a group they won't destroy.

### Identify, Screen, and Place Leaders

Small group ministry rises or falls on the shoulders of great "people people." Because their work is relational and because they have shepherding responsibility, small group leaders are highly influential. And leading small groups is entirely volunteer-based. Whereas in project or task ministry, jobs are simply assigned to the volunteers and the relational risks may be quite low, the point leader has to be much more intentional in selecting leaders for small groups.

Defining small group leadership roles and equipping members for those roles is paramount. One person might be a good small group leader but not be effective as a coach. Another may be a good group leader but need the developmental challenge of becoming an apprentice coach. A couple relocating from another church may be ready to coach right away (every pastor's dream!). Or they might be a leadership nightmare waiting to happen. Sometimes you get the feeling a person is secretly—or openly—saying, "Well, it's about time you realized I'm ready for leadership." The small groups champion has to be savvy enough to respond, "Well, not so fast here. It would serve you well to do an apprenticeship to build trust, see how you lead, and discern your need for development."

The quality of small group ministry depends on leadership screening and placement. Point leaders should oversee the screening and placement process of all critical players throughout the entire system, so they know who is selecting and approving leaders in each area of ministry. Maintaining clear criteria for identifying coaches and leaders is essential, as is involvement in the placement process whenever possible.

### Assure That People Get Connected

Willow Creek is known for programming excellence in and beyond our worship services. Leaders like creating dynamic ministry events. Our entrepreneurial staff and volunteers invent new ways to meet our community's spiritual needs, and they create energy—poignant, fun, or both—in many large gatherings.

That's the problem. A good event with great attendance becomes the measurement of ministry success. So much enthusiasm and energy is created that you believe everything is going well. And it is always easier to count numbers than measure transformation or community building. We know that real change can take place through events and services, or we would not do them. But when we transitioned toward a small group–intensive model of ministry, we stopped measuring our success by how many people showed up in a room to see a platform-based presentation. Instead, we started measuring our success by how many people connected into small groups because of the event.

For those familiar with Carl George's metachurch concepts, assimilating people into small groups is the purpose of the "fishing pond," where you gather people together and "fish" them into small groups. Here's the risk at Willow events. Somebody starts planning a ministry event. They begin with pure intentions—a fishing pond for groups and potential leaders—but the excitement of the event takes over. Afterward people say, "Wow, you should have seen this gathering we had! It was great and all these people showed up, and God was there!"

We used to reply, "Sounds exciting!" Now I (Russ) get the fun job of pouring water on the fire by asking, "And how many people are you expecting to connect into small groups as a result of our having done that?" This question can produce disappointing answers. But it has to be asked. The point leader must make sure that people actually get connected in community through small groups. If it's not happening, we must redesign our events.

"Leadership is a push," goes another Hybelsism. Connecting people is a leadership push, because it is hard work assuring the connection of every person your church can touch. But you need to champion the individual as well as the church to achieve your small groups objective. Chapters 13 and 14 give more details on how to assimilate more church attendees in small groups.

### Monitor Group Effectiveness

Another essential task for a point leader is to monitor group effectiveness. Finding out what goes on during the average small group meeting has been one of our greatest challenges. Tracking quantity has been hard enough; monitoring quality is especially difficult in a church as large as ours. Yet ministry efficacy depends on the quality of community at thousands of tables each week, as well as at informal gatherings between meetings.

The barriers to information gathering appear formidable, yet we must discover the real story. Besides overseeing our coaches and staff, we conduct surveys, focus groups, and leader interviews. In smaller churches, the small groups champion can gather information through casual conversations with leaders and group visits. Point leaders *need* to know. No news is *bad* news.

## The Breakfast of Champions

A family room not far from Willow Creek Community Church's campus provided the scene for a unique meal. The gathering hosted by Mindy Caliguire, currently a church point leader for spiritual formation, attracted guests who had one thing in common. Like Mindy with her spiritual formation banner, each of us at that breakfast meeting is responsible for championing some aspect of our church's life, moving

61

across every department to influence evangelism, extension, small groups, and volunteerism. Since it was a morning meeting, there was only one suitable meal: Wheaties!

Between munches of flakes and milk, we shared the joys and challenges of championing our important causes. We all knew why we need a point leader for each cause, and we felt accountable to serve our church well. We realized again that we are banner wavers and strategists, change agents and influencers. Unless we can mobilize people, deploy them in the right roles, monitor their effectiveness, and discern the next movement of the Holy Spirit in our midst, Willow Creek will not reach its redemptive potential.

It became crystal clear that morning that we have a cadre of dedicated champions positioned to bring small group community into the entire structure of Willow. Our leaders can have an extraordinary impact through their initiatives, which are joining God in the adventure of seeing people connected, formed in the image of Christ, and serving our church and community for eternal impact.

As director of small groups, I (Russ) left the breakfast of champions challenged by my peers' enthusiasm and hearts. And I realized all over again the remarkable impact a point leader can have when a church is clear on where it is trying to go. Imagine churches around the world infused with the energy of men and women championing the cause of community. It is a picture of a prevailing church.

# Chapter 4

# Strategies and Tools for Choosing Effective Point Leaders

We all have seen the impact a key player can have on a team or group. It might be the first-chair violinist who inspires an entire orchestra, a campus leader who transforms the college or university atmosphere, or a sports playmaker whose passion and skill open up championship opportunities for teammates. The same can be true for the small group point leader in a local church. The right person working toward common and clear objectives can revolutionize a local church. We've seen it many times. But you need the right person, one who has essential qualities suiting him or her to the position and skills for performing the job.

## Point Leader Essentials

Given that we have both been point leaders and have evaluated others in this role, we've identified essential qualities for effective point leaders. The point person doesn't need to possess all of these qualities to be successful. Neither of us has all of them. But understanding these essential qualities will help you discern gaps and bring a team together to fill those gaps.

As you review this chapter, remember that we're presenting a composite picture. People who hear us teach, especially those in the small groups champion role, sometimes feel great angst as we unpack the material. They quickly conclude, perhaps rightly so, that only Jesus would match the standards we outline. Actually, these are not standards at all. They are tools for ensuring that you have thoughtfully considered the person to whom you are entrusting a most precious possession, your small group ministry. The Scriptures tell us to look at ourselves "with sober judgment" (Rom. 12:3), a worthy admonition given the high-stakes adventure of building a relational community.

### Spiritual Gifts

We at Willow Creek spend a lot of time thinking about spiritual gifts, talking about each individual's spiritual gift mix, identifying the gifts needed for each role, and analyzing how those gifts blend with other team members to create the ministry impact we hope to have. (See *Network*, the WCCC spiritual gift training resource.) So we always start with spiritual gifts when looking for a point leader. When considering a potential point leader, we seek to understand whether God has made the candidate for this kind of ministry and has gifted him or her accordingly.

We've seen too many churches commit the same error as Samuel, who looked "at the outward appearance" (1 Sam. 16:7) of Eliab and thought he'd seen Israel's next king. Point leaders are chosen more often because of their impressive resumes instead of their spiritual gifts. Beware: the success of your church's small group ministry requires that you get the spiritual gift screening process right. It is one thing to have a track record; it is another to be running in the right stadium. A candidate's success in previous ministry roles may indicate faithfulness, fruit, and commitment, but it does not ensure a good fit. By focusing only on the "external" indicator of past performance, you may overlook people whose spiritual gifts suit them for the job. Assessing and affirming someone's spiritual gifts affords the church a way of looking at the heart of a candidate, trusting God's wisdom and design over our own wisdom and desires.

We've noticed that effective small group champions often have the gifts of leadership, administration, and discernment. Matching roles and gifts or discerning someone's actual spiritual gifts is somewhat subjective, so this exercise can't entirely predict a potential leader's success. Yet reviewing gifts is one way to look at the heart and determine how well God has equipped someone for ministry.

### Leadership

As *Network* explains, the gift of leadership is "the divine enablement to cast vision, motivate and direct people to harmoniously accomplish the purposes of God within the church."[1] This gift helps people see the future, sense their role in shaping it, and begin to move together toward the new direction.

If the point leader does not have the gift of leadership, aimlessness will set in, resulting in frustration throughout the ministry. The small groups champion must clearly stay the course, moving people—including others with leadership gifts—toward the goal. Gifted leaders draw people in and together, captivating them by the opportunity to be part of something larger than themselves. A prevailing small group ministry thrives on vision, motivation, and direction—essentials in attracting other leaders to front-line, high-impact ministry in people's lives. You need a leader of people *and* leaders.

I (Bill) remember asking a potential small groups pastor of a growing church, "Do you have a passion for small groups?" He paused and answered, "Well, I have a passion for life change. I have been a Christian counselor for ten years and love to see people's lives change. Since groups change lives, the church felt that I should lead this new area." Bad start. The church needed a passionate leader who loved developing leaders (not simply individuals) *and* who could move others toward the overall small group vision.

We also see churches that appoint an individual to lead their small group ministry based on evident shepherding gifts. The person might have a track record of being a great small group leader, or might even be an effective small group coach, but yet lack a strong leadership gift.

### Administration

Mentioning the gift of administration often conjures images of filing, typing, and detailed record keeping. Those who discover this gift often think, "Oh no—I hate details!" Soon they realize this gift is often associated with a leadership gift and is not what they had thought. The biblical gift of administration is "the divine enablement to understand what makes an organization function, and the special ability to plan and execute procedures that accomplish the goals of the ministry."[2] It's not about doing tasks; it's about bringing order, processes, and systems to ministry objectives.

A functionally equivalent term from the secular business realm would be "management." It is the ability to get the job done day in and day out. Biblical administration translates vision into practice, motivation into applied energy, and direction into practical results. A person with this gift will bring order out of disorder through systems and processes, resulting in consistent performance across any kind of enterprise. This "organizational architect" can put the right people in the right places, honoring God's design of people while optimizing ministry outcomes. He or she will have insight into why something is broken and design a plan to fix it.

If a church selects a person who has shepherding and encouragement gifts but lacks leadership and administration gifts, the mission will likely suffer. Leaders may feel loved but will lack coherent strategy and tactics. The results will be disorder, poor decisions, ill-defined solutions, and confused, frustrated people.

The gift of administration can have an enormous impact as people see vision transformed into reality, creating a sense of accomplishment, teamwork, and momentum. A well-led and well-administered small group system can bear untold fruit and will provide a sense of order and consistency in the church. When you appoint a leader with the combined gifts of leadership and administration, your small groups ministry will move forward.

### Discernment

A third gift important for effective point leadership is discernment, "the divine enablement to distinguish between truth and error, to discern the spirits differentiating between good and evil, right and wrong."[3] Someone with the gift of discernment can evaluate a situation's spiritual dynamics or look into people and understand the relational dynamics.

Small group ministry is extraordinarily people-intensive. Any person leading the ministry must make constant decisions about leaders, their readiness for their next serving role, and their hidden flaws. Relational breakdown, which is inevitable when flawed people come together, demands the intervention of one who can read between the lines of the breakdown.

Since small groups often include teaching in a decentralized setting, the possibility exists for theological error or spiritual misdirection. A discerning small group champion knows how to separate doctrinal wheat from chaff. As society hands the church increasingly dysfunctional people to enfold into the body, the need for discernment increases proportionately. People considering leadership roles in your church may have **67** developmental deficits, both spiritual and psychological, and someone needs to discern these shortcomings and address them appropriately.

Leadership, administration, and discernment work together to enable the small groups point leader to lead effectively. If the discernment or administration gift is not strong, then surround this person with a team of people who provide support where there are weaknesses. But make no mistake: all three gifts are needed, particularly as the ministry grows and expands. Choose well, and your church's small group ministry will flourish, whether you want to be a church *of,* church *is,* or church *with* groups.

### Leadership Traits

After trying to navigate Willow Creek Community Church's complexities and trying to connect our whole congregation into small groups, I (Russ) was often dazed and confused. Then I met Ron Nobles, the business consultant mentioned earlier. Our conversations showed me how much he and others like him could help us win some of our more complex organizational battles. Over time we formed a serving small group (of course). I would lead a group meeting every other Friday, made up of business executives who spent their time battling Fortune 500 complexities and challenges. It became known affectionately as the RATS Group, an acronym for "Russ's Alternative Team Strategies." I asked this group to help us determine the essential capabilities our best leaders should have. Ron and other RATS taught us about leadership traits.

Traits are inborn characteristics or capabilities. No longer the province of social scientists alone, systematic research into these internal wiring patterns has provided breakthrough insights about how effective leaders function. Researchers have identified several "core competencies" and have explained how they're developed. We used *Leadership Competency Inventory* (LCI), developed by the Hay Group.

The LCI, used with thousands of leaders in hundreds of for-profit and nonprofit organizations, reveals four core traits among the most effective leaders. The innate traits (as we modified them for church use) are strategic orientation, conceptual thinking, intellectual curiosity, and others-focused mind-set. Even if your church decides not to look for leaders with these specific traits, you should define the traits your ideal point leader should possess.

- *Strategic orientation* helps leaders translate disorganized efforts into organized, churchwide outcomes. This trait enables someone to put together organizational pieces so that everyone works together while achieving the church's God-ordained mission.

- *Conceptual thinking* is the ability to connect seemingly disparate facts into useful explanations. Conceptual thinkers aren't confused by abstract or complex circumstances. Instead, they absorb an array of data and information and clarify what is really happening.

- *Intellectual curiosity* is the desire to understand what makes things work. It is the capability to move into various settings and ask questions that extract the information necessary to understanding ministry dynamics. The intellectually curious are relentless information gatherers who keep digging until they can make sense of perplexing situations.

- *Others-focused mind-set* is similar to customer service orientation in a business. Just as a businessperson says, "The customer is always right," an others-focused point leader meets individuals on *their* terms. Such a leader cares more about meeting people's needs than fitting them into predesigned programs. The others-focus means going onto the turf of others and walking in their shoes.

Recent research provides sobering evidence in the age-old debate about whether leaders are born or made. The research indicates most leaders either possess these four traits or they don't, and the degree to which they exhibit these traits doesn't change much over time. You can train people—through strategic planning, creative thinking, information gathering, and service management—in leadership. But the greatest leaders are born with a potential for excellence. Training merely develops what they already possess. That's why you should consider looking for a point leader born with the traits we've just described.

As with spiritual gifts, we don't see trait identification as a litmus test of a current or potential leader's effectiveness. But these traits do give you a framework to understand why a certain leader cannot build the ministry beyond a given level. Understanding a point leader's lack of certain traits will help you build a team that will buttress his or her weaknesses.

### Proven History

Spiritual gifts and traits are primary ingredients, but don't neglect proven experience. What has this person done in other churches or organizations? In other words, have they ever built something organizational that involves people and structure? If a potential small groups leader doesn't have an organization-building track record, how can you be sure they'll be able to build the organization your church needs? Your best bet is to find someone with a proven history of rallying people, identifying and coordinating leaders, and getting everyone to work together for a common goal. Proven experience was foundational for us before coming to Willow Creek.

I (Russ) came to Willow Creek Community Church staff with real ministry deficits, because I had never been in a vocational pastoral role. Few lawyers are skilled at building an organization. Thankfully, I was an exception because God made me a builder. I was serving as an elder with Bill Hybels, who knew that I had built a law firm. Over seven years I had moved from being a solo act to running a law practice with eleven lawyers and twenty-five employees. I understood what it took to provide direction, leadership, and vision and to identify people, screen them, put the right players in the right places, and grow the enterprise.

I (Bill) had built teams in many settings and helped develop a parachurch organization from the ground up. So we both knew what it took to get something up and running. You want people who have a passion and sense of calling to ministry; but you also want someone who has had some experience working with organizational and leadership issues. Their experience will help them get a handle on the challenges facing the church in building a small group structure.

Someone who has already developed an organization is most likely to succeed as a small groups champion at your church. Some of the reasons are common sense. They have made some mistakes already and will not repeat them at your expense. Their instincts will have been sharpened by their experiences. The bumps and bruises of prior circumstances will have honed their abilities to read situations and understand people.

### Spiritual Life

You should also examine a potential point leader's spiritual life. To be clear, all of life is spiritual. But we want to focus on those areas that involve someone's relationship to God. It is out of this relationship that a leader will become an example to others and set the ministry tone. Therefore, the leader's spiritual life will be essential for modeling a contagious, God-honoring life and for developing ministry atmosphere.

*Modeling* is the 2 Timothy 2:2 vision: "And the things you have heard me say in the presence of many witnesses entrust to reliable men who will also be qualified to teach others." Will this person develop other spiritual leaders, who can develop other spiritual leaders, who will develop still others? Some people have strong leadership and administration gifts, the right traits, and a proven history yet lack spiritual maturity. Their impressive outward appearance may conceal deep, unresolved character flaws with destructive potential.

Though you are not looking for perfection (or we wouldn't have jobs), you must pursue someone who is growing in his or her spiritual and personal development and relationship with Christ. Anything less is unacceptable. As Paul advised in 1 Corinthians 11:1, choose someone who follows Christ's example—because others will follow the leader's example.

Only a leader with Spirit-led passion can create the proper *ministry atmosphere*. This passion results from hours spent in prayer, solitude, and other spiritual practices to discern the Spirit's guidance. You want a leader who relies on the Holy Spirit and believes God can work through any crisis. In looking for a leader with the tactical and strategic ability to build community in your church, remember that your goal is not to create a slick, impressive organization. Rather, it is to see the central theme of John 17 become a reality—that the church would become one. We long to see this vision become a reality in our lifetime at Willow Creek, and in churches worldwide. To make this vision come alive for your church, someone—a Spirit-led leader—will need to model a strong spiritual life and create an environment in which dependence on the Holy Spirit is normal.

We suggest you look for a veteran follower of Christ, someone whose character is impeccable, whose leadership is proven, and whose maturity is established. This person's spiritual disciplines should be well established *before* he or she enters into the role of point leader, because it will require every internal resource they can draw from.

## Key Skills for Point Leaders

In addition to essential leadership qualities, your point leader will also need the core skills required to do the job well. These key skills include communicating vision, building teams, and interviewing for leaders. This list is not exhaustive, and these skills can be developed through training and experience.

### Communicating Vision

When I (Russ) became small groups champion, I was used to a twenty-five-person organization in which casting vision was simple. But a church has multiple platforms from which people communicate vision, including pulpits, classrooms, groups, teams, and committees. There are more people, leaders, and volunteers to mobilize, and the stakes are higher. People's spiritual growth and eternal destiny hang in the balance. So I searched for skill-building tools to help leaders cast vision. Sadly, few existed.

Three resources that did help were George Barna's book, *The Power of Vision*, a video by John Maxwell entitled *Casting a Courageous Vision*, and Willow Creek Resources' *Defining Moments* audiotapes on the subject. I also had the luxury of being in a church led by a world-class vision caster, Bill Hybels. So I have had a front row seat at a vision-casting clinic. Find a good vision caster and study what they say, how they say it, to whom they say it, and when they say it. Look for tapes or videos of great vision-casting leaders.

The small groups director must be skilled in the day-to-day communication of vision to large and small groups. Casting vision creates a sense of urgency among church members.

### Team Building

Can your point leader consider the team more important than his or her personal ministry skills or aspirations? Is he or she able to give ministry away? And can the point leader then help *others* lay aside their personal agenda for the sake of the mission? If so, the person is a team builder. For small groups to flourish, ministry leaders will at some point have to sacrifice personal desires to advance the whole mission. And they must motivate others to bring their best efforts and ideas to the ministry.

A youth leader may need to consider how to integrate groups into the youth meeting, doing fewer activities and allowing students to pray together and meet with an adult small group leader. Classroom teachers will need to consider how much time is spent on large group efforts and teaching and how much is spent building community in the classroom and allowing time for group discussions. In the long run, the content discussed in teaching sessions will take deeper root in hearts and minds that are given time to process the material and consider the applications. Time for exchanging prayer requests and caring opportunities will add a rich texture to the classroom environment and promote the formation of caring communities within the class. In this way, all ministry leaders can contribute to the churchwide effort to build groups, working as a team toward a common goal.

Need help in building teams? Find a great coach to mentor you, because people who lead winning teams pull the best out of players for the sake of the entire team. They do not allow one person to break community down by dominating play to the exclusion of others.

### Interviewing for Leaders

We use the term "interviewing" on purpose, though most of us live in volunteer-based settings. Putting the right people in the right places, screening them and orienting them to the vision and ministry, requires asking skillful questions. "Do we have the right person?" "Do we have each person placed and deployed appropriately?" Interviewing requires keen discernment as you delve into hearts and minds.

Human resource professionals can offer tools for interviewing. **73** Consult these professionals to help you design good questions and define aptitudes you seek. Ask them about "behavioral event" interview techniques, too.

## Key Qualities and Skills Working Together

Expect the worst if you try to cheat the system when choosing a point leader. As we've already said, the qualities and skills we've described are not complete, nor should they necessarily be used to disqualify candidates. But we also know churches get better results when they use prayer and sound selection principles. God has always chosen leaders to face problems and challenges associated with his will for the church. Every leader has flaws, and many have been reluctant. But when leaders are gifted to lead, remain spiritually submitted to Christ, and skillfully execute the plan, God moves among his people in profound ways that honor him and bring glory to his name.

Leadership matters. It matters when choosing the one who will lead your small groups adventure into the future. It matters for small group leaders who will encourage and shepherd people toward full devotion to Christ. And it matters for coaches of leaders who shepherd and support them in their role. It is to this critical role—coaching small group leaders—that we now turn our attention. After all, we have committed a few sins there ourselves.

# Chapter 5

# Sin Three:
# Poor Coaching Structures

*Symptoms of Poor Coaching Structures*

 *The small group pastor is approaching burnout*
 *Spans of care are too large*
 *Coaches are unclear about their role and responsibilities*
 *Coaches are viewed as ministry channels, not as people*

We live just outside Chicago, Illinois. For most Chicagoland veterans, the city is first and foremost home of "Da Bearsss." Since winning the National Football League's championship in 1985, when the Chicago Bears taught the world the "Super Bowl Shuffle," reincarnated the "Monsters of the Midway," and unleashed a "Punky" quarterback named Jim McMahon on an unsuspecting public, Da Bearsss have become part of our community identity.

When failure on the football field becomes commonplace, fans wax poetic about the "good ole days" of '85, especially remembering "Da Coach." On the west side of Lake Michigan, "Da Coach" is the moniker of just one human being: Mike Ditka (Coach "Dikka" if you carry the Chicago South Side brogue). Whatever his fallibilities, Da Coach is king, and there are no contenders for the throne. Ditka's coaching prowess and success have earned him undying devotion and esteem among players and fans alike. Championships will do that. Teams lacking great coaches rarely experience championship seasons.

The same is true for small group "teams." Setting clear objectives and choosing the right point leader aren't enough. Winning the small groups game requires that every leader receive consistent coaching. Leaders excel and feel valued when someone invests in their lives and ministries.

But a point leader who fails to build a proper coaching system— defined by healthy span of care within a pyramid structure—will burn

**75**

out. What's more, without a proper coaching structure, group leaders and coaches will feel overwhelmed, small group community will break down, and task groups will remain undiscipled.

Regardless of the small group model you adopt, you will need a coaching structure once you have more than ten or twelve groups. We learned from the experience of Moses and Jethro in Exodus 18 (when adjudicating conflicts became overwhelming) and from the early church of Acts 6 (when widows were being neglected) that leaders who try to care for too many people face exhaustion and ministry breakdown. Moses and the early church needed to appoint leaders of leaders so they could maintain proper spans of care.

Despite these biblical examples, too many point leaders try to do it all. And the results aren't pretty.

### Down in Flames

Burnout. This vintage 1970s term has zoomed from mere euphemism to national health crisis. We replace our desperate need for rest with "power-napping" strategies and watch our continued sleep deprivation degenerate into chronic fatigue syndrome. Burnout is alive and well among small groups staff and laity, mainly because they violate the span of care principle.

I (Bill) unknowingly set myself up for disaster in my first role as a small groups pastor. With forty-five home groups and another sixteen specialized groups, I could not keep up with all the leaders. Combine that with performing weddings, running the adult education ministry, and working on the leadership team of the church, and it was getting intense. I never thought of myself as a candidate for burnout, but I soon became overwhelmed. The exciting ministry voyage I had begun was heading for the rocks. Soon my spiritual disciplines began to slip and I avoided phone calls from anyone that had a problem—I just did not have the energy to deal with them. Potential leaders were being overlooked, and existing leaders were being neglected. I was beginning to fail the people I had hoped to serve—all because I had dramatically violated my span of care.

Now, some of you believe that because it is ministry, you are *supposed* to suffer at the hands of your people, right? You are a "burnt out" offering placed on the altar of ministry. Like a modern-day apostle Paul, you could boast of your trials. "Five times from the congregation I received requests for my resignation; three times I was beaten in golf; once I was stoned (it was the '70s!); three times my proposal was shipwrecked; I spent a day and a night in the deep (in the church basement—we were remodeling my office); and I have been constantly on the move (not always by choice). I have been in danger from elders, danger from deacons, danger from our own choir. Danger in the pulpit, danger in the pew, grave danger at the baptismal font! I have labored and toiled, often without sleep (especially when Mr. Burns was scheduled to sing). I have known hunger and thirst and have often gone without food (usually at our potluck dinners.)"

Well, it may not be that bad, but doesn't it feel good to get it off your chest?

Point leaders often deny their weaknesses. They don't see that they are repeating Moses' error. Instead, they lean into their heroic sense of mission and try to become Superman or Wonder Woman. Attempting to leap the entire small group structure in a single bound, they fly like a speeding bullet into the powerful locomotive called human limits.

Finally these point leaders admit they are a whole lot more like Moses than Superman or Wonder Woman. Their burnout, as well as the frustration among small group leaders and laity, happened because the point leaders ignored healthy spans of care and didn't build a coaching pyramid.

### Healthy Spans of Care

As point leaders wave the small group banner churchwide and groups begin to flourish, it soon becomes clear that they can't care for all the new small group leaders. They risk exceeding their span of care, the ability of one person to effectively respond to the care and development needs of those they shepherd. The solution is to add a layer of leadership between small group leaders and the point leader—a layer of coaches (or whatever you wish to call them). The point leader can now focus their shepherding and development efforts on the coaches who, in turn, will do the same for small group leaders. Coaches become the shepherds of the shepherds, leaders of leaders.

During Willow's first decade of small group ministry (when small groups was a department), we experimented with overseers for some leaders, but we didn't monitor or understand span of care. Some small group staff members occasionally cared for over one hundred groups. It was a disaster waiting to happen. Many churches make similar mistakes and risk losing small group leaders. Fortunately, when we decided to become a church *of* groups, we chose a model that included the coaching tier.

Coaches are usually members of the congregation who have the gifts and the experience to coach a handful of small groups and their leaders. They empower and support the ministry of others who are "on the playing field" of ministry. Coaches derive joy and satisfaction from watching other leaders bear fruit in the lives of small group members. Virtually all these coaches are volunteers, except for some who staff certain task-based ministries.

How many leaders a coach can care for depends on ministry requirements and the coach's other work, family, and life responsibilities. Emulating Jethro's Exodus 18 wisdom—using ratios of 1:5 and 1:10 to ensure care for all without anyone caring for too many—we concluded that most coaches should care for no more than five leaders. Many of our coaches are responsible not only for shepherding leaders but also for *not* leading a small group, so they can focus on the leaders.

When a church ignores the importance of proper coaching, small group community tends to break down. We've seen the difference first-hand at our church. Good coaches meet with leaders, pray for them, visit their groups, and bring them together to learn from one another. Poor coaches treat their leaders like tasks to accomplish instead of people to develop. "Call me if you need me" is the negligent coach's motto. Sadly, one negligent coach can affect the quality of several groups.

When you connect leaders to a coach it's like connecting branches to a vine. If the vine is weak or becomes detached, the branches suffer. Or if too many branches are grafted into the vine, the vine cannot support them, and they wither and die. Good coaches given a manageable span of care can produce fruit ten- and twentyfold throughout the ministry.

But this ministry is not easy. One of the hardest things to do is develop and support good coaches. In many churches the emphasis on starting groups often wins out over building a shepherding structure, **79** so coaches are often the last people on your mind in the early phases. Or you cannot seem to find anyone who thinks they qualify. Or, in many cases, few pastors have been trained for developmental ministry. Most were taught to exposit the Bible and counsel parishioners; few were given the tools and experience needed to build leaders. That is why we will devote time to this in the next chapter. We know this is difficult, so we seek to bring some encouragement and solutions to your situation.

### The Inevitable Pyramid

Mapping your small group structure, showing which coaches oversee which small group leaders, is an easy way to check whether you're committing the sin of poor coaching structures. Your diagram should look like a pyramid. Churches and parachurch organizations that effectively use small groups all share a common strategy—a pyramid-like "leader of leaders" structure. Some people put "metachurch" on the label; others use a cell-church brand. You can spiritualize it (in a good way) by inverting the pyramid so it reflects servanthood as a core value of the kind of leadership Christ modeled. But it is nonetheless a pyramid.

The pyramid takes shape as you accommodate the size of your organization, no matter the type. Churches cannot escape it, because at some point they must be organized to effectively carry out their mission and respond to growth challenges.

Because a growing small group ministry is so leadership-intensive, pyramid dynamics develop more quickly and yield stark consequences if ignored. You sin at your own peril. Ignore the pyramid, and you'll experience Exodus 18 and Acts 6; like Moses and early church leaders, you'll wear yourself out.

The larger the church or small group ministry, the larger the pyramid and the number of tiers will be. At Willow Creek, for example, we have a tier of coaches who care for small group leaders. We also have a tier of division leaders, staff members who shepherd approximately ten coaches, who in turn oversee small group leaders. But no matter how many tiers our church or your church adds, the span-of-care ratios should remain constant.

A recent experience at Willow Creek Community Church highlighted the benefit of having a pyramid with clearly defined spans of care for small group coaches. Lee had been a small group leader for some time. During a challenging spiritual and emotional season, a terrible calamity struck his family. The catastrophe made Lee consider dropping out of group leadership. His coach (a husband and wife team) came to the rescue. They periodically provided meals, helped with the children, and served Lee and his family in simple but profound ways.

The coaches could help Lee because they had a manageable span of leaders to oversee. Their life-giving ministry made Lee more enthusiastic than ever about leading. Because others helped carry his care load, an otherwise fragile leader was rejuvenated instead of burned out. As Lee provided for people in his small group, a coach provided for him—reinforcing the value of community at every pyramid level.

## Love 'Em and Lead 'Em

Simply putting coaches in place with appropriate spans of care is not the end of the story. Neglecting coaches can lead to a multitude of sins. Willow Creek Community Church has sinned in this area often, so we know how costly poor coaching structures can be.

Believe it or not, coaches need just as much care and direction as small group leaders do (and we'll admit our behavior has too often indicated how little we understood this). Coaches need for themselves whatever they must provide to leaders. They also need help to develop a proper coaching attitude and techniques.

### Coaches Are People, Not Pipelines

We tend to forget that leaders are people, too. In our zeal to get on with the next ministry initiative, we have at times neglected our coaches. Once a needed lifeline to sustain the ministry, coaches soon became mere channels through which we could distribute ministry responsibilities. In other words, the coaching structure became a collection of pipelines, a set of impersonal spiritual plumbing used for delivering the next new ministry project.

It sounds like an oxymoron: a "shepherding structure." The structure is needed, but a shepherding flavor must be maintained throughout the system. Coaches need to be pulled aside from their ministry responsibilities for ongoing development, care, and support. The coach must be seen in the same way as a leader—as a person with needs, goals, and concerns. We must remember that the structure supports the people; the people do not support the structure.

I (Bill) have served as a coach in the men's ministry at Willow Creek. Even though I am the high and exalted intergalactic possessor of all small group knowledge for the expanded global network of the Willow Creek Association (Russ wrote that part), I still needed to be treated as a regular guy in the ministry. I know what it is like to have somebody phone to say, "Let's have lunch," or "How are you? How is your coaching huddle going?" or "How are your leaders doing?" Whenever I received these calls, I appreciated knowing somebody was concerned about my needs, wanted me to become more effective, and could answer my questions. I wanted ministry and personal connection, conversation about my family and marriage in equal measure with that about my volunteer ministry. All of us desire that.

### Coaching Attitude

Coaches also need the right attitude to minister effectively to small group leaders, as do division leaders who minister to coaches. We used to debate whether the coach needs to be primarily a leader or a shepherd. Our instincts told us the small group leader needed to have more of a shepherding focus. Perhaps influenced by the leadership testosterone Willow Creek tends to be known for, we thought coaches needed to be primarily leaders. Finally we asked our leaders about the coaching they receive.

Here is what we learned. Our leaders express a strong desire for more coaching. Leaders want even more than they currently receive from coaches, especially personal, life-on-life connection. They desire a "pastor" who is accessible and approachable, someone intimately acquainted with their lives.

The bottom line is leaders want shepherding first, teaching and training second, and leadership (vision, instructions on what to do, how to manage their ministry, and so on) last. Our leaders have a pretty good idea of what makes effective coaching. Basically it honors a leadership rule we have espoused, the "80-20 feed-lead" split. As we often say, "You have to feed leaders 80 percent of the time to earn the right to lead them the other 20 percent." We realized we had to earn the relational authority to disciple and lead our people. Put more simply, "Love 'em, then lead 'em!"

The coaches at Evergreen Community Church in Burnsville, Minnesota, have displayed the right kind of attitude. "There has to be organization in the church," says Mark Bowen, Evergreen's director of small groups. "But we must also embrace the church as 'family.' The church needs structure, but people need family. Our best coaches are relationally connected rather than strategically connected. If coaches do not function with a caring, concerned, encouraging, shepherding bent, small group leaders will feel used," Mark adds. Evergreen coaches extend hands of care through group visits twice a year, and by connecting with leaders one-on-one twice a month. Span of care is carefully monitored; three leaders per coach if the coach is leading a group, and no more than five if they are coaching exclusively. Since Evergreen requires coaches to have led and birthed a group, strong relationships exist with the leaders they have birthed (and are now coaching). "The coach's job is to love their leaders," Mark concludes.

## Three Barriers to Maintaining Great Coaching Technique

Coaching technique complements coaching attitude. Having failed in this area, we now realize how much technique matters. I (Russ) spoke to our coaches and leaders at an annual small groups gathering entitled "First and Ten," signifying a "back to the basics" theme for the ministry year. I challenged each person to stick to ministry fundamentals. So I defined each role in Willow Creek's small group structure and spoke to each role, coaches included. The response confirmed what I had suspected. Our coaches had gotten fuzzy with their coaching technique. You might say too many were running trick plays instead of executing the proven fundamentals that make for successful teamwork. They **83** needed reminders on basic coaching technique.

So I asked the coaches to ponder a question as their small group leaders listened. "If you were to stick to the fundamentals in your role as a coach," I asked, "how would you shepherd, develop, and serve with your small group leaders?" I wanted small group leaders to hear and understand what their coaches were trying to do.

Then I went back to the fundamentals we had adopted when we implemented our current small groups strategy. The fundamental way coaches accomplish their role is through huddles (gathering leaders together), visits (attending a small group to support the leader and encourage the group), and one-on-ones (personal meetings with leaders). While I acknowledged that these fundamentals do not reflect their entire responsibilities, I stressed these three as first-order activities that will produce a healthy ministry. Violating these fundamentals was like carrying the football with one hand; it looks exciting but results in more fumbles than touchdowns.

Then I discussed the barriers—stagnation, discomfort, and superficiality—that prevent coaches from executing the three fundamentals.

### Stagnation in Leader Huddles

Carl George, the small groups guru from whom we drew most of our initial strategy, calls huddles the single hardest thing a coach has to do. Why? Two reasons: first, few coaches do huddles well, and second, huddles are hard to schedule. It is not a regular weekly meeting for leaders and is often scheduled every month around several leaders' calendars.

It takes vision and planning to make a huddle experience worth attending. Great huddles demand creativity, engaging communication, and a better than average aptitude for spiritual nurture and stimulus. We have learned to increase huddle attendance and effectiveness by creating "superhuddles." Rather than laying the entire burden of a great huddle on the coach's shoulders, a staff member organizes a quarterly gathering of several coaching huddles in one room. Here we can relieve coaches of ministry planning and training responsibilities. The result is greater community, more energy, and wider resources and interactions. The rhythm of regular huddles and quarterly superhuddles throughout the ministry season seems to serve the small group leader quite well.

When coaches plan their own huddles, we suggest Willow Creek's *Coaches Handbook* or *Leading Life-Changing Small Groups* for good meeting content. Huddles, when well planned, can become a complementary skill-building arena for small group leaders.

### Discomfort during Small Group Visits

Coaches who visit their leaders' small groups sometimes feel like uninvited wedding guests. Everyone wonders, "Who are you and why are you here? Do we know you?" Encouragement is the best antidote for small group members' discomfort. Coaches visit groups to observe and assess, but these visits are more powerful when the coach goes in as an encouragement maniac. Warmly greeting members as they arrive at the meeting, encouraging the group, affirming the leader in front of the group, and praying with the leader before and after the meeting will raise the comfort level.

### Superficial One-on-Ones

Coaches meeting one-on-one with small group leaders find it tempting to stick to business. They start safe discussions about curriculum choices, group attendance, and church issues. How do coaches overcome the superficiality barrier? Learn to love these leaders. Ask searching questions. What is their love language? Where do they struggle? What would help them grow most? How best can you serve them and their family? Simple acts of service also help coaches remind leaders how much they care.

Huddles, visits, and one-on-ones remain the fundamentals of coaching. Combined with a shepherding spirit, they provide a strong framework for life-giving, fruit-producing ministry. If coaches keep huddles inspiring and useful for leaders, encourage people during group visits, and use one-on-ones to serve and develop, they will see the rest of the ministry fall into place.

Assess your coaching structures on proper spans of care, coaching attitude, and coaching technique. Where you find shortcomings, take notes, because we offer tools and resources in the next chapter. First, **85** however, we want to discuss a specific coaching situation.

## The Challenge of Coaching Task-Based Leaders

It's a stretch to create a high-quality coaching structure, especially when you've committed to build small groups and serving teams across the church. Hard as it is to develop a coaching ministry for affinity-based groups, such as men's or couples' groups, it's even harder to develop coaches for task-based ministries. How you do this may affect the quality of everything from childcare ministry to sound and lighting for weekend services.

Cindy Manning is a Willow division leader, a staff member who shepherds approximately ten coaches, who in turn oversee small group leaders. She works with groups who support our midweek and weekend services, such as ushers, greeters, and information booth attendants. Her objective is to faithfully complete a task while helping these teams develop a sense of community. How do you accomplish that mission in a way that develops coaches and shepherds people? Her story answers that challenging question.

I first joined a Willow Creek small group in my aerobics class, part of the Sports Ministry. I had three goals—get a good workout, listen to some nice Christian music, and make some friends. But as I grew in my journey with God, I realized there had to be so much more we could do with this community of women who were coming faithfully. These people wanted to be there, and yet I felt we were really falling short, that we weren't cultivating this opportunity to gather them together. We were building bridges for people, helping them get to know each other. But we were not structured to *purposely* come alongside these women to develop them spiritually. Soon God brought other people to our team who embraced that vision, too, and I was so grateful. We transitioned that part of our Sports Ministry to connect people into small groups. Now that whole ministry is based on a small group design.

The lessons I learned there proved invaluable. Like how to blend community and spiritual development in an activity that already brought people together. Now I am serving in that part of the church called Service Ministries and am responsible for overseeing a lot of people who perform service-related tasks. We have an ushering and collection team, a communion team (who prepares and serves communion elements), a medical team, an offering counting team, and even an interpretation team to serve the deaf who attend services. So we have a broad spectrum of people coming to the church to serve the body.

It is a challenge to help people see the connection between serving and being connected in a community so they can grow in Christ. It is ironic that I got my small groups start in Sports Ministry, and now my position is a pastoral leader of this ministry. Especially when it has grown from 300 to almost 900 people who come to help complete many important tasks.

The development of mature coaches is of primary concern for our ministry. The coach is not just a pastor, a shepherd, or a leader, but a developer of others. Coaches actually bring clarity, stability, and unity to our ministry and structure. I really see them as the ones who integrate everything we are trying to accomplish. They do much of what a coach does on a football team, or what a conductor does with an orchestra. I have really come to understand the coaching position as the pivotal person to help ministry flourish.

Cindy's story prompts a counterintuitive conclusion. Coaches who combine the task with a spiritual focus help leaders grow spiritually. It is Ephesians 4:11–13 at work: people grow not just by Bible study but by "works of service" as well. Thus, coaches need to give great support and clear instructions. This will be true throughout the church as you extend community to every segment of ministry. Be diligent in assessing your coaching structure against today's realities and tomorrow's needs. If you fail here, poor ministry oversight and neglect of small group leaders will be the result, causing more problems than you can handle.

## Coaches Matter—A Lot!

*The small group leader is the most strategic person in the life-change process.* That mantra reigned supreme during the early stages of our **87** small group transition. It was never an attempt to downplay the role of the coach or any other ministry function. Rather, it was created to emphasize the impact a shepherd can have in each little flock.

We describe the role of the coach in virtually the same fashion: *The coach is the most strategic person in the life-change system.* While the leader has a front-row seat on the unfolding adventure of God's work in someone's life, the coach has a bird's-eye view of the accumulated life change in several groups and leaders. Few roles in the church provide anointed servants with the opportunity to contribute to such a systematic, reproducing engine of growth. Every leader influenced by a coach will, in turn, impact a small group.

Once you resolve the issues related to the first two sins—getting clear on strategy and selecting the right leader—you are prepared to bring span of care into focus, using the coaching material we've outlined. Now, this begs a question or two: How do you select and deploy these coaches? And how do you develop them? How do you build a coaching structure to meet the needs of your leaders? The answers lie just around the corner, in chapter 6.

# Chapter 6

# Strategies and Tools for Rebuilding Poor Coaching Structures

You might think I (Russ) grew up as a football guy, given all the lingo and analogies in the last chapter. I wasn't. I was a track guy. I couldn't tackle, throw, dodge, or for that matter, pitch, catch, hit, kick, volley, shoot, swing, putt, maneuver, lunge, or parry. I could only run, fast and in one direction. So I became a track rat, training all year for the few short weeks that we call "spring" in Minnesota, when our track team could escape the snowdrifts long enough to compete in a handful of track meets.

Running track taught me the lesson of a lifetime about coaching. My classmates and I were the classic bunch of also-rans. As high school juniors we had a coach who focused his energies toward the one star runner on the team, letting the rest of us languish. Our team, if you could call it that, did poorly that year.

Things looked even worse for our senior year. Our old coach changed schools. Meeting our new coach, Coach Soltis, made us feel insulted, because he was an elementary school physical education teacher near retirement age. How could a guy who taught kindergartners motivate high school guys? Resigned to another lousy season, we looked at 1975 as a lost year for the Mound High School track team.

We were wrong. By June our team had recorded several best-in-state times in multiple events. A dozen runners qualified for regional and state championship meets. Had it not been for a couple of injuries and a dropped relay baton, we would have been state champs. The most valuable team member was a senior—as in senior citizen, our nearly retired kindergarten teacher-turned-coach. In that one season, he transformed ragtag underperformers into a cohesive team of determined, conditioned athletes who accomplished what none of us had ever dreamed. To this day, one of my favorite movies is the basketball film *Hoosiers*, because my track adventure was similar (except in era) to that Indiana basketball experience. I learned what a difference a good coach can make.

Good coaches can make or break a small group ministry too. But finding, recruiting, developing, and supporting these essential players is one of the most challenging yet fulfilling aspects of building an effective small groups infrastructure.

Here's the difficulty: coaches are people, so they come in all shapes and sizes. Some are as surprisingly effective as Coach Soltis, some as energetic as Coach Ditka, and others as methodical as famed UCLA's John Wooden. Coaches vary as much in demeanor and temperament as in age and background. Do you wonder how to recognize a good coach? Having made good and bad coaching choices over the years, we believe we can help. This chapter will reveal specific behaviors that identify potential coaches, people who can shepherd small group leaders. We will also discuss how coaches develop leaders and how division leaders (staff) supervise coaches.

## Marks of Effective Coaches

Once you have chosen coaches, you can use our Willow Creek *Coaches Handbook* to train them. But how can you tell which leaders would make great coaches? We've discovered five behaviors that are sure marks of effective shepherding: caring, listening, encouraging, praying, and reproducing.

### Caring

Paul portrays the standard of caring: "My dear children, for whom I am again in the pains of childbirth until Christ is formed in you" (Gal. 4:19). Of course, neither Paul nor either of us has given birth to a child (though Russ secretly wishes he had just for the sake of meeting the challenge). We can only recall watching our wives in pain, the kind that sets the ultimate standard for attention and intense focus. When Paul describes his longing to see believers grow to maturity, he compares it to labor pains. His concern for them is intense and unyielding; he desires their growth like a mother desires to end the pain and bring new life into the world.

Shepherding involves that kind of caring. Good shepherds struggle to see people reach maturity. Likewise, a good coach exhibits strong, consistent affection for his or her small group leaders. Developing **91** people can be as long and painful as childbirth. Coaches—the ones who really care—long to see Christ formed in the leaders and groups they shepherd.

As you scan your pool of potential coaches, seek out those who go beyond empathy or understanding to caring, loving action. When they move from mere words of comfort to "love and good deeds" (Heb. 10:24), you have a coach candidate.

I (Bill) saw this as I began to work with Ken, a men's group leader in my huddle when I served as a coach. He was an intense guy, striving to be like Christ in every area of his life. As I met with Ken, visited his group, and watched him in huddle meetings, I wanted to see if he also had a heart of compassion. So I challenged him one day after breakfast. "Ken—I have seen your disciple-making skills at work; now I want to see the other side of shepherding, the part that cares for people and extends compassion in their pain, love in their brokenness. I'd like to see more of that." Ken was humble and received my words. It was not long before I saw his heart for those who were hurting in his family, in his group, and in the huddle. He prayed with men who struggled, listened to his wife as she opened her heart to him, and spent time with other leaders in the ministry who needed a caring word or a listening ear. I had always known he could be a coach one day—now I was sure.

### Listening

Listening well is hard to do. The Bible exhorts, "Everyone should be quick to listen, slow to speak" (James 1:19). Find a good listener, and you've found someone with high coaching potential. Good listeners have a Philippians 2:4 mind-set; they're more interested in others than themselves.

We have created a core training course on active listening, because we want every leader and coach to master this oft-neglected skill. Be sure to pull your coaches aside on a regular basis and teach specific listening skills through a process of learning, demonstration, practice, and feedback. Coaches must listen intently to small group leaders if they are going to move those leaders toward spiritual maturity. Whenever you observe a caring, attentive leader in action, you have a potential coach. Such leaders tend to shepherd well.

### Encouraging

Encouraging others is the third behavior of effective shepherding. When we said "encouragement maniacs" in the last chapter, we were not overselling the case. Watch the best cheerleaders on the sideline at any sporting event, and you'll have a picture of the consistent encouragement that marks great coaches. Few people receive the encouragement they need. Walk into work on a Monday morning and likely you will not hear your coworkers say they sat all weekend in sackcloth and ashes because they missed you and value your fine contribution.

Coaches must inspire players at all points of the game, whether winning or losing. Encouragement from a coach is like a shot of adrenaline. Jesus understood the difference a shepherd's encouragement could make among a demoralized and confused flock. "Let not your heart be troubled," he said as he encouraged a fearful group of disciples in the upper room (John 14–16). Faced with the reality of his departure, he spoke words of truth and life. He reminded them of his mission, assured them of his presence, gave them an eternal perspective on their grief, and promised them a fruitful ministry. Then he prayed for them (John 17).

Unpack the word "encourage." To encourage means "to inspire courage." The apostle Peter inspired courage among elders and church members who were suffering:

> To the elders among you, I appeal as a fellow elder, a witness of Christ's sufferings and one who also will share in the glory to be revealed. . . . [Be] examples to the flock. And when the Chief Shepherd appears, you will receive the crown of glory that will never fade away. . . . God opposes the proud but gives grace to the humble. . . . Cast all your anxiety on him because he cares for you. . . . Resist him [the devil], standing firm in the faith, because you know that your brothers throughout the world are undergoing the same kind of sufferings. And the God of all

grace, who called you to his eternal glory in Christ, after you have suffered a little while, will himself restore you and make you strong, firm and steadfast. To him be the power for ever and ever. Amen.

—1 Peter 5:1–11

Peter based his appeal to overseers on the greatest suffering in human history—Christ on the cross. He reminded leaders that because we share in Christ's sufferings, we can also display courage in adversity. Peter himself needed that encouragement to face persecution and martyrdom. He and the other eyewitnesses to Christ rebounded from adversity, defiantly shouting, as it were, "Go ahead. Try and knock us out of the game. You can't."

Peter encouraged the church by reminding them that brothers and sisters around the world also share in Christ's suffering. So we should all take courage. We share in his sufferings, but we will be restored and share in his glory as well. Now that is strong encouragement.

According to Peter, frontline ministry leaders shouldn't be surprised by adversity (1 Peter 4:12–13). He said that enduring trials is the way to suffer with Christ, participate in Christ's glory, and inspire courage in others. Coaches will experience plenty of challenges. The key question is whether they'll remain encouragers—true "no matter what" leaders.

I (Bill) led the couples' ministry when I first came to Willow Creek. I can still name couples who inspired our entire church as they exhibited courage through pain and suffering. We have watched them lose loved ones to brain tumors, endure painful debilitating illnesses, live with degenerative diseases, and struggle with terminal cancer. Several still struggle today yet maintain a courageous view of life. Bob and Marie, Tom and Debbie, Rhea and Marty (now with the Lord), and Ken and Phyllis are "no matter what" leaders. Three of these couples have served as coaches. They are the kind of people you would follow anywhere. Willow would never be the same without them.

Just recently Debbie has discovered more tumors from a deadly cancer; Ken has been in the hospital twice in the last two months for heart problems that linger and often defy treatment. As Debbie was given the news of her condition, her thoughts drifted toward celebrating her daughter's twenty-first birthday. Ken continues to pray for the Willow Creek Association in Sweden, his homeland, and for the churches there. He was disappointed about missing a small groups conference we conducted there recently. These leaders continue to express their love for Christ and the church in the midst of very trying times, lifting each of us to new levels of faith.

When coaches display courage, they become consummate encouragers. Perseverance through trials develops character unlike any other factor (James 1:2–4). It helps coaches care for and relate to others in deep encouraging ways.

### Praying

Prayer makes the top-five list not because it seems spiritual or necessary to include but because Scripture and experience demand it. James said that the prayer of a righteous person "is powerful and effective" (James 5:16). An average coach armed with prayer is worth an army of leaders without it. Our coaches are the most seasoned, mature Christians in our church. In the terms of James 5, they are righteous people who minister to others in Holy Spirit power and effectiveness when they pray. Prayer seems like a small thing to most people, a minor activity holding nominal value. But for shepherds who coach leaders, it is an indispensable asset.

I (Russ) do not know how to teach well enough to persuade a coach that prayer matters, so I have relied on modeling. For example, over the past several years I have developed a private team of intercessors who pray for me constantly. Lynn, my wife, works as our church's prayer ministry director. Often Lynn trains coaches and leaders to "weave the threads of prayer into the daily fabric of ministry." They lean into each other as mutual intercessors. Our coaches are beginning to embrace the fullness of this teaching, realizing how leaders long for someone to intercede on their behalf. This one coaching behavior— praying—will ensure significant ministry impact in any leader's life.

It is no surprise that coaches at Evergreen Community Church in Burnsville, Minnesota, are as effective as they are. Every three to six months coaches and leaders participate in a weekend prayer retreat, where they intercede for their ministry together. Friday night's prayer time looks upward, on a leader's relationship with God; Saturday is aimed at praying for their groups, including the "fresh fish." The **95** overnights have been a major factor in reducing leadership turnover. Apprentices catch a vision for leading, leaders understand the purpose of coaching, and everyone begins to believe God for increasing fruitfulness in ministry. Small Groups Director Mark Bowen describes the prayer gatherings as the ministry's foundation and glue, "the reminder of why we do what we do."

"It started slowly," admits Bowen, "but after we persisted for a couple of years, it caught on. It has become a 'don't miss' experience with nearly 100 percent attendance." It's now required of small group leaders. Once an apprentice experiences the retreat, however, they do not object. "It's still a spiritual battle; we just tell people to expect something will happen to distract them from coming. We remind them if they don't 'come apart for a while,' they will 'come apart,'" Bowen laughingly concludes. Evergreen's coaches are using prayer to shepherd well.

As you inquire into potential coaches' prayer habits, look for leaders who welcome the chance to pray for others. Pursue them. James meant what he said: effective prayers from righteous people yield God-honoring results. Prayer, combined with other shepherding behaviors, increases a coach's influence and encourages the work of our great God.

### Reproducing

A shepherding coach's supreme mark is reproducing. Coaches who focus more on strategies, numbers, and structures than on spiritually developing their leaders will drift off course. The whole point of coaches caring, listening, encouraging, and praying is *so that* Christ will be reproduced in others. The best coaches want to develop true Christian community.

Our ministry slogan for coaches comes from Paul, who reminded Timothy to pass on Paul's teachings to reliable leaders "who will also be qualified to teach others" (2 Tim. 2:2). Many call this the principle of spiritual reproduction. Translated into small group ministry objectives, it means coaches should develop other coaches *and* seek to reproduce the life of Christ in them. "Remember your leaders who spoke the word of God to you," exhorts the writer to the Hebrews. "Consider the outcome of their way of life and imitate their faith" (Heb. 13:7).

We make this possible for coaches by teaching them the skills of intentional shepherding. It's part of our investment in their ministry. But we also look for emerging leaders who tend to replicate their spiritual life and leadership in others naturally, even without training. Such leaders reproduce themselves by building relationships of influence, spotting developmental opportunities in people, and helping others grow. Look for leaders who tend to attract and stimulate maturity in other leaders, and you have a coach in the making.

### The Coach's Shepherding Challenge

True shepherding is really focused on transformation. But even for seasoned coaches, transformational ministry to leaders happens slowly. Coaches may commit to caring, listening, encouraging, praying, and reproducing but must accept that all growth takes time and cannot be "microwaved." We partner with God to see people change into the image of Christ (Eph. 4:12–16; Phil. 1:6; 2:12; Col. 1:28–29). God is at work, but his timing is not always ours. His methods are not always what we would choose. Consider the tyranny of the urgent—tasks the coach or ministry must complete—and you'll understand the powerful temptation to seek developmental shortcuts.

The coach who won't allow God time to work will undermine a leader's growth. We've put the phrase "becoming rather than doing" in our Willow Creek Community Church leadership lexicon. Leadership, we must remind ourselves, is first concerned with becoming, allowing the doing to flow naturally from our life in Christ (see John 15). Small group leaders' ministries of leading, shepherding, and discipling are less important than their relationship to Christ. This must be the primary focus of the coach.

How do you know when coaches understand the principal of becoming rather than doing? Typically, such coaches clean up their leaders' messes. It is not unlike potty training a toddler. There will be accidents before reaching the goal. A coach cannot force a leader to get it right any more than a parent can make a child avoid every mess. The coach and parent use influence, but the training is a trial-and-error process, in which success prompts new behaviors. Of course, shep- **97** herding a leader differs from potty training a child. Shepherding coaches soon realize that though God is for us, the forces of darkness are pitched against us in the battle for spiritual transformation.

"Becoming rather than doing" means waiting patiently for growth while dealing graciously with a leader who's still learning. We marvel most at those who coach young leaders, such as junior high school students (ages 12 to 14) who lead children, high schoolers (ages 14 to 18) who lead younger students and peers, and young adults who lead throughout the church. As Bill Hybels says, twenty-somethings have a couple of decades' worth of mistakes in them. Whoever coaches them will need a couple of decades to purge them of those mistakes and their consequences. The more inexperienced leaders are, the more patient coaches must be.

The coach's challenge is to rely less on methods and techniques and more on the Holy Spirit's counsel. This in no way invalidates coaches' training. As we have said, resources like *The Coaches Handbook* are invaluable. Every coach needs a toolbox of skills and resources. But they need the Holy Spirit's leadership and guidance much more. Great coaching structures, once designed, work well because well-trained coaches are "in step with the Spirit" (Gal. 5:25).

Holy Spirit power combined with clear objectives and quality training produces high-impact coaches. It takes a vulnerable, courageous shepherd to say, "I care more about you than about what you're going to produce for me." It takes time for a coach to help a leader peel back layers of sin and confusion, expose their needs and problems, and submit to God's grace. Coaches need the eyes, mind, and heart of Christ to see small group leaders' potential for ministry and growth.

### Oversight of Coaches

Like small group leaders, coaches need supervision, too. Our strategy also requires that we supervise coaches. Caring for and developing coaches requires an investment of staff energy and resources, regardless of church size. Our division leaders make such an investment. Our church is large enough that we need many division leaders, each caring for about ten coaches. Other staff ministry leaders, called "area leaders," supervise those division leaders.

Our church size prevents me (Russ) from directly managing all these staff and volunteers, but Bill Hybels has asked me to do a half-hour "fly-by interview" with any division leader joining our staff, thus providing another check on our hiring process. In a recent fly-by conversation with a prospective division leader, I was impressed by the person's obvious passion for the ministry. I'm aware, though, that passion can override strategy, so I offered a warning. I feared the candidate would forget to focus on shepherding coaches and get wrapped up in extraneous ministry issues that would be the purview of other staff and volunteers.

For the structure to work, we must work it *together*. It is the practical expression of how "the whole body, joined and held together by every supporting ligament, grows and builds itself up in love, as each part does its work" (Eph. 4:16). We cannot afford to have anyone lose the "community" mission, especially staff members. The core strategy is leader development, not ministry activity.

Division leaders can have the most enjoyable job in the world—if they focus on identifying and developing coaches. Imagine picking the leaders you want to develop for ministry, then devoting yourself to them in loving service. If that is not enough, you get to watch them build into leaders who create life-changing groups. Wow! And you get a paycheck for it.

I (Russ) remember the day this strategy became clear for me. Instead of getting distracted trying to orchestrate small groups ministry for the whole church, I began pouring myself into our area leaders. It occurred to me that I could actually get paid to spend the bulk of my time with some of the most wonderful people on the whole planet. The more I did this, the more I felt like I was cheating. I would go home thinking, "This ought to be illegal."

We began taking this strategy systemwide to all area leaders and their respective ministries, naming it "the two-thirds standard." Division leaders should spend about two-thirds of their time, directly or indirectly, focusing on coaches. Encourage your division leaders to walk through their schedule and compare how their time is allocated with respect to the two-thirds standard. Remember, a coach with five **99** leaders shepherds them using huddles, visits, and one-on-ones. Division leaders, overseeing ten or more coaches, will need two-thirds of their time to shepherd those coaches well, developing them (and their apprentice coaches) so that ministry can be reproduced effectively.

We want division leaders to carefully select coaches. To check the quality of coaches being selected and developed simply ask, "Could you see some of your coaches taking your place someday?" That's a good rule of thumb. It is not a fail-safe rule, but it is an indicator. Unless some coaches are able to grow that far, something is amiss with the selection criteria or process.

I (Bill) had a teacher who hammered one principle into us: "Never do ministry alone; always have a Paul and a Timothy in your ministry relationships." A Paul was someone ahead of you, an experienced guide. A Timothy was someone you were bringing along to develop or influence. Division leaders must treat coaches as Timothys, including them in regular ministry activity. "Ministry is caught, not taught" the familiar saying goes. But we often go it alone because of busyness or lack of planning, missing opportunities to pass the 2 Timothy 2:2 baton to others. John Burke, who served with us in the late '90s, often used the phrase "Take Timothy" to remind division leaders to take a coach along when visiting huddles or meeting with a leader. The coach can "catch" behaviors useful during small group visits and one-on-one visits with leaders. A coach can learn a lot from watching a division leader interview a prospective leader, handle a conflict, or guide a huddle meeting. And the coach can bring an apprentice coach along, so that "Timothy takes Timothy, who takes Timothy."

### The Leader's Legacy

Every year, in either September or January, we gather our coaches and leaders for an event planned to capture their hearts for another year of ministry. Sometimes we take a whole weekend; other times a Friday night and Saturday morning. We want to build them up and clarify the mission. After twelve months of running hard, our leadership team needs a pit stop. It's a great challenge in church work to avoid the rut, to keep people from going on autopilot. The last thing you want to hear is, "Well, here goes another year of ministry." Sounds about as exciting as watching paint dry. When creativity wanes and passion fades, leaders approach ministry like assembly line workers waiting for the five o'clock whistle. We come together to feed and inspire one another.

The gathering also unites us in a common mission as a leadership core. We go home with clear marching orders, fresh vision, renewed passion, and shared purpose. Each gathering is defined by a theme or phrase that captures the essence of our ministry for the coming season.

One year we chose "The Legacy of a Leader," to reinforce 2 Timothy 2:2 and remind everyone of the call to reproduce themselves in the life of a Timothy. To mark the moment, we handed out batons inscribed with 2 Timothy 2:2 and the phrase "into the hands of another." That symbol motivates each of us—staff, coaches, and leaders—to train others who, in turn, can pass the baton to others.

Coaches pass ministry batons every day they serve. But the exchange can be mishandled. Batons will be dropped and races lost unless we develop coaches who bear the marks of good shepherds and give them the care and attention they deserve. When we fail to envision and support our coaches, the baton simply represents an elusive ideal, and 2 Timothy 2:2 joins the memory verse pile with other discarded texts.

Choose coaches who will run a good race *and* pass the baton to others. Churches are littered with dropped batons, and for the most part, we church leaders are to blame. Overcome poor coaching structures by getting the right people in the right places. Love, develop, and support them, and your small groups ministry will flourish. Neglect coaches and you'll become one of those burnt out offerings. And it won't be a smell that's pleasing to God.

# Chapter 7

# Sin Four: Neglect of Ongoing Leadership Development

*Symptoms Indicating Neglect of Ongoing Leadership Development*
  *Too many people have no identifiable shepherd*
  *No one knows the leadership development potential in the church*
  *There is little or no teaching about leadership roles and gifts*
  *Senior leaders are not modeling leadership development*

"I'll never forget my first leadership experience at Willow Creek Community Church," says Jon Bodin, former director of our couples' ministries and current director of small groups for Central Christian Church in Las Vegas, Nevada. "I became a Christian here in 1981, so right away I got plugged into a small group. It wasn't long before the leader decided that everybody in the group was going to take a turn leading the small group. That sounded good, until he turned to me and said, 'Jon, next week you're going to do a study on the life of David.' And I said, 'Okay. I've got just one problem. Who is David?' It was true. I had no idea who David was. So he explained David to me as a great leader in the Old Testament, to which I responded, 'That leads to problem number two. What's the Old Testament?'"

Back then, Willow Creek used a stringent test for determining a leader candidate. Our first question for any potential leader was, "Can you fog a mirror?" We sometimes refer to this as the "alive strategy" for developing leaders. If you are breathing, you're a candidate.

We have made many improvements since then but have still sinned regularly along the way. The symptoms are distressingly obvious. When you neglect ongoing leadership development, you'll have two chronic problems: way too many unshepherded people and not nearly enough qualified, prepared leaders. This happens when churches fail to assess leadership "fertility," fail to develop a leadership culture, fail to teach about the gift and role of leadership, or fail to expect key church leaders to model leadership development.

## Defining the Sin

Jesus understood the need for leaders. "Jesus went through all the towns and villages, teaching in their synagogues, preaching the good news of the kingdom and healing every disease and sickness. When he saw the crowds, he had compassion on them, because they were harassed and helpless, like sheep without a shepherd" (Matt. 9:35–36).

It is hard to look at God's people and not feel your heart breaking over their need for shepherding leadership. God wants his flock to be well tended. When you are responsible for reaching, assimilating, and caring for shepherdless sheep, you will always have your antenna up for possible leaders.

But having an insufficient number of leaders is not a sin. The deadly sin is refusing to take responsibility for ongoing leadership development.

Like most of you, we've often had too few qualified leaders. Those in ministry are well acquainted with leader shortages. When speaking to an audience of pastors, we frequently ask, "How many of you need more leaders?" After a unanimous show of hands and laughter, we ask, "How many of you are willing pay for them?" Many pastors would give us cash on the spot, because they know small group ministry rises or falls on the number and quality of leaders. From there we go on to explain how costly it is to invest in ongoing leadership development. Fortunately, it is less expensive than a chronic leader shortage. Chronic shortages stall your strategy, frustrate your point leader, impair great coaches, and close the door on open groups.

At Willow Creek, our leader shortages stem from two main problems. The first is too many new Christians. For Willow Creek's first fifteen years, our *church with* era, small groups were our only way to mature a congregation dominated by spiritual rookies. We put people in groups by the hundreds each year and gave their leaders just one mandate: produce people who could lead more groups of baby Christians. Leaders used a structured two-year curriculum (now the *Walking with God* series) to disciple members. On completion, some two-year graduates cycled out of groups, and others began leading their own groups. Meanwhile, the original leaders began groups with new Christians. This method helped ease our leader shortage.

The second problem arose when we declared, "Community for everybody!" Suddenly, not only did we need to turn those newborn Christians into fully devoted followers of Christ; we needed to have enough leaders to give everyone—whether new Christians or *Walking with God* graduates—a place in a group. A nice problem, but a very big one.

Our history has made one thing clear. Every time we have hit a ministry bottleneck, the cause was leader shortage. If the shortage persisted, it was because we had neglected ongoing leadership development. We confess. We have sinned here, too.

Any church committed to small groups has to take the leadership development challenge seriously and determine a systematic approach to growing their leadership corps. If you are in Christian ministry, you can count on leadership shortages. Like death and taxes, leadership shortages will always be with you. But because God wants all his people to be shepherded, you cannot cheat this rule of the small group game. Neglecting ongoing leadership development doesn't work.

### Assessing Your Fertility

Allow me (Russ) to get personal. Lynn and I had an experience that provides a metaphor for assessing your church's fertility in developing leaders. Like many couples, we had trouble having kids. We had been married for six years when we decided to start a family, but after a couple of years with no pregnancies, we knew something was amiss. After a barrage of doctors, pokes, prods, examinations, tests, procedures, fertility drugs, and vain attempts, we received news no aspiring parents want to hear. We *could not* have children. We had a fertility problem. It couldn't be remedied. In fact, our adoption agency required us to have medical certification declaring us infertile in order to be eligible for their process. So, to our sorrow, we were pronounced certifiably infertile, opening the door for adoption.

God is in control, but he also has a sense of humor and loves to beat the odds. After one successful adoption we later had two wonderful children—biologically! Since the medical tests had declared normal pregnancy to be impossible, we were surprised each time. Even our doctors called them miracle babies.

Just as some churches hope and pray for leaders, we could have waited for miracles. But as aspiring parents, we wanted to know why we were having problems reproducing, so we could assess the situation and take action. Despite later surprises, knowing our fertility potential helped us make decisions to fulfill our desire to be parents.

Does your church have enough emerging leaders? Does your leadership shortage seem chronic? Perhaps you have a fertility problem. You won't know for sure until you assess your overall vision and process of leadership development. For small group ministry to keep thriving, you must constantly ask, "What are we doing to reproduce our leadership?" Let's analyze your leadership development possibilities.

## A Leadership Development Culture

Your church has a culture, a set of beliefs and practices that people embrace and affirm. That culture will determine your ability to identify and develop the future leaders. We both discovered this as young leaders. (We mean young in church years—although church years are like dog years. One year of service translates into seven years in any other occupation!)

We each became Christians through the influence of parachurch organizations. Because parachurch organizations such as Navigators, Campus Crusade, and Intervarsity work with college campuses, they are highly leadership-intensive. Leaders graduate every year and must be reproduced. Therefore, leaders expect to help develop the next generation of leaders. It is part of the ministry culture.

In our early church experiences we searched for people who had led small groups within parachurch organizations. We prayed, "Oh Lord, send us more of these trained people. Wow, do they ever know how to lead small groups!" We wanted to let someone else do the hard work, then pick the best and brightest from them. It was the "find a leader" approach. Not a developmental process in sight.

As we matured in ministry, we realized we should emulate the culture of these organizations rather than simply inherit their leaders. I (Bill) devoted much of my time to imparting a culture that kept **105** leaders flowing into two churches I worked at before I came to Willow Creek. But the pressure to find so many leaders for thousands of people took us off the developmental track for a season. We reverted to the "identify and deploy" model, neglecting ongoing development. It served us for a time, because we were able to pick the fruits ripened by the efforts of others. Soon our needs outgrew the number of quality leaders. That transformed my thinking back to core beliefs I had embraced years earlier.

As we assessed our churchwide leadership development, we committed to creating a ministry that would identify, equip, and send out leaders. We wanted our culture to move from merely saying "I would like to get new leaders" or "I am praying for new leaders," to adding "We are going to develop new leaders. We are going to equip leaders." Hopes and prayers must become intentions and commitments; that's the way a leadership development culture emerges.

Maintaining a fertile leadership culture requires a champion, much the same way the small groups initiative needs a point leader. If it is a core value, it needs a champion, a banner waver. Church ministries all wave their banners, much like states at a political rally. Each says, "We are important; give us attention!" If no one represents leadership development, it will be lost in the sea of competing initiatives.

Can you identify this champion in your church? It might be the small groups point leader, or if you are that person, you might want to challenge someone else to champion leadership development. Whether or not your church has such a banner waver indicates your commitment to becoming a church that develops leaders.

If you choose a point person for leadership development, he or she is likely to feel like John the Baptist, a lone voice in the wilderness. People often respond, "What are you talking about? All we need is four more leaders to keep this Sunday school program going." Or they want to do five more small groups, and the champion must say, "Let's step back. Let's not just look for five small group leaders so we can make incremental gains. What if we talked about producing fifty or five hundred small group leaders over the next five years?" That's a huge paradigm shift you can begin introducing over time. But it takes a champion.

Finally, if you really want to step out into fresh territory, believe that you will one day send leaders to other churches. Instead of a wish and a prayer to import leaders, you should move toward equipping and exporting leaders around the world, serving churches with limited resources. Your ministry might become a leader-sending ministry. It takes vision and a leadership development culture. And it can be done.

## Teaching about Leadership

A church will never develop a leadership culture unless it teaches about the gift and role of leadership. Although gifts are an inherently biblical concept, and Paul tells us not to be ignorant of them (1 Cor. 12:1), few churches and seminaries have paid much attention to them. Thankfully, that is changing. Churches are beginning to place people in ministry based on giftedness and God's design.

### The Leadership Gift

We've learned we cannot identify and produce leaders at Willow Creek unless we consistently emphasize the leadership gift. This is a delicate balancing act, one we haven't always gotten right. Undue emphasis on one spiritual gift can be detrimental to the body, denying the essential and egalitarian role of all gifts. "Gift envy" results, creating division instead of unity. A church can create a fertile environment for leadership by discussing the gift without giving it undue attention.

Willow Creek incorporates use and emphasis of spiritual gifts into our "Ten Core Values," the list of ten statements used to unify our efforts and define our distinctives as a church. One value reads, "We believe that a church should operate as a unified community of servants with men and women stewarding their spiritual gifts." But we have also declared as a church, "We believe that churches should be led by men and women with leadership gifts." Thus we promote the leadership gift as we teach about all the gifts. This helps our whole church remain aware of our need for leadership identification and development.

Some church members do not know they have the gift of leadership. Many mistake the biblical gift for our world's understanding of leadership, namely, the exercise of power and authority over others. Few understand the biblical view of leadership as an expression of servanthood. To consider oneself a leader seems arrogant, so feigned humility drives those with the gift underground. Our goal is to teach the biblical expression of the gift and draw gifted people out of hiding.

Still other reluctant leaders need a challenge because nobody has ever suggested they might be a leader. Teachers, parents, friends, supervisors, and coaches failed to either recognize or affirm their ability by saying, "You are a leader." These are words that bring honor to God and life to the body. How often are those words spoken in the church? Did you ever hear those words? If so, you know what it means to be recognized as a leader and developed appropriately. So please, assess your teaching about the leadership gift. The untapped leadership potential of your church awaits.

### Leadership Roles

Beyond gifts, it is essential to address the *role* of leadership, both inside and outside the church. When talking about leadership inside the church you will encounter another barrier. Most people cannot see themselves as *spiritual* leaders. The typical response at Willow Creek is "Me? A spiritual leader? Like Bill Hybels? No way."

There is a context for the role of leadership in the church, and that context is the biblical emphasis on the priesthood of all believers. When people understand that we are all called to ministry and all play a role in building the church, everything changes. It becomes normal instead of unusual to assume responsibility in the kingdom. Unfortunately, some theologies still espouse a limited view of ministry, allowing only ordained seminarians to do ministry. Others believe ministry is limited to preaching and administering the sacraments. Everything else is viewed as second class. (For more on this subject, read *The New Reformation*, by Greg Ogden.)

When a church combines biblical teaching on the priesthood of all believers with teaching on spiritual gifts, it is clear that the Spirit has distribution rights. We are all responsible for stewarding our gifts to

God's glory and for his purpose. He guarantees the right people will have the right gifts to accomplish the works of service (ministry) he has ordained (Eph. 2:8–10).

The last session of our *Network* class is exciting and affirming for all participants. We encourage everyone in our church to take this class. After learning or refining their spiritual gift makeup, participants line up based on their spiritual gifts. One by one they affirm each other, and the whole group observes how God has chosen to distribute the gifts. Amazingly, there are people representing every category of gifts. Those with the gift of leadership may hear for the first time, "I think God has designed you to be a leader. Maybe you will lead some day." People rise to the occasion as they begin their leadership development journey.

To determine the hidden leaders in the congregation, Bill Hybels taught a four-week series on leadership at our seeker services. He described different arenas in which leadership is exercised, including business, family, and church. Each week Bill reminded us we are all called to some type of leadership, though duration and intensity may vary. As he closed the final session, Bill asked whether any hearts were stirring during these weeks of teaching. If so, he suggested that interested people might like to hear what Scripture teaches about leadership. He invited people to spend ten minutes with him in a room to get further information. Many responded, evidence that Bill's teaching had contributed to creating a leadership culture by "shaking the tree" to see if any fruit would fall off. We might never have discovered some of these people without teaching on the gift and role of leadership.

## Leaders Must Model Leadership Development

You cannot simply declare, "Let's develop leaders!" or just teach about leadership development. You must develop a strategy. If your church teaches boldly and often about leadership yet more leaders aren't being reproduced, the problem may be that your leaders are not modeling leadership development. In other words, don't just teach. Lead!

Nehemiah's life provides a fine example of moving from talk to action, from vision to reality. God gave him a vision to begin rebuilding

Jerusalem. The nation of Israel needed to rebuild Jerusalem to restore God's glory. But Nehemiah did more than proclaim his vision. He put wheels on it. He united people around that vision. He created a plan.

Willow Creek recently formed a small task force to study leadership development so that we could construct a comparative standard and gauge our progress. After meeting with several leaders and studying their approaches, the team met Bobby Clinton, Fuller Seminary professor and author of *The Making of a Leader.* A young male student and a young female professor joined us at the table, making the meeting more than memorable. It was not necessarily what they said that made the difference. It was the fact that these people were living examples of Dr. Clinton's leadership investment. He wasn't just talking a good leadership game; he was playing it—all nine innings. The protégés at the table provided living evidence of a strategy at work.

It's easy to assess your actual leader-to-leader activity. Are your top people (senior pastor, staff, lay leaders) investing time and energy to build into groups of men and women who will represent the next generation of leaders? If so, your church is doing well at creating a fertile leadership development environment.

If not, then the strategies we will introduce in the next chapter will help, but they will be limited in effect until the new behaviors become part of the way you do ministry. Once you diagnose the current leadership culture, your teaching on the subject, and your leaders' actual habits, you will clearly see where change is required.

When a leader steps forward and declares, "Follow me," powerful words sink into the hearts of hearers in whom God is working. When our leaders and teaching pastors talk about the people they are developing as leaders, our developmental fertility increases. Small group ministry is served when key leaders in the church model the developmental activity they long to reproduce throughout the congregation.

To test how leaders are personally modeling leadership development, observe whether they delegate responsibility for meetings and events. Sadly, some leaders are insecure and cannot or will not share leadership. Jon Bodin recalls:

As I was emerging and developing as a leader, I had some insecurity. I'll never forget my very first small group. Talk about a control freak! I led every meeting. I planned everything. This poor habit continued even after I became the leader of an entire ministry area in the church. We held a retreat and I lined up the guest speaker—me! On the way to the retreat, five of my young guys said, "Jon, we've got to talk to you about something." It was a spiritual leadership coup, but a loving one. They sensitively, but truthfully, said, "Jon, we're ready to lead." And looking back, they really were ready. I was just holding on, keeping control. I was insecure about letting them have some responsibility, letting them share spiritual leadership. Fortunately, I had enough humility to say, "You're right." And that was a big turning point in the group, which God eventually blessed. They all became leaders.

Look for leaders who share leadership with others. When leadership is hoarded, development is stifled. Remember the "take Timothy" principle. It might be as simple as asking someone to take you to the airport to pick up the guest speaker for your missions conference. Instead of driving to the airport alone, take someone—anyone! Why not share the experience? Chances are, if there is ministry to be done, there is leadership to be shared. Make it a way of life.

Some of you are thinking, "I don't have a systematic plan for developing a leader. What do I do?" Just show up. Don't wait for the perfect strategy. Begin now to assess your opportunities for leadership development in the relationships you already have.

I (Bill) remember working with a small group leader who had hidden potential that apparently no one had discovered. It was a case of what might be called "role blindness." Because he wore a label—small group leader—we had treated him as one. I remember raising a leadership issue one day at breakfast, and this guy just came to life. He was deeply interested and offered engaging insights. I asked, "What, specifically, do you do at your company?" His answer stunned me. "I am responsible for developing leadership training initiatives for our managers." He had obviously answered this question before, but no one had ever said, "Wow! Maybe you can help us." His leadership potential and passion lay dormant.

Here was a man who loved to help leaders, but we had assumed his sphere of influence was limited to leading a group. Our lack of response to his work activity probably fueled his perception that the church world was so different and spiritual that his experience would be of no help. I met with him regularly for the next eighteen months. In that time he moved from small group leader, to a coach of leaders, to training coaches, to joining our leadership task force.

Assess your perception of people and their *potential* as leaders—taking into account their experience in the marketplace, the home, at school, in government, in other volunteer organizations. You may have limited their spiritual leadership potential based on their personality or current role in the church (usher, greeter, prayer team coordinator, choir member), allowing role blindness to hinder your vision.

## From Diagnosis to Treatment

After you assess your church's leadership fertility, you can treat obvious symptoms and form specific strategies for removing obstacles to reproduction. How fertile is your church for leadership development? Are you likely to reproduce leaders because of your culture, teaching, and modeling? Are you looking at people through developmental eyes? Perhaps your church requires focus on these important issues before moving on to specific strategies to correct an era of neglect. Once you have assessed your environment, you can choose among the wonderful tools available to help you consistently reproduce leaders.

# Chapter 8

# Strategies and Tools
# for Developing Leaders

Ever go to a water park? We have never seen so many creative uses for plastic tubing anywhere on earth: water slides, giant inner tubes, ramps, launches, waterfalls, and "power showers," all designed to channel water for unending hours of delight. The giant slides are the most fun to ride and watch. Each summer kids in creative bathing suits climb the forty-foot platform and sit down, eager for the wild, slippery descent through a large, enclosed plastic pipeline.

Speeding through these tunnels on the ride of your life, you often see only as far as the next turn. Water jets propel you through drops and twists all the way down, emptying you into a swimming pool. Kids climb in at the top, and you don't see them again until they emerge with a splash, laughing hysterically. It is a crazy adventure!

Sometimes, however, there is a delay at the top of the ride, and the steady flow of kids comes to a halt. Spectators watching at the pool don't notice the delay at the top. Instead, they begin to wonder why no one has come out at the bottom. Soon people understand that something—or someone—has caused a blockage at the top of the platform, preventing kids from plunging into the pipeline. It may be the lifeguards are changing places, or an unruly eight-year-old is trying to throw his sister down the slide. But as long as kids keep jumping in at the top, they are sure to come flying out at the bottom. Gravity never fails.

In too many churches most of us are spectators when it comes to developing leaders. At first, small group leaders come shooting through the pipeline in response to the new vision. Needing little training, this first crop of experienced leaders is eager to take the plunge. One day, however, no one emerges from the leadership pipeline to splash into the adventure of leading a little community. No one is coming out the bottom because no one is getting in at the top. Something—or someone—is blocking the way.

When the leadership pipeline dries up, small group momentum stops. We must make sure people get into the leadership development process so that leaders consistently come out the other end. In this section we show you how to keep your leadership pipelines open and active.

First, of course, you must create the conditions for leadership fertility, as we described in the last chapter. You must develop a leadership culture, teaching about the gift and role of leadership and expecting church leaders to model leadership development.

Now you're ready for systematic attention to your leadership pipeline. We suggest you concentrate more on selection than on development as you identify people to enter this pipeline. You can use either apprenticeships or turbo groups to determine which potential leaders in the pipeline are actually ready to splash into the adventure of leading a small group.

## Pay Attention to the Leadership Pipeline

The phrase "leadership pipeline" is not simply a metaphor; we use it to refer to people who have leadership potential. Paying attention to the leadership pipeline requires an intense focus on individuals. Pipeline health and productivity is a key measure of a division leader's effectiveness. Focusing on the leadership pipeline has enhanced the fertility of leadership development at Willow Creek.

You can find rising leaders and apprentices for your leadership pipeline by monitoring spiritual gifts, using special events, and talking with newcomers to your church.

Monitor people who are identifying their gifts through the *Network* process, so you can recruit people with gift sets common to effective small group leaders. Those with shepherding, leadership, administration, and teaching gifts have good potential to care for a flock. Be careful, however, not to miss potential leaders who have gifts not often associated with small groups. For example, the gift of helps is prevalent among leaders in our operations ministries, and mercy gifts abound among our community care ministry leaders, who design group life for broken people needing healing and compassion.

Use leadership gatherings to recruit potential leaders, not simply to equip existing ones. Our best recruiting events for rising leaders are our annual small group leadership retreats and conferences. Often 10 to 15 percent of those attending are nonleaders just checking out what it means to lead. We give these reluctant leaders a vision for ministry during conference sessions, and we gather them together during the event. We encourage them to consider how God might be preparing them for leadership. It is exciting to see as many as 60 percent of these rising leaders enter formal ministry roles within the next year.

A good leadership pipeline includes sensors for those suited for the fast track to small group leadership. One by-product of our increasingly mobile society is that many newcomers to church already have experience leading groups or ministries elsewhere. My own experience here taught me (Russ) the importance of getting to know newcomers.

Lynn and I invested seven years helping to plant a small church in North Dakota, so when we moved to Chicago, we were tired. We wanted to join a small group, but not to lead it. As we started to explore small group opportunities, however, ministry overseers asked about our background. We did everything but lie to avoid revealing our lifelong church commitments, Bible college education, and small group leadership experience. Willow Creek leaders were persistent but never demanding, praying and envisioning us into a leadership role. We were glad we agreed, not just for the investment we made in other couples but for the lesson I've learned to apply to my current ministry.

To this day, I never hesitate to challenge new people to consider the leadership game as soon as possible. In our membership class, I pull no punches about their need to steward the gifts and experiences they bring to this body. I remind them that God expects them to use these attributes to build up his bride, the church.

Using the principle of affinity, you can connect potential leaders to niche ministries quickly. Even newer Christians can be apprentice leaders (a concept we will discuss later in this chapter) in a seeker small group designed to help others like them embrace the faith. Kids' groups and ministry teams are also great places to connect new leaders seeking to serve. With the right coaching and training, these fresh recruits can move into positions of leadership.

## Concentrate on Selection More Than on Development

One of the most fascinating lessons we learned from studying nonprofit and profit-based organizations was to distinguish carefully between leadership selection and leadership development. Mark Miller, vice president of training and development for Chick-fil-A, Incorporated, and also a small group leader at Braelinn Church of Peachtree City, Georgia, drove this lesson home for us. Behind Mark's winsome southern drawl ("I'm just a chickin' saaalesmun") lie a bright mind and an experienced church leader. Mark is responsible for improving the performance of thousands of employees through the creation of a whole new leadership development process. His down-to-earth approach and pithy observations ("with every pair of hands, you get a free brain" and "if you have to decide who to choose, smart is good") make us glad for the time we have spent learning from him. Recently it occurred to us that though Chick-fil-A has had fifty years of uninterrupted success, the firm did fairly well without a formal leadership development system. Our obvious question to Miller: "How did you guys build a billion-dollar company with no leadership development program until now?" His answer changed the entire direction of our work at Willow: "That's easy," Mark responded. "We selected the right people." Then he explained the painstaking screening and placement process perfected over five decades and how they were incorporating this process into their approach to leadership development for the future.

After looking at other successful ministries and organizations, we discovered a common story. Leadership selection played a dominant role in each institution's success. So we decided to clearly state this principle for our people: 80 percent of the leadership development game is about selecting the right person in the first place. This does not invalidate the need to develop every leader you select. There is a both/and to selection and development. But we discovered that the solution to our leadership development problems was on the equation's selection side.

Our church, like most churches we've consulted, had put far more weight on developing anyone and everyone rather than on selecting the right people to develop. This "develop everyone toward leadership" focus is rooted in a discipling perspective, which appropriately focuses on helping every person mature spiritually. We assumed that every person automatically has potential to move beyond spiritual maturity to spiritual leadership, without asking whether we should yet select them to lead. This perspective prompted us to bypass any selection process.

We have begun new conversations about how we will screen for the right people and place them effectively. It has become necessary for us to reconsider the criteria for selecting potential leaders. And you will have to revisit the topic, as well. The decision to put people into the pipeline is commendable, but you will have far greater success if they are the *right* people.

With over forty years of combined experience in developing leaders, we've learned five tips that may help you select the right potential leaders for your pipeline:

*Focus on relationships.* If someone cannot relate well to people, his or her leadership capacity is low.

*Always be working with a few people.* You do not always need a formal group or process. Begin to do something with someone.

*Seize leadership moments.* Be prepared to pull someone aside and say, "What you just did demonstrated real wisdom and insight. I wish many of our leaders had that skill."

*Take calculated risks.* Don't be afraid to place someone in a role or task that requires leadership. Watch their response as they serve. Perhaps they will rise to the occasion in a way that surprises both of you.

*Use books to identify potential leaders.* Any good leadership book will do just fine. Classics like *Spiritual Leadership* by J. Oswald Sanders, *The Making of a Leader* by Robert Clinton, and *Leaders* by Bennis and Nanus are proven to make leaders' hearts beat faster.

## Define the Apprentice's Path to Small Group Leadership

The apprentice method—one unlearned person studying a craft under an experienced journeyman—attracted us to the metachurch model. We used the apprentice leader role as part of our strategy and, to this day, continue to reap much fruit from the practice. Most of us cannot imagine our present small group ministry without apprentice leaders and coaches. Your church can more quickly develop successful apprentices if you learn from our mistakes and follow a six-step process from apprenticeship to leadership.

### Avoid Common Mistakes

We've had a clear apprentice leadership philosophy for years and have had terrific results. Yet we've also made mistakes. Save yourself time by learning from our experiences. The following four mistakes are easy to avoid or correct.

*Blurring the distinction between assistant leaders and apprentice leaders.* Assistants do what leaders do not want to do (logistics, administration, phone calls, planning events). Apprentices do the same things that leaders do. The small group leader with an assistant often thinks, "I need help," whereas the leader with an apprentice ponders, "How can I help this person lead someday?"

*Cheating the system.* Remember when we gave the good news and bad news about cheating? Willow's commitment to connect every member into small groups meant that in 1991 and 1992 we had to retrofit a huge, complicated structure with small groups. We needed rapid acceleration to create far more ways for people to connect into community. So we cheated our system. After the first year we loosened restrictions and allowed small groups to begin without an identified apprentice. Beyond that, if anyone looked, felt, or smelled like a leader, we got them in the game as quickly as we could. We paid for these decisions. Inexperienced leaders made lots of mistakes, and few leaders learned how to develop a leader in training.

*Reaping results rather than selecting potential.* Kent Odor, once Willow Creek's area leader for operations and now director of spiritual formation for Canyon Ridge Christian Church in Las Vegas, Nevada, taught us this lesson. Drawing on small group experience with Lyman Coleman at Serendipity and from directing groups at East Ninety-First Street Christian Church in Indianapolis, Kent made an astute observation about how we selected apprentices. We were choosing apprentices we thought could become leaders overnight—in effect, reaping those who were already ripe. Instead, we needed to select people with demonstrated *potential* to lead.

*Setting the apprentice bar too high.* The number one objection voiced by potential apprentices is the perception that they will be asked to lead a group in thirty days. Over time we have tried to dispel that myth, asking simply that they be willing to be equipped for leadership someday. When that expectation is clear, apprenticing appears attainable.

### Follow a Six-Step Process

Unless there is a clear path for apprentice leaders to make their way into leadership, leaders in training will never realize their potential to shepherd their own flock. Here is a six-step process to move apprentices toward leadership.

*Provide basic training.* Every leader needs a basic orientation on leading small groups. Pilgrimage/NavPress and Serendipity have good elementary training resources. At Willow we designed a class called Foundations of Small Group Leadership, using *Leading Life-Changing Small Groups* as a core-skills training manual. We want every leader to have good facilitation skills and the ability to ask good questions and deal with difficult people. Improve your apprentices' success by giving them four to five hours of foundations class training.

*Involve apprentices in planning meetings.* Allow apprentices to look over your shoulder when you prepare for leading a group. It sounds simple, but actually planning a meeting together with the apprentice can be an effective exercise in leadership development, especially for new apprentices.

*Help apprentices lead a group meeting.* On-the-job learning is enhanced when an apprentice conducts a meeting and the leader observes and encourages. The leader can first delegate a portion of the meeting, such as prayer time or a good discussion question. Later the leader can ask the apprentice to lead an entire meeting. The leader can provide evaluation and feedback, and group members can see the apprentice's ability, building trust for the birthing process. How many meetings an apprentice should lead varies by skill level. Larger groups should form subgroups for part of a meeting, with the leader and the apprentice each taking part of the group—another step toward a healthy birth.

*Teach the apprentice to assess the group's spiritual development.* Leaders constantly evaluate group members' discipleship. The leader can ask the apprentice to help in this assessment. If your church has a framework for spiritual development, such as Willow Creek's five Gs, assessment will be easier. At Willow Creek, our leaders and apprentices often use our Shepherding Plan, a tool for analyzing where a group and its members are spiritually.[1]

*Encourage apprentices to attend specialized courses.* We ask apprentice leaders to participate in the courses any Willow Creek Community Church attendee would normally take. These include the *Contagious Christian Training Course, Network,* and *An Ordinary Day with Jesus.* This training in evangelism, spiritual gift assessment, and spiritual formation helps apprentices mature.

Some apprentices will also need ministry-specific training. Those leading children and students would benefit from training on developmental stages, and those in specialized care ministries need extra preparation for working with hurting and needy people.

*Help apprentices to embrace core values.* At Willow we require all leaders to become participating members of the church. Since the membership process is quite demanding (a five-week class or group process, personal Bible study, and an affirmation interview), this requirement increases the likelihood that leaders-to-be share our church values. Apprentices must also understand basic small group values, including the open chair, birthing, apprentice leadership, authenticity, covenants, and what it means to become a church *of* groups.

This process is not linear and may take several months. But defining the pathway to leadership not only assures some measure of leadership preparation; it also gives the apprentice some sense of progress.

Your process will probably differ. But do create a clear pathway of apprentice experiences and training, so you can keep your leadership pipeline stocked with quality people.

## Use Turbo Groups to Develop Leaders

A "turbo group" combines intentional leadership training with a healthy group experience. Every member of a turbo group is an apprentice, learning skills to lead his or her own group. Turbo groups work especially well when you are in start-up mode, either churchwide or within a department. The structure and process of the turbo group allows you to move inexperienced leaders into leadership roles more quickly, but without compromising quality. Through turbo groups, you can refine skills of those nearly ready to lead, while making sure they align with your church's values and mission.

The turbo group leader provides apprentices the opportunity to practice leadership skills with each other, as well as to observe and practice healthy group dynamics. The leader can divide apprentices into subgroups for prayer and peer-to-peer leadership mentoring. Some turbo group members experience filling the open chair as they or their leader spots others with apprenticing potential, which may lead to walking through a group birthing process. Along the way to "graduation," members of the turbo group should each identify the person they in turn will take on as an apprentice.

Turbo groups function much like regular groups and include typical group essentials: forming a covenant, experiential learning, study, prayer, service, and discussion. Make sure these apprentices experience everything you want them to reproduce in their own groups. Also include skill development, communication of vision and core values, and evaluation by the leader. Each meeting should follow much the same pattern of a regular small group, except that the curriculum is focused on leadership development and leadership issues.

We have developed a twelve-session approach to conducting a turbo group. Because many sessions require more than one meeting, we've found that training apprentices or leaders through turbo groups takes six to nine months. This usually includes half- or all-day retreats, too. If people have some leadership experience and simply need to be oriented and affirmed, a three-month turbo group should work. Regardless of the duration, you'll want to cover these twelve topics in your turbo groups. [2]

*Topic 1:* Get acquainted and form a covenant to reach agreement on the mission of the turbo group. Communicate the vision and values of small group ministry, weaving fun into the process of people getting to know each other.

*Topic 2:* Exchange life stories and pray for each other along the way. Keep reinforcing vision as the apprentices complete the process of getting to know each other. There will not be enough time in one meeting for everyone to share their life stories, so you can include one or two each week in the early stages of the group.

*Topic 3:* Train members to balance the roles of leader and shepherd. Blend role-playing and specific life situations into the learning, and make sure vision and values become embedded.

*Topic 4:* Add the experience of the open chair by incorporating a new member into the group if at all possible. Some turbo group leaders will form their group with potential new members in reserve, or the leader may challenge current members to identify a potential apprentice to join them.

*Topic 5:* Start delegating portions of the meeting to various group members. Give members the opportunity to lead a portion of the Bible discussion. They can do the lesson in pairs or work with the leader to prepare for their session. Make the Bible study real to the group's life.

If possible, have a retreat at this point to speed up the community-building process, to provide more opportunities for practicing leadership skills, and to catch up on storytelling or other aspects of the preparation process. Even a half-day getaway can boost turbo group progress.

*Topic 6:* Experiment with other group meeting elements, such as prayer, spiritual exercises, communion, or worship, to expand experiences for the leaders in training. Divide the apprentices into subgroups when it will enhance the learning. Remember, someday they will likely have to make subgroups in their own groups as they prepare them for birthing.

*Topic 7:* Discuss pastoral care, so members learn about meeting "extra care required" needs, both within a group and by seeking outside help. Real needs within the group may yield teachable moments about caregiving.

*Topic 8:* Begin challenging the group to identify apprentices they can invite to join them when the turbo group ends.

*Topic 9:* Use role-playing to teach conflict resolution skills and techniques, concentrating on implanting the values and practices of Matthew 5 and 18. By now your turbo group likely has some conflicts. Address them so members will know how to manage conflict when they lead groups.

*Topic 10:* Have the whole group design and plan a meeting together, leveraging all the learning so far to challenge each other's thinking. Consider doing this more than once, depending on the skills members demonstrate.

*Topic 11:* Prepare for birthing. Help the group deal with the emotional pain of the anticipated separation, and begin to do final evaluations of their leadership readiness. You may need to increase one-on-one encounters to shepherd members or to shore up their skills.

*Topic 12:* Graduate and commission the new leaders! Allow enough time to make the process poignant and celebrative. Endow each leader with a sense of blessing as they embark on the adventure of leading their own group.

The wise turbo group leader will carefully balance the pace of meetings and topics while assessing apprentice readiness to lead. It is like reproducing children: once you have the responsibility to train them, they will probably need to be kicked out of the nest without absolute assurance they are ready. They will make mistakes when they encounter real group life, yet they will also discover untapped potential on their own. Some will do better than others. The turbo group leader will feel labor pains in the process and joy at the delivery.

And like many first-time parents, some turbo group leaders will become eager for another birth and gather a new set of apprentices. We know small group directors and coaches who maintain a perpetual turbo group process, or birth a turbo group every ministry year. Leaders who were trained in turbo groups may, in turn, reproduce the process with their own apprentices, exponentially increasing the number of prepared leaders. The same principles of turbo groups can be applied to coaching as well, where a turbo huddle of apprentice coaches can more rapidly produce needed coaches.[3]

One word of caution is needed here. Sometimes only 50 to 60 percent of the turbo group moves into leadership roles. View this as positive. First, it allows you to assess your training methods and curriculum and make adjustments for the future. Second, it will help you select future candidates for turbo groups. And third, it will affirm the apprenticeship process. Imagine the 40 to 50 percent remnant of nonleaders trying to shepherd a small group! By first apprenticing them in a turbo group, you weed out those not ready or unskilled as leaders, despite their hints of potential. It's good risk management and healthy discipleship combined. Even the nonleaders in the group will grow, develop, and serve elsewhere in your church. Usually, it is a win-win situation.

### Facing the Leadership Development Challenge

When leadership is honored, taught, modeled, and shared, your church will become a fertile leadership production environment. You will begin to get the right people into the pipeline and then watch them come splashing into the pool of leadership. Believe us—they really do make a splash! And, yes, sometimes a few group members get wet. But if you work at it—like Jesus and Paul before you—be assured your pool will become filled with modern-day Timothys, Peters, Priscillas and Lydias. You might even find a Moses or Deborah swimming around.

You'll remember what these people were like when they climbed the tower, sat down on the slide, and looked into that long, dark tunnel called leadership development. Would they take the ride or let fear overcome them? Would they do something stupid, disqualifying themselves and keeping others from the adventure? Then you saw them take the leadership plunge and come out laughing with a joy only God can give.

Some of your people may be afraid to enter the pipeline, so you will **125** have to show them the way. And by God's grace, you will. The words of Christian singer-songwriter Steven Curtis Chapman, from his song "Dive," will spur you on:

> *I'm divin' in, I'm goin' deep,*
> *In over my head I wanna be.*
> *The river's deep, the river's wide,*
> *The river's water is alive.*
> *So, sink or swim, I'm divin' in!*

It's a wild and wonderful ride. We've done it many times. So we'll be at the bottom cheering you on. In case you don't recognize us, we'll be the guys with the video cameras and the big smiles. We promise not to show your kids! So what are you standing there for? Get on your bathing suit, grab a towel and some sunscreen, and climb that tower. Then just add water.

# Chapter 9

# Sin Five: Closed Group Mind-Set

*Symptoms of a Closed Group Mind-Set*
   *No vision exists for filling the open chairs in a group*
   *Leaders have not been trained how to invite people to the open chair*
   *Groups have little passion for seekers or fear having seekers in their
     groups*
   *People don't know how to relate to lost people when they come to
     groups*

Our small group leadership retreat in September 1999 was a "can't miss" event. Our leadership corps had grown to three thousand people, and we couldn't find an affordable Chicago-area facility for the retreat. So we trekked two hours north to Milwaukee, Wisconsin, and hoped God would make the commute, too. He did, and he blessed us with rich community as we worshiped, learned, huddled, and partied together. As the closing session neared, we had high hopes for a great ending to our time together.

We often introduce a guest artist at the retreat, hoping a fresh worship approach will impact the entire congregation. We've been privileged to expose our people to the likes of energetic Darlene Zschech from Australia and to Tommy Walker, who left with icicles dangling from his Southern California tan. Each led us to a new expression of worship to our great God. Darlene helped us discover and embrace a more vibrant and expressive worship style; Tommy opened our hearts even wider to the grace of God and his unending joy. So in 1999 we invited Alvin Slaughter. But we must admit, we were unprepared for what God would do in us through him.

It all began as anticipated. Alvin's joy-filled presence, vocal energy, and African-American musical influences inspired everyone to "give it up" for God early on. And then God showed up in a big way. I (Russ) will never forget looking around the conference hall as our generally conservative, white, suburban church folk unleashed a heartfelt—and unprecedented—stream of musical honor to God. Back then, only a few expressive people ever raised hands or offered spontaneous applause during our services. Alvin changed that. I was sitting next to Bill Hybels, just before his final message for that retreat. Choking back tears, I said, "Did you ever think you'd see Willow worship like this?" We laughed, shook our heads in wonder, and reengaged in celebration. When it ended, Bill stepped up to the podium.

"I *never* thought I'd see Willow worship like we just did," he admitted through a quivering voice. We knew how difficult it was to speak after such an incredible experience. Thankfully, it was Hybels and not me who had to figure out where to take our audience. I knew Bill was struggling as he told our leaders about our brief exchange. That's when God took hold of him.

"Everyone look up here at me. Arms stretched *upward,*" he said, as he lifted his normally staid Dutch hands, "should always end up being arms stretched *outward.*" He moved his arms and hands slowly downward, and stretched them toward the audience as wide and welcoming as he could physically manage. Repeating the gesture, he froze the picture in time for every one of us. "God knows nothing of a people who stretch their arms upward to him yet don't in turn stretch them out to those he loves so much. So much that his Son stretched out his arms to make it possible for them to be touched." For the next forty-five minutes Bill challenged us to be "radically inclusive" people, having arms stretched out as much as arms stretched up.

The dark side of falling in love with community is our inclination to form a holy huddle, intentionally or unintentionally. We love the fellowship of the body so much that we become addicted to it, closing our doors to those outside. Yet when *we* are on the outside looking in, we long to be invited into community. Once invited, we fully believe we would freely offer this gift to others. Sadly, we don't. We hoard it, protecting our newfound treasure from any interloper who might compromise our experience. Our arms stretch upward in the holy huddle we have discovered but never extend toward those still searching for a place at the table of community. Sin 5 has set in.

A closed group mind-set is a death sentence to true community. The dying is slow and initially imperceptible, like a degenerative illness whose outward effects are not yet fully manifest. But this truly is a **129** deadly sin. And it must be recognized and remedied.

The symptoms of closed group mind-set include lack of spiritual growth within groups and within the church as a whole, many attendees or members who aren't in groups, and groups that practice spiritual sugarcoating rather than authentic intimacy. Closed group mind-set happens because churches don't understand the open chair and are insensitive to seekers.

## Turning an Empty Chair into an Open Chair

What Bill Hybels gave our leaders in Milwaukee that day was renewed vision for the heart of God. As much as God loves uplifted hands, he may love outstretched hands even more. Our God is radically inclusive. Listen to the angel's announcement: "I bring you good news of great joy that will be *for all the people*" (Luke 2:10, emphasis added). Listen to the Savior's plea "that *all* of them may be one, Father, just as you are in me and I am in you. May they also be in us" (John 17:21, emphasis added). Outstretched arms, radically inclusive community: that's our standard. We follow one who purchased us with his arms stretched out on the cross.

If your church isn't living up to the standard of outstretched arms, chances are your church hasn't caught the vision of the open chair, misunderstands its use, or hasn't mastered the open chair's relationship to small group apprenticeship and birthing.

### Opening Their Eyes to the Open Chair

Without a clear vision for the open chair, groups don't grow spiritually. Nor do they reach their highest potential for serving the congregation as a whole. The average small group leader, running fast just to keep pace with life, feels relieved when members simply show up. After some socializing, one icebreaker, and an incomplete Bible study, he or she encourages everyone (despite their furtive glances at their watches) to remain for a closing prayer. As the meeting ends, the leader is grateful for any signs of growing friendships or met needs. With a few handshakes and hugs and a reminder to be on time next week, members hurry off to babysitters or to a favorite TV show. Relationships are fair and most members seem to enjoy the time. What's the point in challenging the group to do anything more?

As I (Bill) travel the world to work with small group ministries, group leaders ask the same questions. "How can we be expected to add people to the group while trying to get to know the ones we already have? How can we go deeper with new people coming all the time?" Groups like these—without knowing it—can actually function as secret societies. A few people meet, close the doors, settle on their ground rules, learn the secret language (churchspeak), and embrace the belief system (what we could call "groupthink"). People who leave are viewed as dissenters or as uncommitted, and no newcomers are added.

Certainly not all closed groups act this dysfunctionally, but we see it far too often. It is a rare group that never adds new people yet attains new levels of spiritual growth and challenge. More often, the leader assumes the status quo and carries on business as usual. He or she is unaware of these dynamics or doesn't see how they'll hurt the group.

Working with our RATS ("Russ's Alternative Team Strategies") serving small group, taught me (Russ) why the open chair is vital to a group's ability to serve the church. It would have been easy to settle for a closed group mind-set, because just gathering these busy executives was hard. Demanding jobs and limited time required us to combine task and community. People came late, left early, and battled ringing cell phones and buzzing pagers. Helping them shift gears from their competitive, intense worlds and embrace community was one of my toughest ministry challenges. While I was glad I'd invited these gifted players to help us make sense of our complex ministry, leading them was no cakewalk.

From the start, we agreed that the group was experimental, that we didn't know how it would work. Some people cycled out of the group when they realized it was not a fit for them, while others dropped out due to life circumstances or relocation by their company. Since we knew some members might leave, our experiment included keeping an "open chair" in our circle. The open chair represented our desire to invite potential members to a meeting. During the entire time the RATS group existed, we filled this chair again and again.

One Friday afternoon—three years after the group started—I looked around the circle and had a startling realization. Of the eight people present, only two of us had been there from the start (not unusual for a high-task strategy group). A half dozen members had come and gone. (I checked my deodorant; it wasn't because of me!) Our group would have died if we hadn't filled the open chair. And the loss would have been far worse than eclipsed community. That group helped Willow Creek launch an exciting vocational ministry internship. It helped our church redesign ministry responsibilities for optimal effectiveness and sanity. The RATS team also inspired two major evangelistic initiatives that reinvigorated our church. I could go on and on about what that group helped our church achieve—because the open chair kept the group alive.

What was true for the RATS team is true for most groups. Our mobile culture and life tragedies or circumstances all work to pull people from groups. Groups with a closed mind-set are guaranteed a short life span.

Every group needs to embrace the *vision* for a radically inclusive community. However, *reality*—not vision—will shape most small group leaders' thinking. The gap between vision and reality will indicate how you are doing with respect to this sin. That gap is your opportunity. So take heart. Where there is great sin, there is great opportunity. ("So," you ask, "shall we sin more that opportunity may abound?" May it never be!)

### Do They Know How to Use It?

Clear vision must turn into practice. How you describe the open chair will directly affect whether and how small groups make it a regular part of their experience. We were able to correct our leaders' vision, but we did not do so well in correcting how they used the open chair.

In our zeal to communicate the vision, we had assumed everyone knew how to actually fill an open chair. Wrong assumption. Some leaders thought we would send people to them as we had done in our previous small group program. We fostered this assumption by sending them lists of names—people who had expressed interest in a group. We did not ask permission, we simply sent names. Groups thought we were telling them to immediately invite these unknown folks to their groups. "Use the open chair" began to mean "Here is a guy; take him." Group leaders feared they might get an axe murderer or a *Jerry Springer Show* alumnus.

Groups needed the ability to participate on their terms. We had to ask their permission before we introduced new people to them. Even better, we had to shift our focus to encouraging them to fill the open chair from their own relational networks with unconnected people. Soon a compelling vision was combined with sensible practice, and that started to resonate with leaders.

Assess how your church communicates the vision and practice of the open chair. Neglecting either one will foster a closed group mind-set that creeps into all your groups.

### Solving the Right Problem

The open chair is just one of three interrelated dynamics in small group ministry, along with birthing and apprenticing. By filling open chairs and developing an apprentice leader, a group can eventually birth a new group. Often half of the group joins the apprentice (who is about to become a leader), and the other half of the group remains with the original leader. Rightly used, the open chair culminates in the birth of two healthy groups where there once was one. Fending off a closed group mind-set is like a three-legged stool: the open chair, birthing, and apprenticing combine to make open groups work well.

But here's where we lacked some wisdom. In our efforts to grow the ministry, we emphasized all three legs of the stool equally. There was only one problem with this. Our groups averaged five members at the time. We had done a great job getting groups started. But they were too small to birth new groups. We had almost 2,200 small groups in the church, so if we just added one person per small group during one ministry season, we could connect 2,200 more people into community. We needed to fill open chairs!

That is called leverage. We could increase average group size to seven or eight people, adding thousands to groups, without even having to identify a leader, interview them, get them into church membership, train them, or have them get an apprentice. We had constructed a wonderful net with which to catch people but had not used it to our advantage. Rather than emphasize filling the open chair, which would have fit our group size circumstances, we stressed apprenticing (an acceptable thing, since quite a few groups lacked one), and kept highlighting birthing—which has to go down as one of the real bonehead plays in small groups history. Groups of five birthing? Duh!

Most churches we work with face the opposite problem. They have a shortage of leaders, their groups lack apprentices, and most people are reluctant to birth. As a result, the average group has fifteen to twenty members. Since groups are saturated, the small group ministry begins to stall out, waiting lists increase, and the staff begins begging anyone with a pulse to lead a group. Churches in these situations must emphasize leadership development and apprenticing before waving the open chair flag.

Churches must also assess the potential *audience* available for small groups—the unconnected people in your church. Back when Willow Creek's small groups averaged five members, we surveyed our congregation's spiritual condition and commitment. We discovered that almost 3,800 Christians regularly attended our weekend services but weren't connected in a small group. Nor were they tied to any ministry, volunteering, pursuing participating membership, bringing their lost friends to church, or meeting the needs of the poor in our community or downtown Chicago. And they indicated no intention to change their patterns of church participation, remaining satisfied with weekend attendance and no more.

It was tempting to get angry with these uncommitted "stuck" believers. Instead, they represented an opportunity and showed that our system was far from saturated. But to reach and connect these people, we had to teach and practice the open chair. To the extent that we could move people to extend arms up *and out,* we had plenty of folks to connect.

When you carefully diagnose your vision for open groups, your use of the open chair, you, and your group's size, you will see how a closed group mind-set can limit the impact of small groups in your church. And you can design the right strategies for opening groups to an unlimited audience of available people.

## Making Room for Seekers

Our church has been known for its evangelistic passion far longer than for its passion for community. For years "reaching seekers" and "Willow Creek" were synonymous to many observers. As our passion increased for connecting people to groups, the evangelism and community values collided—at the open chair. The people who'd discovered community within their small group grew reluctant to share it with those on the outside. Ironically, closed groups that try to hoard community will destroy it. Meanwhile, groups that practice the open chair—especially those open to seekers—will find true community. Dietrich Bonhoeffer's dictum rings true. "He who loves his dream for community more than community itself, destroys the latter."

If your church has cast a vision for the open chair, yet groups don't grow spiritually or numerically, the reason may be that your small groups are insensitive to seekers. Both believers and seekers lose out when any of the following ten closed-group behaviors are displayed. (If groups display these behaviors, they will often have a hard time with connecting believers, too!)

### Group Hasn't Agreed to Embrace Seekers

Filling an open chair with a seeker won't work unless the entire group—not just the leader or an evangelistic zealot in the group—agrees to the decision and its implications. If only one person invites seekers into the group and others do not embrace the vision, things get scary real fast. "I can't wait for my seeking friend to meet the Christians in my group!" thinks the zealot. Meanwhile, the Christians are thinking, "Who invited this heathen to infiltrate our group? He doesn't fit in or understand the faith. He acts in carnal ways and will probably disrupt the group. What are we going to do?" Soon the seeker senses the negative and awkward atmosphere, feels unwelcome, and never returns. All must agree to embrace seekers or it will become a point of contention and conflict.

For example, a Bible study designed for established believers may alienate seekers. Meetings devoted exclusively to certain seeker issues may feel shallow to believers. Everyone must face this tension to understand the sacrifices required to accommodate seekers. When there is consensus and commitment, however, most groups at Willow Creek can engage in discussions from either viewpoint with authenticity and engagement.

### Group Has No Heart for Seekers

As harsh as it may sound, some closed groups may not care about lost folks coming to faith and entering the community of Christ followers. They decline to pursue "seeker" training so they can relate better to lost friends and relatives, learning how to speak truthfully but relevantly to them. These groups aren't yet willing to emphasize seeker needs and priorities and consider others better than themselves (as Philippians 2:3 instructs us to do). It is not a lack of consensus, but rather a lack of conviction.

### Group Values Events over Process

Many people have been trained in event-focused evangelism, which aims to identify the lost, invite them to an event, and quickly deliver the message. People who like this approach don't expect to see the invitation recipients again. ("If they don't respond, they must not be elect!" goes the rationalization sometimes.) Others try "contact evangelism," making contacts and sharing a standard evangelistic message or tract. Closed groups feel more comfortable with event-focused or contact evangelism than with a long process of getting to know a seeker. But these quick-fix tactics make seekers feel like targets for someone's evangelistic arrows. Group members inadvertently send seekers the message, "We will accept you in this group when you become a Christian." Pressure strategies and "turn or burn" presentations ignore the relational and process components of evangelism, creating undue pressure on the seeker to trust Christ. In contrast, many seekers need time in the safety of a loving community to ask questions, wrestle with truth, and express fears and doubts. Most seekers simply want to feel loved for who they are, not for what they believe.

### Group Is Shocked When Seekers Act Like Seekers

Closed groups seem to forget that because seekers are not regenerate people, their conduct is consistent with nonregenerate worldviews and values. (Sometimes seekers behave more consistently with their value systems than we do with ours.) As seekers start to feel comfortable with the group, they may share an off-color remark, and pristine Christian ears respond, "*What* did she just say?" Or seekers might describe their party weekend, momentarily taking the group on a virtual reality tour of the prodigal's life. The world of the seeker (and of some Christians!) is not necessarily real clean or real churchy—just real.

### Group Sugarcoats Problems

Seekers can sniff out the slightest whiff of hypocrisy. Most seekers recognize when Christians sugarcoat problems or spiritualize complex issues. "We found marijuana in our teenage son's room, but we are living in the Spirit, seeking God's joy and his perfect will, knowing that he makes all things work together for good." A seeker thinks, "C'mon, give me a break! You were never angry or sad? Didn't you feel some disappointment? Don't you feel deceived?"

Any kind of veneer, something many of us tolerate among Christians, will become palpable when seekers are present. In contrast, when people move deeply into each other's lives with authenticity, acceptance, and care, everything changes. True community—not very prevalent in our day— is the result, acting as a magnet that will draw them in. When non-Christians observe and taste community, it has transforming power. *My, how they love one another!*

But here's the irony for most small groups. It is this longing for community that actually keeps them from inviting seekers. They assume the presence of seekers will destroy their group's hard-won intimacy. However, when we interview believers who have opened their groups to seekers, we find a common thread of experience—the authenticity factor increases, creating deeper intimacy and relationship.

(As you assess openness to seekers, learn from those who have actually taken the risk of connecting seekers into their community, not the presuppositions from those who have never tried.)

### Neglects Logistics

Groups already comfortable with their own routines don't go out of their way to appeal to seekers, especially those newcomers who prefer to observe without being forced to participate. Closed groups can handle meeting on cold metal folding chairs in a church basement. They don't necessarily mind whether meetings start and end on time, respecting schedules and honoring commitments. By contrast, a group open to seekers pays attention to simple logistics, such as comfortable chairs, a friendly room, enough space, refreshments, and regular breaks. Just as you might do when inviting a new friend to dinner, groups open to seekers consciously create a warm, inviting atmosphere so that belonging and participation feel normal and desirable.

### Uses Churchspeak

Closed groups use language that assumes everyone present is not only a Christian but also a Christian of a specific sort. Closed groups love Christian lingo. They use phrases like "How's your walk?" "Isn't it great to be under the blood!" and "He's my Ebenezer!"—unaware or uncaring that any seekers present will think of their feet, their gall bladder operation, and Uncle Scrooge. These groups would rather force seekers into a theologically cross-cultural experience than translate key theological terms that are so important to believers but scary to seekers.

### Intimidates with Scripture

Some groups fail to think about their use of Scripture. Never shy away from Scripture because seekers are in a group. The Bible is the source of redemptive truth, the foundation for the faith, our guide for life and ministry. So every group should use Scripture, whether or not seekers are present. Unfortunately, closed groups use Scripture in a way that intimidates, rather than intrigues, seekers. You know the type. Their Bibles have every other verse underlined, contain margin notes, and are highlighted in nine colors. Some of these people love Bible trivia. Such leaders routinely say, "Open up to Amos, chapter two," blithely assuming that everyone present has a Bible and knows where to find Amos. In a seeker-sensitive group, however, the leader provides everyone with the same edition of the same Bible version. These leaders say "Turn to Mark 10, that's page 356, where Jesus is speaking to a rich young government official."

### Chooses Esoteric Study Topics

Closed groups often love esoteric topics, especially those based on Revelation. If they cared more about being seeker sensitive, they could choose among curricula that are both wonderfully beneficial to Christians and accessible to seekers. Some of these studies address everyday concerns, such as worry, stress, money, or relationships. Other seeker-sensitive groups start with questions common to all seekers: who is God, what about the presence of evil and suffering, does life have meaning, are all religions the same, does absolute truth exist? Groups that move from study to action inspire growth and demand engagement. Seekers see their need for Christ and also observe acts of kindness and service toward others, demonstrating how Christianity can meet real-world needs. Groups that combine study and compassionate service are often more seeker friendly than most people think, having a dramatic impact on nonchurched attendees. (The next chapter will present many excellent curricula suggestions.)

### Doesn't Have Any Other Seekers

Another closed group tip-off is that any seeker who does happen to wander in won't find another seeker present. Imagine being the lone seeker in a group of committed Christ followers. If you can't imagine it, then go to your local mosque and attend a service or, better yet, a discussion group on the Koran. Now, imagine taking three friends with you. Feels better, right? The safety factor increases, and you don't feel like such an outsider. Inviting other seekers creates dialogue that is open to the honest investigation of truth.

By raising the value for openness to seekers, you will force your group to wrestle with the question of openness in general. On many occasions groups are not yet ready to connect seekers. As they aspire to do so, however, they become open to inviting unconnected believers as well. In a women's group at Willow, two seekers had been invited to join the group—or so the group thought. After the first few meetings **139** it became apparent that one was indeed a believer who had never been developed. Because she lacked a basic understanding of the faith, it was assumed she was an unbeliever. By being open to connecting seekers, you may stumble upon a few believers who need a home.

## Contagious Communities

Determine whether your small groups are catching your vision for openness and the opportunities it affords them. Make sure you have described how to use the open chair, and emphasize it appropriately in conjunction with apprentice development and birthing. Then diagnose the potential for groups to be open to seekers and believers alike.

We long for you to discover the redemptive potential of small groups. Once discovered, boldly develop a strategy to open your groups and watch God do amazing things. He will create contagious communities like the community in Acts 2, where "everyone was filled with awe" and "every day they continued to meet together," while "the Lord added to their number daily those who were being saved" (Acts 2:43, 46–47). But what would you expect? When God's fingerprints are all over the community, it functions as he intended. "Jesus replied, 'Love the Lord your God with all your heart and with all your soul and with all your mind.' This is the first and greatest commandment. And the second is like it: 'Love your neighbor as yourself'" (Matt. 22:37–39). That's arms stretched upward *and* outward!

# Chapter 10

# Strategies and Tools for Transforming Group Mind-Set

I (Russ) practiced law full-time for fifteen years before devoting myself to my current role. My experiences within law firms were even more exciting than in the courtroom. After serving as partner, then managing partner, of one firm, Lynn and I set out on a high-stakes adventure, leaving behind security and position to start a new firm. It would change the course of our lives forever.

Motivated by a sense of calling to be involved at Willow Creek, we risked all we owned and moved to Chicago in 1995, starting a new law practice from scratch. After we managed a few harrowing escapes from business disaster, our fledgling enterprise got off the ground. We found a unique niche in the Chicago legal services market, and our future looked promising. Although our office was thirty-five miles outside Chicago, we recruited great personnel from large downtown firms. We were poised to build a sophisticated practice in a convenient suburban location. Our competition was light, since most suburban firms focused on smaller, routine legal services. Only one obstacle kept us from forging ahead: some team members were stuck in a suburban mind-set.

As the firm's founding and managing partner, I needed to expand their vision so we could be more than also-rans. A compelling concept began forming in my mind. By taking advantage of our location near the increasing numbers of companies that had moved out of Chicago, we could compete with larger downtown firms. I started casting the vision for us to "build a downtown firm in the suburbs."

As the idea caught on, clients and staff began to feel part of something bigger, something exciting. We attracted top-notch legal talent and soon converted a lackadaisical suburban mind-set into an aggressive, high-potential frame of mind. Vision changed our direction and actions toward a new, energizing future.

Vision changes people—in business and in the church. But it isn't easy. Small group leaders locked into a closed group mind-set reinforce community closure and rob energy from church ministry. Transforming closed group mind-sets into open hearts for seekers requires following a compelling vision with a dynamic strategy.

In the case of small groups, there are two strategic battlefronts. The first vision battle involves changing the entire church's view of small groups. The second battle will be fought in the groups themselves, transforming them from their closed and inward-looking orientation to becoming contagious communities focused on the plight of those on the outside looking in.

## Empty Seats at the Table of Community

God is an open-chair God. None of us would be Christ followers today were it not so. So his church must reflect his character and passion. That means an all-out assault on the tendency toward isolation. It takes everybody—elders, board members, a committed senior pastor, the staff, small group leaders, and key volunteers—to make it happen. You must address many issues to fill empty seats at the table of community.

### Teach about Community

Nothing reinforces the call to openness like sound biblical teaching. Fortunately, the Bible contains a treasure trove of potential teaching content. God's approach has always been to gather a people unto himself for the purpose of redeeming the world.

You may need to do an entire message series on the theme of community, highlighting God's desire that none should perish (2 Peter 3:9), but that all people would repent, believe the gospel, and enter the new community. At Willow we have taught entire series about "Enlisting in Little Platoons" or doing "Life in a Little Community."

Sometimes we weave a theme throughout an entire teaching season. As we write this book, John Ortberg is teaching through the Old Testament in ten months, from September to June. Dubbed "The Old Testament Challenge," the focus is on God's work with and through the nation of Israel, building a community to reach the world for his glory. Sometimes, however, John pauses to link small group community to God's broader plan. This community—as conceived by God—can only realize its redemptive potential by being deeply committed to him *and* profoundly dedicated to reaching outside itself.

### Talk about the Open Chair

I (Bill) remember first casting the open-chair vision to a group of leaders. Many were stunned, some sat motionless, and a few were downright antagonistic. The broad response indicated we had a lot of work to do. "Evangelism" made sense, of course. But what was this open chair? We used this phrase to evoke a picture for our audience, an image to remind them of their mission. Though not everyone interpreted it correctly at first, they soon got the clear message that this was a new day, and groups would regularly assimilate new people.

Whatever phrase you choose (open chair, empty chair, a seat at the table, each one reach one), it must communicate the vision in clear, simple terms. It serves as a constant reminder that the churchwide cause is each group's responsibility. On occasion we introduce fresh language to complement the open-chair concept and to remind our small groups that they should fill chairs. During one ministry season we employed the theme "Community with a Cause" to highlight how we band together in small groups to connect everyone at Willow Creek into community. Bill Hybels has challenged our people not to "stockpile" community but instead to reach out to "strays," while Lon Solomon, senior pastor of McLean Bible Church in Virginia, has exhorted his people to "be channels, not vaults."

When your language changes, actions follow. Ministries begin exploring strategies for implementing the new vision, and members recall the ultimate cause for which Christ died—world redemption. The right words matter.

### Model Openness

Bill Hybels often tells stories about "strays" he invites into his community, modeling the practice for our congregation. Teaching Pastor John Ortberg led a one-year seeker small group (in which a Christian leads a group of spiritual seekers through a study that addresses their questions) and created renewed energy for others to embark on the same adventure. The openness quotient rises and falls according to how the most visible leaders model it.

Some churches require that leaders grow and birth a group before becoming a coach, so that they have modeled the ministry before working with others. Coaches who speak from personal experience can authentically encourage their groups to become more open.

I (Bill ) have trained many small group leaders at Willow Creek and other churches. They always ask about the open chair, especially, "Do you practice what you preach?" Russ and I can both answer a resounding yes to that question. We must do our best to live out this ministry value.

### Find Apprentices

While other strategies to attack a closed group mind-set are up to senior pastors and teachers, finding apprentices rests squarely in the hands of coaches and small group leaders. Coaches reinforce group openness by holding leaders accountable for identifying apprentices. Coaches increase the entire church's connectivity potential by helping leaders spot possible apprentices within their groups. Likewise, the small group leader keeps a group fertile for birth by investing in an apprentice.

Since the apprentice's presence is a constant reminder to grow and birth, a group that does not add members yet has an apprentice becomes dysfunctional. The apprentice cannot lead unless the group grows. One of two things must happen: either the apprentice will leave to start a new group, or he or she will force the group to add people to the open chair.

In one group I (Bill) led with my wife, several members had a closed group mind-set. After I introduced our apprentice leaders and cast a vision for group reproduction, Paula, a Ph.D. in communication, confronted me with what she affectionately called "the birthing thing." My skin still quivers when I recall the exchange. "I'm against the birthing thing, I don't like the open chair, and I think breaking up groups is terrible." I thought, *Okay, tell me how you really feel!* Calmly (but carefully) I asked, "How did you get into this group?" Looking perturbed, she replied, "You asked me, remember?" "And how long had you and your husband been waiting for a group in this area?" She **145** thought and said, "About a year." Then I took a risk. "I wonder what might have happened if there hadn't been an open chair for you in *this* group. Or I wonder if your wait would have been shorter if every group had an apprentice and a few open chairs. Perhaps there would have been more groups and more places months ago for people like you. Ever wonder about that?" I waited for a stinging rebuke or objection from this opinionated woman. Instead, she said, "I get it!" and walked away. In time her fears gave way to the realization that no one should wait a year for a seat at the table of community.

### Select Curriculum

Selecting the right curriculum is critical so that groups can maintain entry points for newcomers. We've noticed two issues. First, groups tend to welcome new members only when they begin a new study. So when they select a series that extends for two years, their likely openness to new members is slim. It's better to choose topical studies of shorter length, such as the six- to eight-week studies available from InterVarsity, Zondervan, or Serendipity. (More recommendations are listed in appendix 5.) It is also easier to assimilate new group members when the curriculum dovetails with a preaching series, since everyone is exposed to the material weekly.

Second, groups that intend to invite seekers must choose curriculum that connects with believers and seekers alike. In fact, authenticity and learning increase when Christians and seekers discuss the tough questions that seekers ask but Christians rarely consider—such as evil and suffering, or why we believe the Bible is true, or what other religions teach. Studying together challenges unbelievers to face the truth. It also strengthens Christians' faith, increasing their courage to share with seekers outside the group.

### Tell Stories

Stories connect truth with life. Jesus used them to teach the gospel, convict people of sin, encourage the weak, rebuke the legalists, and teach wisdom. Stories of groups filling the open chair can do the same. Sermon illustrations, videos, newsletters, tapes, live interviews, or a "my story" segment in the weekend service all work to make the point. When pastors share how they personally use the open chair, people think, *Our pastor is doing this, not just talking about it.* Then, when other members of the congregation describe their experiences, people realize that "average" members fill open chairs. It's exciting when former seekers tell how an open group moved them toward faith in Christ— now, that's a motivator!

We remember when Scott and Keri told their story in the early days of our small group transition. Many people were still wondering whether real groups and real people actually filled open chairs, invited seekers, developed apprentices, and birthed groups. Maybe it was just a mirage. But Scott and Keri dispelled the myths and fears. These two had invited seekers who came to faith, invested in them as apprentices, and then birthed them as leaders of new groups. Then they did it again. And soon the groups Scott and Keri birthed began to reproduce the process. (At one point we counted twelve to fifteen groups that came from Scott and Keri's original group.) Birthing moved from theory to reality pretty fast; so much for the closed group mind-set.

## Creating a Contagious Group Mind-Set

The full potential of an outward-oriented community will be real-ized when groups move from an open group mind-set to a *contagious* mind-set. At Willow Creek, we use the term "contagious" to signify a person or group that reaches spiritual seekers with our church's touch and, ultimately, with the gospel. We encourage every person at Willow Creek to experience the *Becoming a Contagious Christian* training course, and we encourage church leaders to digest Mark Mittelberg's book, *Building a Contagious Church.*

### Snapshots of Contagious Groups

Willow Creek has committed to maintaining a contagious Christian mind-set. Yet I (Russ) hadn't really noticed how it applied not just to our sixty seeker small groups but also to our entire small groups ministry. Then the Willow Creek Association asked me to teach about groups at an international conference. Garry Poole, Willow Creek's director of evangelism, was supposed to teach on evangelism and seeker small groups at the same conference. At the last minute, Garry wasn't able to attend. His substitute? Me, a person whose evangelism gift finishes dead last in any spiritual gift profile I've ever taken. But as Garry and I huddled to figure out how I could do the training, I started to see the enormous potential to combine contagious Christian concepts, including Garry's teaching about seeker groups (some of which follows in adapted form), with the life of every small group in a church.

Let us give you three snapshots of how a group's mind-set can move from open to contagious, so the group extends its hands to Christians and seekers alike. Each snapshot will give you an idea of how our groups vary in scope and formality. Besides setting up a strategy for building an open group mind-set, the stories will begin to set up sin 6, narrow definition of a small group. Observe how each group becomes contagious, and then learn how contagious small groups can be built.

The first snapshot is a men's small group. Every other Thursday, five guys gather over dinner at a local restaurant. They share what is happening in their lives, discuss a book, and pray together. These men do all the things many small groups do.

But periodically the leader asks what each guy is doing evangelistically. Each member talks about relationships he's building with lost friends, about opportunities to tell someone his spiritual story. They discuss inviting these nonchurched people to Willow Creek's seeker services and pray for their relationships with these friends. The mutual accountability and encouragement spurs members to maintain their evangelistic edge, helping the group become increasingly contagious.

The second snapshot is a group that lives in the world of motorcycles, a less formal approach to a small group but representative of the variety of groups at Willow. The bikers and their bikes come in all shapes and sizes. Luxurious touring motorcycles ride next to loud cruisers, and elaborately tattooed Harley riders travel beside young, aggressive sport bikers. But they have one thing in common—they ride together as Christian friends, building community along the highway of life.

**148** This group has taken a risk (beyond cycling with Chicagoland drivers); they have turned pleasure riding into an opportunity to build a growing network of non-Christian, motorcycle-owning friends. Amazing things have occurred during their evening rides for ice cream, morning rides to breakfast hangouts, or long trips through the American countryside. Some seekers have found Christ through that group of cycle-loving Christians, and others are attending Willow Creek seeker services. This group has turned a leisure activity into an evangelistic adventure, doing an activity together that many riders would have normally performed solo. This group has stepped from discussing their individual evangelistic efforts to pursuing group evangelism—becoming a contagious community.

The third snapshot—if you look carefully—is not really a group yet. It consists of married couples that met through what they have in common—children, school, sports, and neighborhood activities. One couple has been at our church for years, while another just began attending. Another couple is devoutly Catholic and loyal to their church, but they might be open to joining a neighborhood Bible study. The fourth couple is on the spiritual fringe, respectful but evasive when the discussion turns to church or faith.

The Willow Creek couple plans to initiate conversation with the small group they lead about the possibility of inviting these friends someday. They envision how welcomed these nonchurched friends would feel in the company of an ongoing small group, and how it could be a good place for their friends to investigate Christianity in the context of safe relationships. If the group is willing to make its open chair available to seekers, it will go from being an open community to being a contagious small group.

### The Three Levels of Contagious Small Groups

These three snapshots picture three kinds of contagious small groups. One assists its members to be more active in reaching seekers. Another actively reaches seekers as a group, through a series of social connections where Christians and lost people can be grouped together to create spiritual interaction. The last will come together in the context of their small group time to help seekers move individually and together toward Christ. In effect, they represent three levels of contagious small groups, so let's take a moment to unpack how a previously closed group might progress from the first to the third level.

### Level 1: Groups Talk about Individual Evangelistic Efforts

In level 1, contagious small group members regularly talk about their individual evangelistic efforts. They hold each other accountable for next steps to build relationships or share their faith. It is an explicit part of the group's covenant to have such discussions and to pray regularly for each other and their lost friends.

These level 1 groups are different from average small groups in four distinct ways. First, they provide a strategy for mobilizing all members for evangelism. If you can get every group focusing on lost friends, building relationships, sharing their own story, and praying, evangelistic fruit will result. In the typical group, however, too few people understand how to build relationships with nonchurched people, let alone share a verbal witness of their faith in Christ. Evangelism is understood as the job of the senior pastor or those with evangelism gifts. Accordingly, group members rarely produce evangelistic fruit.

Second, level 1 contagious groups impact members with stories of eternal significance, celebrating the transformation of those who have come to faith. Many groups have good stories; members of level 1 groups can tell *great* stories.

The third reality is that evangelistic activity injects new life into the group. By contrast, most small groups become stale with age. The best way to inject new life into groups is to get them to experiment with being contagious. Groups have a life cycle. Unless they experience fresh energy through evangelistic activity, groups plateau and lack full spiritual vigor.

Finally, level 1 contagious groups sharpen members' long-term evangelistic edge. Members who leave the group will recall being energized through increased evangelistic activity. Few people think of group experiences as evangelistically empowering, because huddling with other Christians too often dulls their evangelistic edge. Level 1 contagious groups, however, create a legacy that outlasts group life span.

And by the way, every small group in a church should be able to function at the first level of being a contagious group. Once they fall into the rhythms of regular sharing, accountability, prayer, and fruitfulness, they'll pass the point of no return. They'll forever defeat closed group mind-set and will move from being open to being contagious.

### Level 2: Groups Do Evangelism Together

After functioning at the first level, some groups move from individual sharing and accountability to doing evangelism together. A group entering level 2 can take four steps to create their first joint evangelistic effort.

*Cast the vision.* Study God's heart for lost people. Read Luke 15 or study an evangelism curriculum together. In the context of the study, prompt members to consider group evangelism. Members can name fears and concerns, identify obstacles, and relate their past experiences doing evangelism alone. Together they can begin to envision what could happen as they work together to reach their lost friends.

*List and pray.* Each group member should name one or two friends they could invite to join in safe, fun activity with the group. Pray for God to draw people in and for the Holy Spirit to prepare lost friends for a social connection with the group. Such interactions will build trust and generate spiritual discussions.

*Get equipped.* Check one another's ability to effectively share the gospel with someone. Discover your abilities to build relationships with lost people and share a verbal witness to the faith. In this way you can discern readiness. The group can also improve skills through a group-focused *Contagious Christian Training* study.

*Throw a party.* When the group feels prepared to take the last step in being a level 2 contagious group, it should brainstorm ideas for a social gathering they can do together. At Willow Creek, we call this a "Matthew Party," based on the Luke 5 description of Matthew inviting his tax collector friends to his house for dinner with Jesus and the disciples. There his friends might rub shoulders with believers and be influenced spiritually. Once the Matthew Party is planned, it is simply a matter of the group enjoying the social setting they have created with their friends.

Groups at Willow Creek have used all kinds of activities to step up to level 2. Going to dinner and a movie, attending a sporting event, or gathering for a backyard cookout are just a few examples, but the opportunities are unlimited.

Level 2 contagious small groups require no specific agenda other than preparing yourself to discuss "the hope that is in you" (1 Peter 3:15) and brainstorming social gatherings to build relationships. The Holy Spirit will be at work, softening hearts, and opening opportunities. New relationships will likely form, setting the stage for more social interaction. Now the foundation has been laid for level 3 group activity.

### Level 3: Groups Fill Open Chairs with Seekers

Now it's time to fill open chairs with seekers, those for whom you have been praying and with whom you have built some relationship. The group has progressed from building personal accountability for evangelism and pursuing evangelism together, to including seekers as part of their small group community. For some groups, there may be a couple of other stops along the way to filling the open chair with seekers.

One means toward this goal is to maximize seeker events at your church. These may be special Christmas or Easter services, special outreaches or presentations, or guest speakers who know how to speak to (and with) the spiritually curious. A group should discuss the role of seeker events and strategize how to use them effectively with their friends.

Another approach involves what Garry Poole has labeled a "party with a purpose." The party with a purpose is a discussion-oriented social gathering, where invitees have been told that part of the time together will include a spiritual purpose. Host a dinner party and ask, "If you could ask God any one question, and you know he would respond, what question would you ask?" We have years of experience with groups using that question to generate profound discussions. There is no need to resolve all the questions that may arise; simply allow seekers the opportunity to discuss their spiritual concerns.

As a result of this preparatory work, and taking into account the readiness of non-Christians you have met, you can make room for seekers in the group. The group may decide to shift the focus of the group for four to six weeks, or continue their ongoing routines if appropriate to the seekers they will welcome. Some Willow groups invite seekers every other week while believers continue coming weekly. They use the first and third weeks of a month to meet as a believer group, and then use a separate study for seeker friends they invite on the second and fourth weeks. This lets Christians discuss "believer" issues and pray for their seeker friends in confidence. As seekers come to faith, it also creates a place for them to meet for further discipleship without removing them from the small group and their seeking friends.

Moving from a closed group mind-set to a contagious community is exciting, and sometimes the results are overwhelming! Our statistics indicate that when seekers participate with believers in small group community (and stay with it), 80 percent become followers of Christ! We are seeing this phenomenon across the globe. Churches are rediscovering the power of community-based evangelism, where believers' lives, combined with gospel truth and Holy Spirit power, transform unbelievers—forever. Where the closed group mind-set once sowed the seeds of death to a community, contagious groups now plant seeds of perpetual life. *Wow!* Sounds like Acts 2 all over again. Count us in!

# Chapter 11

# Sin Six: Narrow Definition of a Small Group

*Symptoms of a Narrow Definition of a Small Group*
  *Using a "one size fits all" approach to group life*
  *Failing to provide a range of entry points into groups*
  *Limiting what counts as a small group*
  *Potential leaders are overlooked because of lack of group variety*

Glaucoma is a disease that causes pressure to build up in eyes, thus narrowing vision and, ultimately, causing blindness. My (Bill's) father had the disease for years until recent surgery permanently relieved it. Since glaucoma is often hereditary, I have my eye pressure checked regularly and take an annual field-of-vision test to detect whether my vision is narrowing. Narrowed vision means the disease has progressed to dangerous levels. If caught in time, however, glaucoma is easy to treat with daily eyedrops, preventing permanent damage.

The field-of-vision test takes only a few minutes. You rest your chin on a support bar and stare into what looks like an eighteen-inch white saucer peppered with tiny pinholes, each about an inch apart. The machine randomly shines light behind the holes, one at a time, covering the entire range of normal vision. Each time you see a pinhole light up, you press a button. You learn quickly that "narrow is bad" and hope your peripheral field of vision remains broad. Each year I have passed the test and, thankfully, do not yet have any early signs of glaucoma.

Many churches, however, seem to view their small groups through eyes narrowed by "spiritual glaucoma." By limiting their definition of a good small group, they miss opportunities to connect people into community. Narrow definitions also lead to turf wars, frustration among small group leaders, and fear among leaders of ministries that don't use groups. So let's assess how narrowly we view small group life and acknowledge the degree to which we have committed sin 6. (Yep, it's that time again. Join us at the confessional.)

### Don't Confuse "Narrow" with "Good"

You can see the average Christian's tendency toward spiritual glaucoma whether you study church life, personal spirituality, or small groups. The pattern is remarkably consistent: Christians have a noteworthy desire and capability to make things narrow. We sacramentalize church practices, formulize the "right" way for doing things based on others' spiritual successes, and oversimplify ministry for lay leaders. Even when churches try to broaden the range of acceptable activities and behaviors, groups within the church engage in turf wars.

Perhaps this tendency results from the misperception that narrow is biblical. After all, we are to "enter through the *narrow* gate," for "small is the gate and *narrow* the road that leads to life," said Jesus. "Narrow is good" becomes the mantra. And soon narrow thinking that makes sense in a few areas—like core doctrines—is applied to all areas of church life. Soon there is only one acceptable Bible version, one form of music, and one color combination for choir robes. (Like the church that insisted on green and gold robes—green for the Tree of Life and gold for the heavenly throne. Sounded good, but it inadvertently shifted people's attention from the sermon to the Green Bay Packers.)

In striving to become pure we instead become narrow, limiting the potential for innovation and creativity. Our field of vision shrinks without our realizing it. But if you take a step back, you'll see glaring evidence that it is so. Worship wars used to erupt when congregations narrowly interpreted what was musically permissible, but now most churches vary styles, lyrics, and instruments. For decades Christians defined "personal devotions" only as prayer and study. Only recently have many accepted spiritual practices such as silence, solitude, journaling, and reflection.

For too long the term "small group" implied a home-based Bible study with some prayer and dessert. Or, on many college campuses, it meant a systematic training system designed to impart doctrine and win converts. The definition of small group life was often limited to several people at a table, Bible in one hand and fill-in-the-blank curriculum in the other. Other church gatherings were viewed simply as "fellowship," because they didn't count as the kind of spiritual development (answers to Bible questions) that scored points with God—at least in many people's minds.

In the last fifteen years, however, as worship styles and spiritual practices have expanded, cutting-edge churches and leading curriculum publishers have helped broaden expressions of life in community. Some local churches have begun blending true fellowship (*koinonia*) with sound small group strategy. This revolutionary change is yielding rich spiritual growth as more people connect with each other.

Your definition of a small group will directly influence how many people get connected into a little community in your congregation. Building an ever-increasing network of small groups depends on extending and adapting community values and practices to all aspects of church life. It requires offering multiple entry points into small group life and addressing turf wars among different kinds of groups.

### Limited Community Bandwidth

Technology has introduced us to bits and bytes, floppy discs and hard discs, WYSIWYG, CD-RWs, ISPs, dot-coms, dot-nets, dot-orgs, and dot-whoknowswhatsnext. People today need computerese as a second language. With a working knowledge of modem speeds, search engines, and the latest web sites, we can use Internet technology to access from home or business virtually any person, place, or thing we desire. Our access to the vast array of technological innovation is only limited by one reality—bandwidth. Bandwidth refers to the amount of information we can transmit at high speed; the wider the bandwidth, the more we can do and the faster we can do it. Widening bandwidth increases our capacity to tap into new technologies and services.

At Willow Creek, it took ten years in one group model before we learned to apply the bandwidth concept to our small groups structure. For ten years we had a narrow small group bandwidth: we had only one kind of small group to help scads of new Christians take their first spiritual steps toward maturity. All our official small groups met often and focused on in-depth Bible study, prayer, and accountability. This limited definition of a small group didn't offer nonthreatening entry into community life for people who desired basic fellowship or introductory spiritual information.

But after embracing the metachurch strategy in 1992, we widened our bandwidth. Because we wanted to introduce small group life to every Willow Creek department and ministry, we began experimenting with new kinds of groups. We created terminology to help volunteer teams and staff understand this new wide bandwidth. We adopted language from American higher education, which designates introductory classes as 101-level courses, more rigorous classes as 201- or 301-level courses, and senior-year classes as 401-level courses.

Thus we have informally designated our groups as 101, 201, 301, or 401 groups, depending on spiritual intensity and meeting frequency. The 101 entry groups focus on connecting people to one another and to the church, helping them discover basic fellowship and explore introductory spiritual development. Groups at the 201 level begin to introduce a regular curriculum or study and encourage members toward a moderate level of openness and accountability. Our 201 groups provide a net of care for people, a basic support system in times of need.

Our former one-type-fits-all "disciple making" groups were the prototypes for our current 301 groups. These groups meet regularly for in-depth Bible study, prayer, and accountability. Members of these groups place increased importance on learning and see their groups as places of primary care and longer-term relationship. Finally, 401 groups take everything a step further, meeting weekly, connecting between meetings, pursuing intentional development and growth, and exploring leadership roles in the body. "Doing life deeply together" is a phrase we use to describe the community experienced in the 401-level group environment.

These are not hard and fast categories, and we do not use these labels publicly. (No one at the church would say, "I'm in a 301 group.") Rather, these terms help us, area leaders, and division leaders to assess bandwidth within any ministry area. The greater the bandwidth, the greater the opportunity for people to enter community.

### *"Us versus Them" Turf Wars*

As you attempt to widen bandwidth, however, you'll probably need to address a common negative thought pattern. "Us versus them" turf wars erupt between different kinds of groups or between small groups and ministries that don't yet use small groups as a core strategy. This problem is most common in churches moving toward the church *of* groups model. (In a church *with* groups, both types of ministry efforts are generally validated. It is both/and, not us versus them.)

We first noticed this negative thought pattern during Willow Creek's transition toward becoming a church *of* groups. Our existing 301 groups—remember, the only kind of group we had at that point—met three times a month, two hours per meeting, and followed a structured curriculum. In 1991 and 1992 we launched 101-level "community groups," in which we offered people initial places to connect, especially for those not ready to commit to a two-year Bible study. We thought if we could get them connected, then we could start them on the path to 301-level commitment.

We underestimated the significance of this change. Viewing the 101-level groups as rather soft and loose, the 301 groups declared, "You don't want to see people grow up in their faith. You just want to socialize." Not to be outdone, the community groups pointed back and charged, "Well, you just want to fill people's heads with knowledge; you don't really care about people unless they are Scripture-memory zealots and leadership candidates." Like two kids arguing over whose bike is faster, they lost sight of the vision. We had to confront each group, dispel the myths and misperceptions created by each, and validate the contribution of 101 and 301 groups. Now we can laugh about the skirmishes, but "us versus them" thinking indicated we had to move away from our narrow definition of group life. A narrow definition of what is acceptable can tempt people toward spiritual inflation, in which one group begins to feel superior.

Once when Muhammad Ali was getting on a plane, the flight attendant asked him to buckle his seat belt. Declaring "I am the greatest" to remind her of his boxing fame, he refused to put on his seat belt.

"Muhammad Ali is the greatest fighter of all times. I am the greatest—I am Superman. And Superman don't need no seatbelt." She calmly and directly replied, "Superman don't need no airplane!"

Spiritual inflation can take place whenever there is change. One group feels superior to another. It can also result between Sunday school or adult Bible fellowship (ABF) leaders and impassioned small group champions. As churches experiment with groups, two camps can form, competing for resources, people, and the title of "I am the greatest!" Will it be classes or groups? Who will win? Who is better? Soon leaders assume that an increased small group emphasis must deal a deathblow to ABF and Sunday school. That's "us versus them" thinking getting in the way.

You will notice the narrowing effect when ministries begin to compare and contrast their groups with one another. Even in churches with less than twenty small groups, people become experts in the comparison game. This is true especially in churches that build small groups based on affinity. For example, staff members say, "Our men's groups are strong, but our couples' groups don't seem to be as committed." They're using meeting attendance as the prime measure of success. They're forgetting that men can meet weekly at lunch, before work, and almost any evening (except during the Olympics or during baseball, basketball, and football seasons.) Getting couples together twice a month involves overcoming childcare issues and work schedules. Though both groups may provide community and growth, the staff views one type as superior. Unless you address this, ministries with many 301 and 401 groups will feel superior and devalue ministries with 101 and 201 groups.

Groups are needed at every level to connect people throughout the congregation. And any ministry that starts to value certain levels of groups more than others will be less effective with their target audience than if they were ready to connect people at any level. Don't miss the opportunity for whole-church ministry. Discourage ministries from focusing too strongly on 301 and 401 groups, or from starting only 101 and 201 groups. Keep the bandwidth wide.

One tool to use when you see a comparative mentality is to conduct a "group audit" to see what the 101 to 401 array is in a particular ministry or division. By placing all groups in the ministry on a continuum, you can test for a narrowing of small group definition. And connecting people at the 101 and 201 levels will, in our experience, be the best means for them to begin to *hunger* for 301 community and beyond!

## Inertia and Drift

As the transition at Willow took root, a healthy array of small groups developed along the entire bandwidth, from 101 through 401 levels. We thought we had embedded the bandwidth philosophy into the DNA of our ministry.

But then a mysterious thing started to happen. I (Russ) saw it for the first time during a conversation with one of our division leaders overseeing small groups in our women's ministry. During an informal discussion about the latest developments in her division, she related how glad she was they had successfully shut down a set of moms' playgroups. She was proud to tell me their entire division now had nothing but weekly Bible studies. An alarm went off in my head.

Why? My wife had been in one of those moms' playgroups while mothering our three boys. I knew it had been a spiritual lifeline for her and for every other playgroup mom. Playgroups gave those women a weekly time to connect for adult conversation, mutual prayer, and support for their parenting challenges. While they didn't open a Bible during their time together, they had more accountability and depth of community than some 301 and 401 groups.

After questioning the division leader, my alarm shut off and a lightbulb went on. We had narrowed the definition of groups again, retreating once again to the place where only 301-level groups counted. We soon noticed a similar dynamic had occurred in other ministries. The cause was simple: the wonderful legacy of discipleship groups had an anchoring affect among some volunteers and staff. They had forgotten the significance of maintaining an array of groups to meet people where they are. It was time to confess and take action. Now we are back on track, but we must continue to watch for slippage.

Once you achieve a wider bandwidth in your small group ministry, do not declare victory too early. Instead, beware of inertia and drift created by old definitions.

## Unclear Definition of a Small Group

When confronted with an unclear definition of a small group, church leaders tend to fall back on narrow definitions. For example, small group leaders rigidly define expectations for their members' spiritual growth, then reap failure and frustration. Leaders of "unconverted" ministries—departments that don't yet use small groups as a core strategy—see small groups as a single confining model that will stunt their fine-tuned programs.

If you encounter discouraged small group leaders or resistant department heads, then chances are your church needs to more precisely define spiritual expectations and essential small group elements.

### Impatience with Spiritual Development

Everybody knows the mission of a small group leader is to disciple group members, right? Over and over we told our leaders exactly that. Develop people toward maturity, make disciples, move people to full devotion. We beat that drum on a regular basis. What do average small group leaders begin to think when that message is driven home so frequently? They believe they are supposed to turn a carnal Christian into Mother Theresa in two years or less. We inadvertently communicate that leaders who haven't moved their groups through the entire 101–401 pipeline haven't quite cut it; they have failed.

Our carelessness in setting discipleship expectations pushes leaders back to a narrow definition of groups. Christian growth takes time; we all know that. And it usually takes place through a variety of influences and experiences. Yet we sometimes give leaders the impression that they are responsible for delivering in their groups everything a person needs for growth. We all know that is impossible. Often all you can do is help people take the next step in their faith, one step at a time. That is how small group life works. It is about moving people to the next step of their spiritual development. And it will take a variety of group experiences over time to move people forward.

For example, a person might begin in a 101-level group serving on a ministry team. After completing their ministry task, group members continue conversations started during their community time. As a sense of safety grows, a member or the leader takes a risk. "Hey, how about we come another fifteen minutes earlier each week so we can have a brief devotional as a part of our time?" they say. The group agrees, and the move to becoming a 201-level group begins. Good group experiences tend to foster a hunger for more—more prayer, study, community, and life together. Good leaders allow the natural process of development to guide the group into deeper levels of growth and activity.

### Unconverted Ministries Fear Small Group Structure

If you are retrofitting an existing church with small groups (instead of planting a new church with groups at the core), you will have to decide which ministries will be built on a small group foundation. You will eventually need to strategize how community will touch every department of your church. The process may take a long time. It has taken us almost ten years to implement the vision throughout the church. Some think that is fast (because we are contemporary and can move at lightning speed compared to established churches); others think that is slow (because we are so large and it takes a long time to turn a battleship around). How long it takes actually depends on neither of these realities; rather, it depends on how quickly each ministry embraces the vision and gets on board.

How quickly the vision is embraced depends on two things. First, departments must recognize that while authentic small groups share essential elements, groups can take widely varying forms. Second, they must also recognize that adopting a small groups structure can improve, rather than destroy, a well-run ministry.

### What Counts as a Small Group

The ultimate weapon in the battle against an ever-narrowing definition of small groups is a precise definition of what will and will not count as an official small group within your church. Without a clear definition of small groups, your frustrations will never end.

Our current definition of a small group is included in appendix 6 for reference, but here are the critical elements of any detailed group description:

*The role of the leader.* The leader is the cornerstone of our definition. There is no such thing as a leaderless group, and any collection of people without an identified leader is not "official." All our eggs are in the leadership basket.

*The nature of connection.* Focus on how people will relate to one another and to the leader. The ability to build a lasting community depends on frequency and level of connection, which in turn determines group commitment and longevity.

*A community of care.* One of the sure tests of "groupness" (or what some group experts call "cohesion") is what happens when one of the members encounters a storm in life. When the group provides compassionate help and support, a community of care has been created.

*Spiritual next steps.* Spiritual parameters, expectations, and next steps provide each group with a developmental goal. When discipleship objectives and opportunities are clear, leaders can move group members toward healthy growth and change.

*Willingness to extend community.* It is essential that groups understand and declare their intentions regarding newcomers. Groups must decide how and when community will be extended to those seeking a small group.

Other elements of our current definition of a small group are significant, but these elements define small groups at Willow Creek Community Church. We want to build communities of care in which leaders are connecting people to community and taking members to their next step spiritually. These groups can function in all kinds of settings, as we will describe in chapter 12. But making the definition clear prevents small group bandwidth from narrowing.

### If It's Not Broke, Why Fix It?

Some ministries remain unconverted precisely because their current strategy is effective. After all, if it's not broke, why fix it? At Willow

Creek we've found that when ministries properly understand the essentials of a small group, they can use the strategy to make good ministries even better.

For example, our marriage ministry used a highly effective couple-to-couple mentoring approach to prepare engaged couples for life together. We didn't want to mess around with this sound and fruitful strategy. But we did want to make a great strategy even better, by introducing a small groups approach. Open-ended discussions with the ministry's leaders to explore various options gave birth to an idea. What if a mentoring couple took responsibility for two engaged couples and formed a small group as a means to complete the mentoring process? We piloted the new approach, and it worked. Mentoring couples increased their capacity for counseling, and the small groups that began in premarital sessions—initially having only two couples—became places to send other newlyweds in the months that followed. Soon many groups were up and running.

Here are two more examples of how ministries can be transitioned, not destroyed, while widening bandwidth. Besides launching a variety of small groups, our women's ministry included a strong one-to-one discipleship element. As we moved toward becoming a church *of* small groups, many mentors wondered if we would shut them down. We did the opposite. We proposed moving from a one-to-one pure discipleship focus to a one-to-three leadership development focus, a modified turbo group strategy that would profoundly increase the mentor's impact. After a few trials, this approach is working and is still in process as we write. But a more robust mentoring ministry is emerging, honoring the past but aligning with our overall vision for the future.

Our financial counseling ministry, Good Sense, is another excellent example of how transitioning to a group approach can improve a well-run department. Since its inception years ago, Good Sense has deployed scores of counselors who assist church attendees on a one-to-one basis with budgeting, planning, and managing financial distress. Thousands of counselees later, we have decided to revise the strategy. Not because it wasn't working, but because it could work even better.

164 "We're transitioning to a group-based approach," says Jim Riley, director of Good Sense, "and the response has been overwhelmingly positive. It's brought a whole new group of leaders forward and has resulted in new energy for the volunteers (as well as for the director!). Our plan is to have two Good Sense counselors/leaders at tables for every four to six families, leading them through a ten-week curriculum. After some large group teaching for the entire class, these small groups will focus on discussion and prayer at their tables, as well as on financial help." Leaders will continue with their groups after the initial curriculum. At least thirty counselors will become small group leaders within three months, adding small group leader training to their current counseling expertise.

Leaders of unconverted ministries often have narrow definitions of small groups. They'll tell you why small groups won't work in their ministry and remind you how effective the current strategy is. If you work hard to explore win-win strategies with these leaders, you may be able to dramatically expand the definition and current conception of how groups can work. It will open the door to even more small group gains and will likely enlarge their ministry beyond what they ever imagined.

A clear definition of small groups protects from accusations that "you only care about numbers" or "you only care about people who are in small groups." Staff, boards, and elders will benefit from a focused definition of small group life and how it fits into the church's overall mission. During crises or opposition to the vision, clear definitions allow you to have a united front without needing to become combative. Because definitions clarify, they can also unify. When the definition is broad enough to allow a variety of expressions of community, you make it possible for everyone in the church to enter community life and the opportunity for spiritual growth.

### A Leadership Opportunity

Increased opportunities for leadership development have resulted from our defining groups along the 101–401 continuum. Not everyone is ready to join a 301-level small group—and not many leaders can lead one. Once you create a full array of groups, you increase entry points for leaders based on their development and training. Entry-level groups can be a good place to guide people into their first leadership assignment. Intensive Bible study groups at the 401 level, however, **165** really do need someone with experience to lead them. Community and serving groups beginning at the 101 level require less expertise in Scripture, allowing leaders to grow and be developed until they can shepherd a 201- or 301-level experience.

By tackling the issue of group bandwidth, you will not only make leadership gains, but your church will grow in its ability to meet the multiple needs presented by people eager to connect to the community. Most are seeking a place to belong, not an event to attend. They need friends and guides, mentors and confidants, caregivers and disciplers. It is unrealistic to expect everyone to sign up for traditional Bible studies in which only the strong survive. It is unfair to say that people who don't choose such studies are "uncommitted" or "can't handle it."

Jesus said, "He who does not take his cross and follow me is not worthy of me" (Matt. 10:38). But, remember, he also said, "Come to me all you who are weary and burdened, and I will give you rest" (Matt. 11:28). Some need to be challenged, some need to be comforted; but everyone needs a place.

Examine all opportunities to connect people. Look out for sacramentalized small group practices or formulistic definitions that have become narrow and lifeless. Consider a broader concept of community. Your 301 groups might be housing leaders who could take on a 101-level shepherding challenge. They just need a place to try. Or you might resurrect some ministries that got buried when you raised the bar for spiritual growth. Perhaps you'll find remnants of 101- and 201-level group experiences for the right people—people who need a nudge, not a push, toward spiritual growth. Or perhaps now that you have fresh lenses through which to view group possibilities, you'll see great opportunities where you once saw only disappointment.

The next chapter will provide many options for stimulating creative brainstorming by you and other leaders. We think you will find that broadening the bandwidth is actually quite fun—for you and for your people.

# Chapter 12

# Strategies and Tools for Broadening the Range of Small Groups

We have spent the last few years staging an all-out assault against narrowness. Providing our people with a broad range of group options remains central to becoming a church *of* groups. Multiple entry points and leadership opportunities are becoming standard practice, assuring that everyone can find a place in community under the watchful care of a trained and loving shepherd. Experimentation is our key strategy for maintaining a wide bandwidth of small group connections.

In this chapter, we offer a quick overview of principles for small group development, a list of Willow Creek groups that support every part of our mission, and tips for designing your own groups. We do this so you can translate our experience to fit your context and design your own group experiments. Many churches discover they have not yet tapped the varied options for small group life when they look over the fence at places like Willow Creek Community Church or other congregations even more creative at creating numerous expressions of small group life.

One other preliminary word: many of the small groups or teams we describe in this chapter blend community with a task, passion, need, or other basis for initial connection. You might conclude from a review of these descriptions that these are random groups of people working on tasks together or that they are connected through the desire for support or the opportunity to serve. They are not. Each one of the places in community is just that: a community of people who have found their way into relationship, mutual encouragement, and spiritual development in this stage of life together.

## Overarching Principles for Small Group Development

Three overarching principles have guided our development of small groups across the church: a common developmental framework, a common structure, and common ground.

Our common framework—the five Gs—gives us a paradigm for guiding and assessing spiritual growth. We have become much clearer about the kind of Christ follower we want to develop and how to shepherd their growth process.

That common framework is then placed within a common structure—the adapted metachurch model, in which each leader is shepherded by a coach. Accountable, equipped shepherds ensure that the five Gs are taught, practiced, and integrated into the fabric of weekly group life.

The third principle—common ground—is achieved by leveraging affinity. Groups at Willow Creek are organized around affinities, those things people have in common. Affinities are not intended to represent the complete expression of community life in the body. They are simply a means of gathering people together so that little communities can begin to form. It's relatively easy for anyone in any stage of life or level of maturity to find an affinity-based small group. We soon discover, however, that people within a given area of affinity are very different. Affinity groups answer our innate desire to connect with others. Within these groups we must exercise love, resolve, and intention to become a Christian community.

Most groups fall within four major small group affinities: age/stage-based, interest-based, task-based, or care-based. We use these categories to assess bandwidth and to describe the wide variety of group experiences possible at Willow Creek. (For more about these categories see appendix 2 in *Building a Church of Small Groups*.)

Given that for decades most cell-based churches and house church models have organized around geography, some people question why we used affinity as our primary organizing method. In fact, we do use geography in some situations and have launched a regional church strategy to help people connect within a given geographical context. Even so, affinity-based groups provide the right kinds of variety throughout our small groups so that we can meet people where *they* are ready for connection. Sooner or later, all geography-based models add affinity groups to accommodate the substantial numbers of people 169 who cannot connect through neighborhood- or geography-based systems. (Task groups are the best example of this.)

Regardless of your approach, when you combine readiness for connection with someone's interest or passion and then determine where that intersects with an actual or potential church ministry, small group community is possible. We hope you will use the ideas generated so far at Willow as a foundation for the creativity you can employ in connecting people into the kaleidoscope of relationship they can find in the church. If we all continue exploring the varied means for small group connection, we will create a never-ending set of new methods to give people an excuse for getting together for connection, care, and spiritual transformation.

### Entry Points for Every Affinity

Here are some examples, listed alphabetically, of how people have discovered true community in small group life at Willow Creek.

*Accounting/Finance.* This ministry safeguards the financial integrity and good stewardship of the resources entrusted to Willow Creek. Small groups have formed among those who count the offering and manage the daily routines of accounts receivable and payable, payroll, bank requisitions, and financial advisory services. Not only has it provided a valuable service to the church, it has been a means of connection for men and women with these skills or passions. As with many of the task-based group descriptions that follow, those in the accounting ministry often have their small group time before or after serving, according to the group's covenant. Groups range from a share-and-prayer time lasting twenty minutes or so, to long-term groups that provide not only consistent, weekly Bible study but also a lot of connections between meetings where they are "doing life together."

*Axis.* We started Axis several years ago to help our church reach and enfold the postmodern generation, but its primary focus is helping people ages 18 to 20-something experience Christ-centered community. Axis

**170**

has groups for couples, singles, men, women, serving, programming, production, extension, and evangelism. They have also experimented with house groups, in which several groups meet together in a home and divide into subgroups for their specific time together. The subgroups engage in the same content the larger group has studied, participating in an application-oriented discussion of the passage. While there is no fixed formula, groups *and* subgroups will decide the rhythms of connection and learning they wish to follow.

*Camp Paradise.* Willow Creek's summer camp in Michigan's Upper Peninsula provides a place for student, father/son, father/daughter, and other camp sessions. Not only has it created serving small groups that regularly travel to the camp to work there, but it has also been a catalyst for student and men's groups throughout the church.

*Campus Operations and Development.* As with many of the serving small groups and teams described in this chapter, these groups focus on mixing task with community, community with task. They take all forms, from groups that meet for a time of connection, sharing, and study one week and serving the next, to the team that leverages the scheduled serving time for varied levels of discipleship-oriented group time. As we have described elsewhere, we entrust the details of each group's agenda to the leader through the covenant process. Meanwhile, the coach monitors and aids the serving team leader in the group's evolution. Included in Campus Operations and Developments are:

*FAST. (Facility Set-up Team).* These leaders contribute to a distraction-free environment at Willow Creek through staff and volunteer serving small groups who clean and set up rooms, bus tables in our atrium eating area, support audiovisual preparation, set up offices, perform daytime security, and assure building safety.

*Grounds.* The parklike atmosphere of Willow Creek is carefully manicured by several dedicated teams, including Adopt-a-Bed groups (who care for specific flower beds or trees), indoor plant teams, landscaping, lawn care, snow removal, and vehicle maintenance serving groups. These teams also partner with Extension Ministries for off-campus ministry opportunities.

*Trades and Engineering.* People of all skill levels serving in a ministry that offers a valuable community experience while maintaining our building's excellent appearance and function.

*Traffic.* These men, women, students, and children are now famous at Willow Creek for their orange jackets and traffic cones. Their teams provide a safe welcome for everyone who comes to Willow Creek.

*CARS.* Groups of mechanics, car detailers, tow-truck drivers, and the like have emerged as a heroic community at Willow Creek. They coordinate donations and repairs with the Community Care Ministry. CARS groups provide vehicle maintenance, detailing, and repairs for single moms and families in need, with meeting time acting as a bookend to serving opportunities. Since our groups set their own meeting content, it can be varied according to the needs of their individual members, even within a ministry like CARS. The expanded variety yields diverse bandwidth.

*Communication Arts.* Artists connect in community to build awareness of Willow Creek and its ministries through written and visual arts that communicate efficiently, effectively, and with excellence. Writers, editors, print and web designers, illustrators, photographers, and a variety of other visual artists contribute to this community.

*Community Care.* These groups care for people in times of crisis or extreme need. Not only does this ministry meet the care needs of its group members, it also employs subject-specific curricula to meet the spiritual or discipleship needs they face. Many groups include a brief teaching or storytelling time from which discussions will emerge. Groups are formed to connect people who desperately need the touch of our church in the following areas:

*A Safe Place.* Provides information and support to help men and women grow and heal from sexual, emotional, and relational struggles associated with same-sex attractions.

*Cancer Support.* Supports people with cancer and their families as they move toward hope, healing, and wholeness.

*Careers.* Offers perspective and practical help for people in career transition.

*Casework/Benevolence.* Provides care, encouragement, and support to those seeking help through Community Care.

*Christians in Recovery.* Provides support based on Scripture, small group interaction, and twelve-step principles in a Christ-centered group for those struggling with alcohol or chemical dependence.

*Counseling.* Provides a referral network of Christian counselors in the Chicago area.

*Divorce Recovery.* Supports those going through a divorce.

*Domestic Violence.* Provides support, encouragement, and resources to women who have been victims of violent or abusive relationships.

*Faithful and True for Men.* Provides support and encouragement to men seeking to maintain sexual purity and integrity in a sexually charged world.

*Faithful and True for Women.* Provides support and encouragement to women struggling with their own or their partner's sexual integrity.

*Food Pantry.* Supplies food and affirmation to those going through financial difficulties.

*Grief Support/Children's Grief Support.* Brings comfort and hope to those grieving the loss of a loved one.

*Hairdressers.* Touches the lives of those who cannot afford the luxury of a hairdresser's services.

*Healing Hearts.* Offers support to women who are survivors of sexual abuse and/or sexual assault.

*Homeless Ministry.* In cooperation with Chicago's Northwest Suburban PADS, provides shelter for those who are homeless.

*Hospital Visits.* Provides comfort and encouragement to those who are hospitalized or bedridden and have no existing small group support.

*Lay Ministry.* Assists the teaching pastors in the "bull pen" area after services by listening to and giving spiritual direction to attendees.

*Marital Restoration.* Engages in the process of healing troubled marriages.

*Medical Ministry.* Serves medical professionals and promotes health **173** care for those in need.

*Oasis.* Provides support for children (birth to high school age) who are hurting from the breakdown of their families.

*OCD (Obsessive-Compulsive Disorder).* Provides perspective, encouragement, and support to people struggling with obsessive-compulsive disorder.

*Pathfinders.* Encourages those struggling with a chronic illness and provides support to their families.

*Past Abortion Healing.* Supports women seeking comfort and perspective after an abortion.

*Pastor of the Day.* Offers a listening ear and spiritual direction to those who call or come to the church with spiritual questions or concerns.

*Phone Care.* Provides comfort in crisis situations and assists callers by connecting them with Christian counselors and community resources.

*Postpartum Depression.* Walks alongside women experiencing emotional changes and challenges after the birth of a baby.

*Self-Help Groups.* Facilitates traditional twelve-step meetings for those recovering from an addiction.

*Someone I Love.* Provides support for family members and loved ones of homosexuals.

*Special Friends.* Befriends and assists the developmentally challenged, both children and adults, and their families.

*True Hunger.* Provides support for those struggling with weight loss.

*Couples' Ministry.* We offer many groups to help couples grow in their marriage and family relationships. Groups will covenant to use a published curriculum, inductive Bible study methods, or message-based discussions for the spiritual development component of their meeting times. Meetings often include sharing, prayer, and other spiritual practices, with the sharing of food an integral part of meeting time! Some groups are connected based on geographic proximity, but others connect based on affinities, such as:

*Intergenerational Groups.* Brings families and singles together, including children in the small group experience.

*Marriage Preparation.* Helps couples build Christ-centered marriages through seminars, personality profiles, and mentoring relationships with married couples.

*Marriage Enrichment.* Offers practical teaching and interactive learning through seminars designed to keep marriages on solid ground.

*Newly Married.* Connects couples beginning their marital journey.

*Parenting.* Offers activities and small groups whose focus is learning more about raising godly children and developing parenting skills.

*Senior Ministries.* Meets needs of seniors (couples or singles) through social gatherings, small groups, and serving opportunities.

*Evangelism.* Groups in this area help people take initial steps in their spiritual growth. Sometimes these groups begin as a class, other times as an affinity-based community out of which groups are formed. Leaders may use a curriculum such as *Tough Questions* or may initiate discussions out of the training they receive for conducting seeker small groups (the Willow Creek Association sometimes offers such training at various conferences). Included in the various groups of the Evangelism ministry are:

*TruthQuest.* Coffeehouses and small groups for people who are searching for answers to tough questions about Christianity. Leaders then move these seekers toward small groups.

*International Connection.* Seeks to meet the unique needs of international people at Willow Creek. Small group opportunities, gatherings, and language tutoring are offered, sometimes through the initial connection of language interpretation available during church services.

*New Believer Small Groups.* Helps new believers pursue spiritual growth with others who have similar interests and questions.

*Seeker Small Groups.* Provides a safe place to explore Christianity with others who are searching. In these groups seekers can discuss spiritual questions, express thoughts and opinions without judgment, hear what other seekers are thinking, and learn what the Bible has to say about life today.

*Sports Ministry.* Provides regular opportunities for seekers and believers to participate in such activities as basketball, volleyball, softball, bicycling, and football through teams organized to function as small groups. Team captains don't just supervise a team; they use pre- and post-game time, as well as time during the off-seasons, to keep team members focused on what they term the "real game," advancing beyond athletics into the spiritual progress of both believers and seekers.

*Event Services.* These groups are well known at Willow Creek Community Church for doing more than providing support to the church and its ministries by assisting in event scheduling, design, planning, and execution. They also meet at specific event serving times for Bible studies or other community spiritual focus.

*Extension Ministries.* Volunteer teams are mobilized to meet the needs of underresourced people. As with other task-based communities, these groups do more than connect to get a job done. They combine a passion for extending hands of mercy with growing hearts of love for God and each other. Leaders are trained how to take a collection of servants beyond their focus on others into a *dual* ministry—to each other as well. Groups work in areas that include:

*Extension Construction.* Develops groups of adult volunteers, ranging from novices to tradespeople, to work on the campus of Willow Creek as well as the H.O.M.E.S. Ministry, Habitat for Humanity, and other partner ministries in local, urban, and international areas.

*International.* These groups partner with churches and organizations in the Dominican Republic, Mexico, Costa Rica, and elsewhere in the world and prepare Willow Creek attendees to serve in short-term ministry teams with these partners.

*National.* Partners with churches and organizations, along with an emerging set of Willow Creek Association churches, to meet needs of underresourced communities around the United States through short-term teams.

*Urban.* Partners with churches and ministries in Chicago that minister to the homeless and incarcerated, single parents, seniors, the hungry, and gang members. Also provides tutoring to children and immigrants.

*Local.* Partners with churches and ministries in the northwest suburbs of Chicago by building relationships and allocating resources. Works with facilities for seniors, children, families in crisis, the homeless, youth, AIDS patients, and incarcerated youth and adults.

*Good Sense.* As described in chapter 11, groups of people gather for the purpose of being educated about biblical financial principles and their application to personal money management.

*Harvest.* Willow Creek's food-service ministry includes people in serving small groups who manage the food court, catering, conferences, and decorating. Harvest small groups do more than just fill plates; they often join the guests they serve—after they finish their task—for a time of consuming spiritual food together.

*Human Resources.* Experts in personnel matters connect to encourage and affirm the call of God on peoples' lives into vocational ministry, but do so in community.

*Information Systems.* Through the Computer Connection, this ministry has created serving small groups comprised of technology lovers who provide hardware, software, network, and telephone support to the church. The Computer Connection now does a quarterly outreach event for computer users.

*Marketplace.* This ministry is actually a cooperative effort of our women's and men's ministries. It connects people into groups through events and classes designed to help men and women live out their faith in the workplace. They include the following:

*Applying Faith to Work.* This thoughtful Bible study focuses on "moments of truth" at work. The topics covered include success, balance, pursuit of plenty, servant leadership, stress, dealing with **177** difficult people, office politics, honesty, lust, and winning.

*Making the Most of Life@Work.* Groups can choose from three short Bible studies designed to help people flourish at work—Cornerstones Work for Calling, Framing Your Ambition, and Ethical Anchors.

*ExecuServe.* This ministry is designed to meet the needs of men and women who work as senior executives, CEOs, business owners, and vice presidents.

*Groups in the Loop.* "The Loop" is the Chicago term for the commercial district of the city. Groups in the Loop is an informal medium-sized gathering of men that provides a central point of contact for those wanting to join a small group that meets during the workday. A speaker introduces a topic for the day, which is then discussed within small groups. As new relationships form, some discussion groups become more permanent small groups, meeting at days, times, and locations convenient to the participants.

*Men's Ministry.* Men's groups sharpen men for life change in Christ through small groups that include men who are single, married, and with or without children. Also includes groups designated as "Dads' Groups."

*Ministry Services.* This ministry is in transition but has provided services needed by various church ministries. Along the way, each of these areas has moved their volunteers into teams that combine their unique tasks with regular, spiritually transforming community and relational care. Included in Ministry Services are:

*Call Center.* Groups of staff and volunteers connect callers to the right person or resource within Willow Creek.

*Child Protection Ministry.* Provides a safe environment for minors at Willow Creek by screening adults who work around children.

*Data Connection Team.* Helps manage the online records of people who connect with Willow Creek.

*First Steps Ministry.* Helps connect people with small groups and volunteer opportunities by providing general information about Willow Creek through the information booths, building tours, seminars, and conversations at the welcome center. These groups own the "front doors" of Willow Creek Community Church.

*Membership.* Helps Willow Creek attendees enter into membership and periodically renew their participating membership.

*Network.* This seminar helps individuals discover and explore their spiritual gifts. Groups of volunteers sponsor classes examining the purpose of the church and help attendees find a place to volunteer.

*Prayer Ministry.* Prayerfully intercedes on behalf of anyone who makes a request known to the church. Prayer small groups also pray for specific ministries, the church, and the world.

*Training and Development.* Provides ongoing learning opportunities to the church body through Willow Creek Institute classes. Volunteer teams develop and deliver training for group leaders and coaches, as well as for other needs throughout the church.

*Volunteer Services.* Coordinates volunteers in serving small groups for churchwide events and conferences.

*Production/Programming.* A community of artists creates all public worship services for Willow Creek Community Church. Organized into small groups, these artists build a community who together unleash the arts to create transformational moments in the lives of seekers and believers. Since many of these groups have to serve in multiple services when they are scheduled to serve our church, they schedule alternate times to meet in community for sharing, prayer, study, and the like.

*Production.* Handles the technical support for events and church services at Willow Creek. These teams set up, control, and store sound systems, staging, cameras, and lights.

*Programming.* Creatively uses the arts to plan and implement weekend and midweek services. Instrumentalists, vocalists, actors, writers, administrators, producers, and behind-the-scenes people share their time and talents while connecting in groups within their ministry areas.

*Promiseland.* Children from birth to fifth grade receive biblical teaching and practical application through large and small group presentation. Creative communicators present biblical truths through music, puppets, teaching, and media, which leads to a small group time led by student or adult leaders for every child age three and older. We have had a front-row seat to the impact these groups have had on our own children. In fact, our kids can no longer think of church without thinking of their small group as an integral part of church life. Our kids think small groups are as normal as worship services and biblical teaching. In their minds, a church without community is not a church— and small groups are a big part of developing that community!

*PromiseTowne.* Groups of people provide childcare for those who come to volunteer at the church or attend special classes during the day. Children participating in PromiseTowne are on their way to a small group connection, while the adults watching over them are part of a growing community of those who give care to kids and to each other.

*Regional Ministry.* Our new satellite campuses provide locations for Chicagoland residents to experience Willow Creek via live and video-cast services. We expect that the kinds of small groups in this list will now find expression in multiple localities. The first regional site— Willow Creek Wheaton—opened in November 2001.

*Seeds.* Staff and volunteer small groups provide resources for spiritual growth through our bookstore, tape production, copy center, and mail processing in the context of a community that shepherds, cares for, and spiritually disciples each person who serves.

*Service Ministries.* Serving teams and groups provide a safe, distraction-free environment for our guests and attendees at public worship services. Their responsibilities include counting attendance, collecting offerings, preparing and serving communion, planning and serving conferences, greeting, ushering, hospitality, and interpretation for the deaf. These groups not only connect in community around their serving times, some of them meet for a twenty to thirty minute share-and-prayer group time, others meet for a semiweekly intensive Bible study. These groups also present a "front door to community" for every attendee at Willow Creek.

*Single Adults' Ministries (SAM).* Meeting the relational and spiritual needs of singles creates numerous affinities, each with its own identity. Each of the following singles' ministries has large group gatherings, social events, serving opportunities, and small group connections. Most of these ministries offer singles a progression of small group experiences, starting with a discussion group at the larger gatherings and leading to a longer-term small group committed to Bible study and personal discipleship. SAM groups include:

*Champions.* Ministry to the children of those involved in Single Parents, which meets concurrently with Champions.

*Firm Foundation.* This class on basic Christianity leads to connection into small groups.

*Graceland.* A spiritual community for people in their twenties who are looking to grow in their relationship with God and each other.

*High Point.* Ministers to single adults ages 35 to 45.

*Inductive Bible Study.* A Bible study to deepen spiritual understanding and sharpen Bible skills through small groups.

*Late-Night Connection.* A late-night spiritual discussion group.

*Lord, Heal My Hurt.* A support group for those in pain.

*New Horizons.* For single adults ages 45 to 60.

*Marketplace Seeker Small Groups.* Connects single seekers within the marketplace.

*Single Parents.* Serves full-custodial, joint-custodial, or noncustodial single parents. Teaching and small group study focuses on parenting issues and relevant topics.

*The Gathering.* Ministry to single adults in their thirties who want to gather on Sundays.

*The Arts Group.* A community for serious-minded single artists.

*The Edge.* Saturday meetings that connect single adults ages 30 to 40.

*Travel and Tours.* A community for single adults who enjoy travel.

*Women's Group.* A community that takes a holistic approach to being a godly woman.

*Sonlight Express.* For students in sixth through eighth grades. Meets Saturday mornings, September through May, and connects students to small groups under the leadership of adult shepherds. Group studies are rooted in the theme for each week's large group gathering, with an emphasis on age-suitable application.

*Student Impact.* Students starting high school graduate into Student Impact, which meets Sunday evenings, September through May. Some small groups meet before or after the large group gathering, but many meet during the week to connect students in community under adult and experienced student leaders.

*Willow Creek Association (WCA).* WCA serves and encourages like-minded churches and leaders throughout the world by enlisting many volunteers connected into serving small groups. As with our other serving teams, WCA volunteers integrate small group rhythms with their tasks, enjoying varied levels of group life (covenanted by each group).

*Women's Ministry.* Similar to Men's Ministry, Women's Ministry helps women of all ages learn and understand how God's Word can change their lives. Support is given through Bible studies and discipleship small groups, within homes and in the marketplace, based on subaffinities of life situation:

*Career and Professional.* Part of Marketplace Ministry, this small group connection enhances relationship building among career and professional women who gather for quarterly forums and in small groups. Their mission is to build community and integrate biblical principles in the marketplace.

*Moms' Ministry.* This ministry has groups that provide support and encouragement through every stage of motherhood. Some groups are organized geographically, meeting during the day or in the evening. There are groups for mothers of preschoolers, grade-school children, and teens. Special-interest groups include Moms through Adoption, Moms in Single Parent Roles, Moms and Dads of Blended Families, Twenty-Something Moms, and Moms in the Marketplace, which serves moms trying to balance career and home.

*Neighborhood Small Groups.* Meeting during the day, these groups provide an opportunity for community for women, usually within a geographic area. Groups are also available for women investigating the claims of Christianity, providing a safe place to explore and discuss what women believe about God.

*On-Campus Bible Studies.* Held at the church on various mornings, each weekly session begins with insightful biblical teaching, followed by small group discussion time. These small groups remain consistent from week to week, providing the opportunity for women to build lasting relationships. Studies are offered from September through April.

*Reaching Out Together.* For women of action who like doing things for others, groups in this ministry are focused on serving opportunities. Like-minded women build strong bonds as they serve in third-world countries, inner-city homeless shelters, or other areas of outreach.

*Spiritually Single.* Women who are married but "spiritually single" (married to an unbeliever) face a challenging life situation requiring much wisdom. In these small groups spiritually single women can grow spiritually as they find support and encouragement from women in similar situations.

*Women Doing Life Together.* This weekly on-campus evening study helps women learn through teaching and small group time. Registration is not required and groups are always open to newcomers. This study brings together women of all ages and from all walks of life and is often a great starting point in Women's Ministries.

## A Final Word of Caution and a Few Tips

Overwhelmed? We are too. We have so many groups, in part, because Willow Creek is so large. Mainly, though, this wide range of group possibilities exists to initially connect people, not to fragment the church. Consider them entry points and points of contact with the outside world. People who will not darken the door of your church or feel safe coming into your home may connect to a group that reaches out to them. Our passion to connect the unconnected and build community compels us, even when the variety seems crazy.

At one management team meeting, I (Russ) presented a proposal for four new community care ministry efforts. The management team's elder representative asked us how many ministries already existed. As we described the twenty-five current initiatives, her eyes started to glaze over. "How many more of these do we anticipate pursuing?" she asked. Smiling, I responded, "As many as it takes!"

I wasn't being irreverent to an elder in that moment; I was being pragmatic. Every time we identify where people want to connect, whether around a need, task, interest, or life stage, more small groups form, more care is delivered, and more spiritual development results. In many ways, we stay on the lookout for any excuse to get people together—*as many as it takes.*

After pastors realize the breadth of possible connections and group experiences, they often get so excited they start fifteen new initiatives in the first week. Pulpit announcements, sign-up sheets, and organizational meetings clutter the landscape of church life. Soon activities and newcomers pop up everywhere. Then reality hits—where do we put all these people? Who's in charge? Why are three events scheduled for the same day and time? Why did Mrs. Johnson receive five pieces of mail this week, each recruiting her to a new ministry?

To provide opportunity is a wonderful thing—unless you provide no leadership in the process. So here are a few guidelines:

*Pray for wisdom and opportunity.* Ask God to show you the best places to experiment, and then seek people who share the vision.

*Never start a ministry without a leader.* This is a creedal statement at Willow, one we invoke because of hard lessons learned. When you create ministry activity without a leader, guess who gets the phone calls.

*Tap into people's passions and strengths.* Don't simply identify a target audience (single moms, for example); find someone who loves single moms.

*Start small.* Look for a few strategic places to begin and start a pilot group in each one. After three to six months, pause and evaluate, make improvements, and then move forward more aggressively.

*Use medium-sized groups.* In these larger settings you can meet basic needs, really get to know the audience, use subgroups for connection, and identify emerging leaders for the pilot groups mentioned above. As we emphasize elsewhere, however, a medium-sized group is not the ultimate goal. Until people find a connection to a small group, they are not at the destination of enjoying small group life.

Paying attention to these basics will allow you to expand the ministry without exploding it. Once you identify new places and strategies to connect the unconnected within your grasp, moving them into small groups remains the final challenge—the assimilation challenge. It is a challenge that we, like many churches, have faced again and again. And yes, we have committed some sins along the way. Failure to create a workable assimilation strategy is the final deadly sin.

# Chapter 13

# Sin Seven: Neglect of the Assimilation Process

*Symptoms Indicating Neglect of the Assimilation Process*
   *Newcomers feel isolated and have difficulty finding their way*
     *to a group*
   *No system is in place for collecting data about newcomers*
   *No clear process or pathway exists to connect the unconnected*
   *No one follows up with people in the assimilation process*

We were trying to figure out how to take our small group ministry to the next level. We had a clear strategy, a point leader in place, a coaching structure, rising apprentices, and increasingly open groups. We'd even broadened our bandwidth of group options. Yet not enough people were connecting. Our growth had started to plateau. What was the problem?

Then Greg Hawkins, our executive pastor, said, "We have to watch the flows as much as we watch the buckets." *Buckets versus flows*. In his inimitable style, Greg crystallized an issue we had too long ignored while expanding our community emphasis throughout the church.

The buckets are small groups, "containers" into which we place people who come our way. We had done okay at containing many of the folks who call Willow Creek Community Church their home. But Greg suggested we needed a much better understanding of "the flows," the process of assimilation by which people move into and through a church.

It's easy to understand why churches neglect the assimilation process. Most of us invest our limited resources on existing small groups. We become absorbed with supporting leaders, writing curriculum, delivering training, building infrastructure, and understanding group dynamics. These issues are fundamental to effective group life and often help develop the magnetic appeal of groups. But focusing all your attention on these issues will only help you pluck the low-hanging fruit from the assimilation tree. Unless there are clear and functional pathways for people to connect into group life in your church, people will remain out of reach. Growth will plateau. Too many people will remain outside your reach, far from small group community.

Assimilation—the art and process of moving people into your church—is a bewildering conundrum. You cannot assimilate people into your church if you focus solely on buckets and ignore the flows. This chapter will help you understand assimilation's complexities and assess how well your church is doing on the three major steps of assimilation—collecting vital data, following up, and handing off interested people to ministry leaders. We've included detailed flowcharts of Willow Creek's assimilation process. Though you might design a different system, looking at ours will help you determine which assimilation steps you've neglected.

## A Complex Problem

So far in this book we've focused mainly on the "containers" (small groups) and the already connected. But to address sin 7, neglect of the assimilation process, we must shift focus to those who are far from community, viewing the action from the grandstands. We need to understand the pain of their isolation and commit to developing a process to reach and assimilate them.

### Isolation Hurts

Sooner or later every person experiences the pain of not belonging. Some learn it early in life, feeling isolated during kindergarten naptime or on the playground when they get picked last as kids choose sides for a game. I (Russ) faced it during high school. Until then, I'd spent my whole life in the same safe school system, church, and neighborhood. I knew most everybody I crossed paths with each day, and they knew me. I belonged, and I never knew what it felt like not to belong.

All that changed dramatically when my family moved from Minnesota to Colorado in the summer of 1971. Suddenly, with little preparation, I was in a strange place where I didn't know anybody. Being a shy kid, I didn't make new friends very easily. Even when I started to get to know people, they all knew each other already. They belonged, but I didn't.

Things got worse when we moved again in the summer of 1973. A new high school and a new town, plus adolescent angst, pushed me into isolation. I barely spoke a word for the first six weeks of school, cloistering myself in the library, so any sense of belonging was out of reach. I hated being alone but lacked the wherewithal to even try. If an extroverted girl hadn't forced me to talk to her and some friends, I might still be ensconced among the books at that high school. I eventually escaped the library but never lost the feeling of what it's like to not belong.

Given my current occupation, I now know God brought isolation into my life so that I'd understand the pain of others who don't belong. The key to assimilation is meeting people at the point of their desire to belong. Assimilation is not merely about growing a small group ministry or designing systems to mobilize and connect the masses; it means wanting to provide people a place to belong, a chance for community.

### Assimilation Doesn't Just Happen

It is hard to connect people who are unconnected. How do you find them? They appear inaccessible, and it's hard to figure out what might move them toward community. On one hand, people long for connection and love. On the other hand, they avoid opportunities for community like the plague, citing burnout, stage of life demands, or a myriad of other excuses. Are they schizophrenic or simply afraid? In the words of the old television commercials, "What's a mother to do?"

After Greg Hawkins challenged us to watch the flows, we began studying how people moved into our church. We looked at where they tended to show up first, second, and last, and when they might be ready to connect into a little community. We examined why some men, women, students, and children remained disconnected despite being on our doorstep. While learning about our buckets and flows, we experimented with new ways to connect people into our church.

We also noted two sides of the complex problem of assimilation. Understanding the need to belong is the soft side of connecting people into groups. The hard side is understanding that assimilation is a *process*. Having open chairs in groups is necessary, but it takes churchwide systems and processes to fill those chairs. This assimilation process often involves multiple people linking with an individual as they move from the front door to a small group. Since the process can be fragmented among many people—the usher who greets newcomers, a visitation committee, small group leaders preoccupied with existing group members, or a senior pastor with too many names and faces to remember—you must assess your assimilation processes through the eyes of newcomers.

Key laypeople helped us develop our assimilation process at Willow Creek Community Church. Believe it or not, there are process professionals (no, not slide rule and pocket calculator types) who devote their careers to understanding how people flow in and out of organizations, including churches. These insightful people helped us diagnose how we work together to connect people to Christ and his church. Though our assimilation flow may be more complex than your church requires, it will help you analyze the gaps and breakdowns in your process.

### Capturing Vital Data

Many churches neglect the first step of collecting information when a newcomer first encounters their church. (See figure 1 below; appendix 7 includes written descriptions of the three-stage assimilation process.) These churches haven't thought about the ways someone might first learn about them. It might be through a service, a program tear-off, or even a web site or a conversation with a friend who attends the church. Some people meet a church at their point of greatest need, perhaps the death of a loved one, a divorce, or a serious illness.

No matter how or why a newcomer first meets your church, you can't get them into your assimilation process unless you collect simple information, such as their address, telephone number, and e-mail address. As we assessed our assimilation process at Willow Creek, we were shocked to learn how often we failed to capture basic data from newcomers. We lost track of many newcomers because we didn't gather contact information to connect and *stay connected* with them.

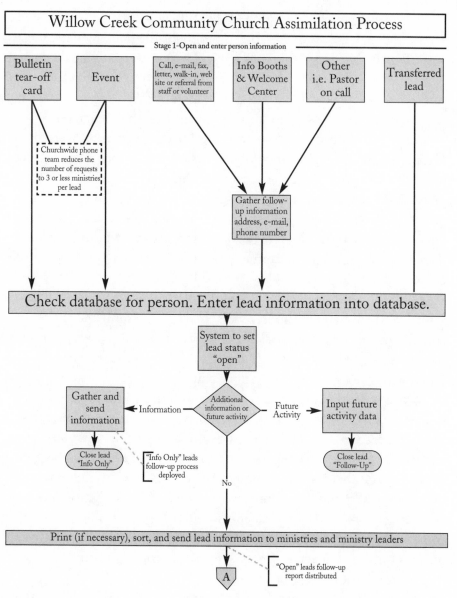

## Willow Creek Community Church Assimilation Process

Stage 1-Open and enter person information

Gathering and tracking such information meant we needed a system to contain the data. Data management may seem about as exciting as watching cheese age. But it's complex, and the right tools for data management in churches are still evolving. We have tested several manual and computer-based programs for tracking data, most recently a customized version of Oracle, a high-end relational database system. Smaller churches will find FileMaker Pro or Excel spreadsheets sufficient. We are modifying our system as we write, because our needs are changing and the system must accommodate those changes.

But don't get bogged down waiting for the perfect software. Bill Hybels is famous for his anticomputer disposition (though he has now made the foray into the Internet, a move he describes with great flair, pride, and even gladness—to our surprise!). Still, he won't allow our team to lean on software problems as an excuse for not tracking people. He reminds the technology-dependent among us that a three-by-five-inch card and a pencil can capture a remarkable amount of data that is also easily filed and retrieved.

Gathering and managing initial data isn't enough. You must also assess your church's responsiveness to each person's questions or concerns. Some newcomers ask for only basic information—the answer to a question, written materials about a ministry, or simple directions on how to take their next step at our church.

Nor is meeting initial needs enough. You need a follow-up system to keep track of people so you can address their next needs and questions. We realized that if the simple information we first provided was insufficient—and if we neglected to follow up—newcomers became confused, and their assimilation into the church was erratic. Since we organize most groups by affinity, we designed our assimilation process according to ministry area, such as couples, singles, men, women, community care, or evangelism. We assigned key staff and volunteers to monitor the connection process, moving people into small groups in their ministries.

Assimilation cannot work without collaboration. We evaluated the process each ministry used to connect people, assuring that each "hand-off" went well. After capturing people at stage 1, we could not afford to get sloppy and lose them. We determined the best practices in each ministry area and communicated those ideas and processes to all the ministries. By identifying successful patterns, we created follow-up strategies that worked throughout the church. Once we knew each ministry could handle the initial steps of connecting people, we could complete the last part of stage 1 and put each person into the hands of our ministries.

Handoffs are determined by asking people about their potential interests. For example, in a family new to Willow Creek, the parents might want to explore connecting into a couples' small group, but the mom might also be interested in a women's group and the volleyball league, while the dad might check out a men's group or a serving small group in Operations. Meanwhile, their children need connection into Promiseland, Sonlight Express (junior high), or Student Impact (high school). We look at each interest as an individual lead requiring follow-up. Each can be centrally addressed but also needs ministry-specific attention. So the same person is often handed off to multiple ministries.

The handoff isn't over when we pass a lead to one or more departments. The process may break down unless we check how those ministries are following up. After experimenting, we settled on a centralized team to track how people are progressing. This team provides accountability to decentralized ministries that actually contact and help assimilate newcomers.

## Follow Up Early and Often

Many churches lose the chance to connect people because they fail to follow up within a month. The stage 2 diagram may appear daunting, but it simply details how each ministry should assess and follow up on leads they've been given. At Willow Creek, we remind ourselves that God sent these people to us, so we can't afford to overlook any step of assimilation, no matter how small. It is our responsibility to follow up on every lead, every person with whom there is a point of contact.

### Inquire and Assess Lead

The top half of the diagram defines steps for a ministry to contact someone. During our ministry evaluations, we discovered that if a person seeking connection did not hear from a specific department within three days, they became far less likely to take the next step. Also, there appeared to be a thirty-day window for beginning successful assimilation. Think of it this way: you have no more than one month to make a significant connection with someone your church has contacted (or who has contacted you).

We refined what we now call our "three call rule" by noting what yielded the right outcomes. Each department makes three telephone calls to the people they are following up on. Calls must be made at least twenty-four hours apart to avoid the temptation to simply make three calls and fulfill the obligation. We encourage callers to phone at different times of day, ensuring maximum potential for contact.

Why get so specific? We needed it. Through trial and error we learned what works for us. Large churches (and even some larger ministries within the church) may receive fifteen or twenty leads after weekend services, especially if the message tapped a particular need. Though the follow-up challenge seems overwhelming, real lives and families are at stake. That's why ministries need clear, not haphazard, strategies and processes for contacting and following up on leads.

### Know When to Quit

Some people choose to drop out of the assimilation process. As the stage 2 diagram shows, we fully recognize that some will not respond to our overtures, or will decline our help in getting connected once we contact them. We attempt to strike the delicate balance between providing encouragement to connect and respect for personal choices. Some people respond to a message, conversation, or event and, in the emotion of the moment, take a first step toward the church. But later when we attempt to follow up, we discover their interest has cooled, evidence that a real spiritual battle is brewing. Our assimilation teams are trained to expect "battles," and we are working to contact people accordingly. Yet we acknowledge it makes sense to stop calling people who aren't interested.

Once a ministry contacts a person potentially interested in the ministry area, the ministry works the bottom half of the stage 2 diagram.

# Willow Creek Community Church Assimilation Process (page2)

Stage 2-Inquiry and assessment of lead

Phone team makes first phone call within 3 days-All three attempts made within 30 days

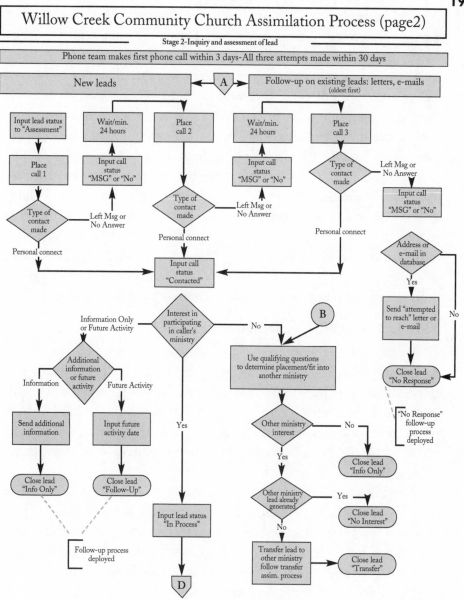

Many newcomers simply want information about that particular ministry, a request easy to accommodate. But as with stage 1, we do not want to end the process there. Instead we ask, "Would you mind if I checked in with you in a couple of weeks to see how you are doing at getting connected?" Most people respond favorably when someone cares enough to ask and will usually give permission for further follow-up.

Because a person may express interest in more than one ministry, callers sometimes discover the person is already connected elsewhere. A mild competition takes place as each ministry team works to assimilate people into their area. Newcomers feel very affirmed when two or three people contact them, offering them a way to enter church life more fully. So if a caller discovers that a particular ministry has already made the connection, then we simply hand the person to them. When a follow-up caller discovers that no contact has been made by a ministry where need or interest has been expressed, we send the person's information to that ministry so they can complete the stage 2 process.

Once a person is ready to connect with a ministry area, we diagnose their specific situation before handing them off to a small group leader.

### The Final Handoff: Connection to a Small Group Leader

It takes a lot of work to get someone to stage 3. And if you begin paying attention to stages 1 and 2, you'll have far more people ready for stage 3. But your church will miss the payoff unless you monitor, track, and report the step of connecting an interested newcomer with a ministry leader. Remember, if you watch the flows as much as the buckets, the number of people you actually connect into community will increase significantly.

Moving people through stage 3 becomes a shared process as the ministry contact person hands off the interested newcomer to a small group leader. The contact person finds out what, if any, prerequisites the person has for placement in a small group. These include scheduling concerns, geographic proximity, group focus or purpose, or other special needs. Understanding personal expectations and needs helps the contact person make the best connection with a specific small group leader, thus maximizing the potential for a fruitful link to a loving group.

# Willow Creek Community Church Assimilation Process

Stage 3-Person is in process then handed off to
ministry leader

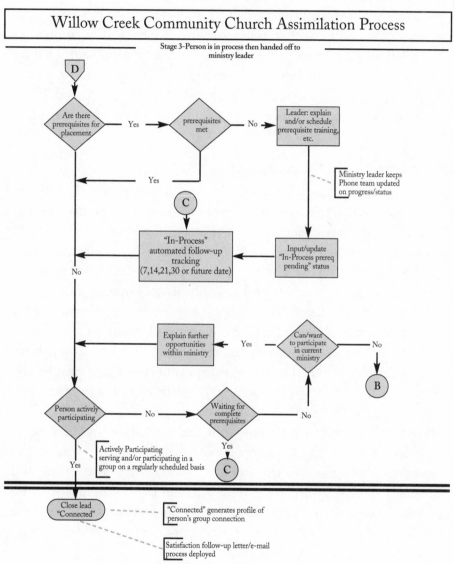

Now the small group leader becomes the primary assimilator. But it is still valuable for the ministry team to track the progress of the person seeking connection. Stage 3 assumes that small group placement happens through the group's efforts, while the ministry department maintains a weekly pulse on the progress. The ministry's assimilation team maintains communication with people until we are sure they are in a small group. As the old adage says, "If at first you don't succeed, try, try again." People's spiritual lives are placed in our trust, and we want to be sure they find a home before we stop the follow-up process.

## Connected . . . and Connected Again

When the pieces of the assimilation puzzle come together, people get connected. By knowing when and where the connection has occurred, you can celebrate the work of everyone involved. Mapping and diagnosing each step of the assimilation process will produce the desired results—connected people and a church where no one stands alone.

Two more follow-up strategies will help you improve your assimilation process. First, continue to track how people move within your church. Inevitably someone will disconnect—they move, a group ends, they connect to another group, become a leader in a new group, birth from an existing group. Use these occasions to ensure that each person is reconnected. For example, if a group of ten people stops meeting, how will you know where and when they connect elsewhere? If you follow up with them, you can determine your next assimilation activity.

Second, by talking to people about what they experienced in the connection process, you will establish a consistent assessment and diagnosis of your assimilation system. It can be as simple as a letter, perhaps even a phone call, to ask a handful of questions. Most people feel flattered when you ask about their experience, because such follow-up declares that your church cares.

You'll need this tenacity to ensure that everyone who calls your church *home* finds a place in community. Assimilation can be confusing and frustrating for newcomers. If your church assesses and maps an assimilation pathway, you'll learn what really works to serve people and connect them to community. Then, when you design strategies to increase the flow of people into the assimilation pipeline, you can be more confident your efforts will pay off. And believe us, you do not want to invest in the ideas and tools described in chapter 14 without being sure they'll pay off.

# Chapter 14

# Strategies and Tools for Improving Assimilation

Go to the high school yearbooks of the key leaders of Willow Creek Community Church and you will find that most were chosen "least likely to be in ministry." None of us had a clue we'd be here today. It started with a produce salesman turned senior pastor (Bill Hybels) and a programming director (Nancy Beach) formerly employed by a Big Six accounting firm. Add to that mix a converted banker (Bill), a former lawyer (Russ), and a consultant (Greg Hawkins, our executive pastor) who retired at the ripe age of thirty and followed God's call to become a church intern. Practically every morning we pinch ourselves, trying to figure out how we got here. Though we bring a wide range of formal and nonformal ministry training to the table, our differences and inadequacies are offset by our combination of unique perspectives.

A few years ago, another "least likely to be in ministry" candidate joined the team—Dick Anderson. Dick was a health insurance executive whose job focused on buckets and flows, on discovering how to identify and connect with people his company was *not* serving. Dick left that job to direct Willow Creek's operations area and later became our director of adult ministries. His expertise in service organizations and experience as a local church volunteer helped us understand large-church complexities, such as assimilation.

Dick helped us better serve our church—and those far from it—by introducing us to a new language for our assimilation flows. Four terms describe the primary tools and strategies every church can use to improve assimilation:

*Mobilize* means moving people from a seat in the service toward connection to a serving or community group.

*Connect* involves ensuring that people become a member of a little community somewhere in the church.

*Develop* refers to helping each person reach maturity in the faith so their ongoing connection is rooted in biblical values.

**200**   *Retain* means capturing people as they prepare to move out of their existing community so they don't slip through the cracks.

In what follows we'll describe how Willow Creek accomplishes each function. We hope our experience will get your creative juices flowing and prompt you to generate fresh ways to mobilize, connect, develop, and retain.

## Mobilize

The key to mobilization is seizing opportunity. There will always be more people to connect into existing or new groups. Some are seated in your sanctuary, and some are in the neighborhood; but you'll only be able to connect them by discovering new opportunities. Your job is to find where people are already gathering and strategize how to enter those gatherings and mobilize people toward a church connection.

Here's the problem. Current routines and structures often mask new opportunities and strategies. But if we dust off the lenses that are clouding our vision, we will see these places differently—as mobilization settings—and use them to challenge people toward a next step in our churches. It's possible to make much better use of "front doors," worship services, and medium-sized gatherings.

### Front Doors

A "front door" is a point of contact with newcomers to our campus. Front doors at Willow include the information booth where newcomers obtain printed materials and answers to questions, the welcome center for longer conversations about the church and spiritual issues, and the tear-off card from our weekend bulletin, which triggers a phone call from a Willow Creek volunteer to answer specified questions. Some of these front doors lead to church tours or newcomer receptions that orient people to our ministries.

When we evaluated our front doors, we found they were working just fine within narrow purposes. Up until this point we had been content to be nice, answer questions, and give help. But we were missing an opportunity to mobilize people toward formal connection to community. Opportunities for assimilation had been staring us in the face, but we hadn't seen them.

We began training volunteers to find out where individuals were interested in further connecting. Questions were asked about special interests, felt needs, family structure, stages of life, and spiritual journey. We encouraged newcomers to explore Willow Creek's ministries. By understanding people's needs more fully, we became better at handing them off to a ministry that could help them. In effect, these front-door strategies allowed people to move from stage 1 through stage 2 and directly to stage 3, where they could more quickly tie into an existing small group.

Wherever someone comes in contact with the church, make sure you connect them to a person, a process, and if possible, a place. The person you connect them to may be someone on the assimilation volunteer team who will be sure to get a name and basic information. The process will help determine the next step (a phone call, a mailing), and the place will be an event, class, or ultimately, a group. But the first step is to analyze how the front doors are being used. Every church has front doors. We hadn't been making the best use of ours. Is your church fully using the tools that could mobilize unconnected people who enter your doors?

### Weekend and New Community Services

Sometimes our creativity confounds us. Our services often surprise attendees with the unexpected, create profound spiritual moments, and stretch us to apply biblical truths in new ways. But sometimes in our effort to be creative we neglect the routine, like how people can take their initial steps toward connecting with our church. The drumbeat of regular reminders seems to violate the desire for creativity. Despite the shortcomings we sometimes experience in our main services, some newer ministries—such as Axis and our new regional service site—have done very well at walking people from the front door to a small group. They leverage weekly services to mobilize people by clearly communicating how newcomers can connect to these ministries.

When we ask churches how they use services to assimilate new-comers, we discover how often churches miss opportunities to connect people. It is a sin we all have in common. We ask, "How clearly do you define the initial steps for each person in your congregation?" Improving mobilization through your weekly services might be easier than you think, if you see these services as an assimilation tool. Communicate next steps from the platform each week, make sure your assimilation team follows up with those who respond, and use a wide array of creative services to keep people interested in moving forward.

### Medium-Sized Gatherings

In chapter 3 we discussed "fishing ponds" and the point leader's role in assimilation. Both the point leader and your whole church need to ask hard questions and create an array of places from which service attendees can explore connection, perhaps through Sunday school classes or adult Bible fellowships (ABF). Small groups need not be at odds with such ministries. Rather, these larger gatherings can develop small groups within them or can assimilate newcomers and then move them toward a small group setting later. At Willow Creek we have adult classes but no formal Sunday school or ABF structure. However, we have numerous medium-sized groups where people gather regularly, from which they are then introduced into little communities. These prime opportunities include special classes, outreach events, celebrations, and extension (missions) events. Such gatherings are never ends in themselves, but they can be a means to a greater purpose.

Let's assume your church, like ours, already creates assimilation events. If you start asking questions, you might be surprised to learn why and how these events are offered. Churches are famous for having events "just because it seemed like a good idea."

Once I (Russ) asked a ministry leader whether people were getting connected as a result of an event he'd organized. He evaded the question and finally said, "Well, we're doing it because it is just a fun thing to do." He didn't see beyond the event itself to the fun being missed by those who attended the event but were on the outside looking in. "Fun" was defined by event sizzle, not by whether the unconnected ever found a home at Willow.

Events can also become institutionalized. Do it once, it's a great **203** idea; do it twice, it's a habit; do it three times, it's a tradition! And you know how people respond when you stop a "tradition." The faithful arise in protest, and you become the target of their criticism. Events become habits and soon become the ministry's identity. Stopping the event leads to a personal attack.

Third, we have found that some ministries expand the fishing pond's function far beyond our original intentions. A medium-sized gathering is not intended to become the final stop on the road to community. This is like being a sports fan who thinks he is on the team just because he went to the game. We're trying to move people out of the stands and onto teams. Assimilation events are not little communities. But people will try to treat them as such. This dynamic inevitably happens when you create places to fish. Remember, fishing pond events are designed to catch fish, not to collect water.

To evaluate our progress, we try to track an event's connection rate, checking whether people really do move toward a group. Sometimes we connect a few people, and sometimes none. But when events are effectively organized and assimilation processes are in place, events work extremely well, reminding us of our potential to do better.

A few years ago, our women's ministry launched some open houses after a major outreach event. At the outreach event women were invited to attend one of fourteen simultaneous open houses hosted in various homes throughout the community. Through that process we identified 112 unconnected women who desired to be in a women's small group. How many of that 112 do you think got connected? Wrong. All 112 women—100 percent connection! We now know the maximum potential of an assimilation event. It really is possible to connect every fish in the pond.

The right kind of medium-sized gatherings can be created, but you must evaluate them well to maintain their effectiveness. If you don't, these gatherings will become ends in themselves, never reaching their assimilation potential.

## Connect

As silly as it sounds, at Willow Creek we have had trouble deciding **204** what the word "connect" means. You might think it is obvious; we have been confused.

When exactly is someone connected? Is it when we have responded to their questions? Or when we have given them the information they requested about a ministry? Or are they connected if they actually attend an event or visit a small group? Or must they attend the small group more than once?

Defining terms matters—especially in churches where several people take responsibility for assimilation. Where there is confusion, the flow of people is interrupted. For us, connection has come to mean that a person has become an official member of a small group. Someone is an official member when they and the leader both agree that it is so. That person is connected. Anything short of that means they are mobilized but not yet connected.

When determining the level of connection for people in your church, consider the essential functions of "handholders," assimilators, and division leaders.

### Handholding

You can increase mobilization activity without knowing exactly how well it is going. We had improved our front doors, worship services, and medium-sized gatherings, but we had little to show for our efforts. We needed to track people's progress beyond simple database or software systems. We needed to get up close and personal.

Soon we began to describe tracking an individual's progress as "taking the hand" of someone. Once someone began to move toward the church in any capacity, we wanted to take their hand and walk with them—until moving them to the next person in the process, who would in turn grasp the hand and repeat the process, as long as it took, until the newcomer was connected.

So you might say we are in the hand-holding business. Every church needs a process for tracking people while remaining warm and personal along the way. Handholders generate lists of newcomers through the various contact points, such as services, classes, and groups.

### Assimilators

Assimilators make sure that newcomers on the list are tracked and connected to a specific serving or community group. Assimilators have the responsibility of ensuring a connection for everyone. They hold a person's hand until someone in our church—a ministry area or small group—has taken their other hand.

This role has evolved over time. Initially, we thought connections would be made simply by keeping our groups open and having great fishing-pond events. Unfortunately, that was not the case. As small groups began to spread throughout the congregation, connection frequency decreased. We created a specialized role for people whose passion is connecting others.

We have worked with other churches that have also seen how assimilators act as catalysts for making the connection process more fluid. They help people take immediate action on their intent to join a group. Some attendees will feel motivated to seek small group life after a motivating service or event. But unless someone is there to help them act on their desire, the motivation will fade. Assimilators help people take steps they would otherwise ignore or avoid. Newcomers find it easier if someone is there to help along the way.

Never allow assimilators to administer a process instead of holding someone's hand, or they might prevent the move toward full connection. There must be accountability for the outcome *and* process.

### Division Leaders

At Willow Creek, accountability and responsibility for the connection process also lie with people called division leaders. When we added the division leader (DL) role in 1992, there was some confusion about the day-to-day activity he or she was to perform. With oversight of 500 people (ten coaches with five small groups of ten people each—10 x 5 x 10 = 500), these DLs function as coach developers, pastors to a flock, small group catalysts, and much more. Although the role continues to evolve, we have asked our DLs to be "monitors of last resort," to assure connection of those we are mobilizing toward community.

That requires them to have some sense of each group's status, which groups are ready to fill the open chair, where there might be greatest relational fit, and how to approach the leader about adding someone to their group. The assimilator can push from outside the group structure, but the DL needs groups to pull from the inside.

Be sure the person who is most responsible for the DL role (a small group pastor or seasoned volunteer) is always ready and willing to pull people into community. It may be a matter of helping new groups form or working with existing groups to open up a chair. Once someone is connected, our focus turns to development, the next function of assimilation.

## Develop

Why is it important to develop people once they are connected? Is development really an assimilation function?

The goal of development in assimilation is to embed the group life value in the soul of every person in the church. Until a person regards small group membership as an ordinary part of their spiritual and life experience, they are always at risk for *dis*connection from their little community. If you can convince people to pursue true community, all aspects of that person's assimilation become much easier.

For most Christians, church attendance is normal. So is sound Bible teaching, worship, evangelism, observing the sacraments, and fellowship. Many others cannot imagine church without a Sunday school program. Still others view certain spiritual disciplines like solitude or prayer as standard procedure for the Christian life. Whatever the case, we want to develop people to the point where small group participation is as customary as weekend church attendance. To help our people view small group community as normative, we consistently use two processes—the five Gs and participating membership.

### The Five Gs

By now you are familiar with the five Gs—our developmental framework—but we want to describe their importance in assimilation. Helping individuals embrace the five Gs ensures a permanent connection to small group community.

206

One reason is obvious: the third G stands for *Group*. Our people know that the Group G is rooted in God's nature—his self-described communal nature of Father, Son, and Spirit. The Trinity experiences a **207** perfect three-in-oneness, and Jesus prayed that his disciples would not only emulate this but also participate in it (John 17). This value, described in the Group G, reinforces a central component of the Christian faith—community with God and others. To the extent our members commit themselves to develop in the five Gs, they automatically embrace the Group G, now and in the future.

The remaining four Gs each express attitudes and actions that culminate in participation in the Group G. *Grace* connects them with the gospel but ultimately with others in a seeker group or in friendships where spiritual questions can be discussed. After conversion, the likely next place for connection is a new believer group.

*Growth* emphasizes the various relationships, experiences, and practices each person must develop if they are to mature. Small group participation encourages this development, and biblical teaching about spiritual growth necessarily involves relationships that help a person mature. (A brief look at Proverbs, Romans 12–16, 1 Corinthians 12–13, and Ephesians 4–6 should convince any skeptics of this fact.)

Henry Cloud and John Townsend, in their book *How People Grow*, drive the point home: "If you are going to help people grow, you *must* understand the necessity of relationship for growth. Often people in the church who are teaching others how to grow eliminate the role of the Body. In fact, sometimes these people teach that their students don't need people at all, that Christ alone is sufficient or that his word or prayer is enough. They actively and directly lead others not to depend on people at all...Years of research and experience back up this biblical reality: *You must have relationship to grow*."[1]

The Gifts G will lead people to serving. Since all serving at Willow Creek is done through serving teams and small groups, any person who lives out their giftedness will find community in the process. And the Good Stewardship G moves people beyond merely giving money. Christ followers are called to use all they have wisely and to give generously to the needs of others, particularly the weak and underresourced. Once again, our extension ministries function in little communities in which people depend on one another as they serve the poor. The road to development in each G leads to community life. It's unavoidable.

Whatever framework you choose to describe how someone matures, be sure it includes an emphasis on community and that the balance finds expression in various forms of group life. To the extent values change, assimilation becomes the automatic response of each person in your church.

### Participating Membership

Both in this book and in *Building a Church of Small Groups* we have described how church membership can be a tool to enhance a church's discipleship process. It is a key incentive and resource for developing people in the assimilation process.

Participating membership achieves two goals: it reinforces the five Gs as a means of growth and involvement, and it allows us to monitor the ongoing commitment to group life in particular. Tracking systems help us identify people disconnected from groups. So does our membership renewal process. Every three years we ask current members to formally reaffirm their commitment to Willow Creek using the five Gs as a guide.

In our church, membership is never a solitary event—it is a commitment to a set of values and a body of believers in a local church. It calls people to a way of life in a community, not simply to membership in an organization. The only privileges associated with membership involve the right to affirm elders and board members and to affirm the call of a new senior pastor. Otherwise, the only real privileges are those received from participation in the body. There are no special powers, just the opportunity to grow and the responsibility to serve. When renewing membership, a person reviews a brief Bible study based on the original participating membership curriculum and then reflects personally and in an interview with their small group leader on their ongoing commitment to the church and five Gs.

Sometimes the renewal process becomes an "assimilation moment" for people who have drifted from community life since their last membership affirmation. If they have no small group connection when they reaffirm their membership, our membership team partners with assimilators to reconnect them. Even if they are still in a group, they have an opportunity to evaluate their commitment to that little community. If someone drops out of a group, we ask the leader to communicate that to our membership and assimilation teams using a quarterly small group profile that gives a snapshot of group membership. These teams are responsible for following up on the person in an effort to make sure that they get reconnected. Of course, it is ultimately up to the person to respond to our efforts to reconnect them.

Imagine the conversations that take place when small group leaders meet with members during reaffirmation. The doorway to discipleship swings wide open, and development opportunities abound.

By solidifying your framework for spiritual development, whether or not you use the five Gs, and by then connecting that framework to a solid membership and reaffirmation process, you will complete the development function of assimilation. For those individuals you develop, little will be needed to retain them.

## Retain

No matter how good your groups or leaders are, and no matter how effective your assimilation process, people will get disconnected. The more mature your small group ministry, the more important it becomes to address retention in the assimilation process. How do you keep people connected for the long haul?

For years at Willow Creek we directed a disproportionate amount of energy to the front end of the assimilation pipeline—getting people connected. In the process, we often failed to pay attention to the back end. In the early days we cheered loudest when new groups formed, when old groups birthed, and when any group filled the open chair. We ignored attrition. After all, we were in the building phase, casting vision and corralling leaders.

Then some of our ministries started measuring attrition rates and the cheering subsided; the party wasn't over, but let's just say we'd run out of cake and ice cream. We learned that in some places annual turnover was 10 percent. So if we hoped for 10 percent net growth, we would have to assimilate 20 percent more people into groups. If we could do a better job at retaining the 10 percent, we would not have to work ourselves into a frenzy trying to connect people. We had to see retaining people as an integral part of assimilation. And retaining people means more people using gifts, sharing Christ, serving the poor, and developing toward maturity.

### Follow-Up

In an effort to lower our turnover rate, first we had to ask people, "Why are you leaving your group?" Responses revealed both good and bad news.

The good news took a couple of forms. Some groups ended naturally and redeployed their members into leadership roles in various small groups throughout Willow Creek. In effect, these groups functioned much like turbo groups, training leaders for the future. Other members left groups because of job changes or retirement to warmer climates (a sure sign we had enhanced their intelligence!). Many of these people found new churches and began leading small groups. Once again, informal leadership development was happening.

But here's the bad news, news that prompted significant changes in our ministry. Some groups ended poorly, fueled by relational breakdown. In these cases, we had to initiate a reconciliation process. Sometimes the breakdown involved leadership issues. Leaders who were functioning below acceptable standards had to be relieved of ministry responsibility. Over time, we found problematic churchwide patterns of group life—role confusion, poor curriculum selection, lack of alignment, and the like—and addressed them at leadership gatherings, such as huddles and our annual conference. People were impressed when we asked about their experiences, and they allowed us the chance to reconnect them into new small groups. Assimilation happened because we took steps to retain people.

Take time to simply ask the *why* question. It may yield keen insights into how people connect and *stick* to the group structure. And it will probably lead to conversations that enable you to effectively retain people in groups throughout your church.

### Transfer Assimilation

Some ministries have retention problems because *disconnection* is built into the design. It is normal for people to leave the group after a period of time. Community care groups, for example, are designed to help people through a short-term crisis or need, which prepares them to join a task or community group after the crisis ends or some healing has occurred. Seeker and new believer groups likewise graduate their members. And Promiseland, Sonlight Express, and Student Impact groups lose members as kids grow up and move to the next age group. After taking a closer look at these time-sensitive groups, we discovered their great potential to foster assimilation from one area to another. It was simply a matter of recognizing the opportunity and tracking the process so that no one fell through the cracks.

Your church probably has ministries geared to moving people naturally toward their next step in spiritual development and community connection. Keep watch on your congregation's transfer dynamics so that you won't miss some obvious ways to retain people in group life.

### Reassimilation

Sometimes the process comes full circle. A person is assimilated into a group where they connect and are developed. They move on to another group three years later. Then, for whatever reason, they might be disconnected, with no one holding their hand. Depending on how you track people throughout their small group experience, you can eventually identify these people and grab their hand again. You might reassess their needs and start the process all over until they are back in a group. Thus you ensure they remain connected, even if for a season they are not in a group.

## The Ultimate Service Organization

People like Greg Hawkins, Nancy Beach, Bill Hybels, and Dick Anderson spent much of their marketplace careers in customer acquisition and retention. So did we. And the parallels to church work are hard to ignore—except the stakes are much higher. That's why we feel such urgency. We sat in conference rooms with other bankers, consultants, lawyers, business owners, and executives strategizing how to reach the next customer and retain the ones we had. Does not the local church, with its eternal mission, demand at least as much energy on our part? How can we refuse to redirect our assimilation energies to the organization with the eternal mission?

In our former endeavors, it was just dollars and cents. Connecting people to the product or service meant linking them to the bottom line. But when we talk about assimilation and connection, salvation and transformation, the stakes are as high as the heavens. We can't escape the knowledge that every assimilation breakthrough might have eternal consequences. It keeps us working to consider every strategy and tool that God might place at our disposal.

# Conclusion

On January 28, 1986, at 11:38 eastern standard time, I (Bill) had just finished an exam in graduate school, and I (Russ) was standing in the television section of a department store in Bismarck, North Dakota. We expected it to be a day like any other. Instead, it would be a day that shocked a nation and grieved the world. In a matter of seconds a dream became a nightmare. American schoolchildren were watching the events live on television in classrooms all across the country. This day, for the first time in history, an ordinary schoolteacher, Christa McAuliffe, would embark on an extraordinary journey into space aboard the space shuttle *Challenger*.

But sadly, only seventy-three seconds into the flight, the *Challenger* exploded, killing all seven crewmembers. The world stood by in shock and horror, unable to comprehend the gravity of the moment. Perhaps even more disturbing was the ensuing investigation that revealed the disaster could have been avoided. For those involved in the space program, it would prompt a new set of questions regarding our purpose in space, the role of politics in space travel, and how mission effectiveness is evaluated.

At first, many conjectured that a severe malfunction had taken place, something of monumental proportion, a major systems failure. This was not the case. A closer look revealed that a series of leadership decisions regarding a relatively minor part had caused the catastrophic incident. This tragedy yielded inherent leadership lessons.

The space shuttle is connected to a massive external fuel tank containing hundreds of tons of liquid propellant. On each side of the fuel tank is a solid rocket booster (SRB) that contains 1.3 million pounds of solid rocket fuel at ignition. These SRBs propel the shuttle and its external fuel tank beyond the earth's gravitational pull. Once empty, the SRBs fall to the earth and are reused for future flights. An O-ring, a thirty-seven-foot rubber circle designed to seal booster sections and prevent hot gas seepage, protects each solid rocket motor joint. These O-rings operate like a large washer or gasket, ensuring that rocket parts form a tight seal when joined together. Fifty-eight seconds into the flight, an O-ring failed to seat and seal properly, which allowed 5800-degree combustion gases to leak from the right SRB and burn through the external fuel tank, igniting its contents. Just seconds later, *Challenger* exploded.

The failure of the O-ring was attributed to many factors: faulty SRB design, insufficient low-temperature testing of the O-ring material and the joints that the O-ring sealed, and lack of communication among NASA management levels. Warning signs of impending disaster were everywhere, but they were ignored. Here are a few:

- O-ring erosion was discovered after only the second shuttle flight in November 1981, and the worst O-ring performance was exhibited during the January 1985 flight.

- Almost half of all shuttle flights had experienced some O-ring erosion.

- There was insufficient data to confirm proper performance of O-rings below 40 degrees; air temperature at launch was 36 degrees. Managers cited the insufficient research data as a reason *not* to delay the launch.

- Economic and political pressures forced a hurried launch schedule.

Instead of the historic flight of the first teacher into space, the *Challenger* flight became an historic disaster. The cost of manufacturing and testing an O-ring is negligible compared to the hundreds of millions spent to put the shuttle into orbit. It was not lack of money that caused the problem; it was pride and ignorance. The failure to implement and follow basic troubleshooting procedures and an unwillingness to address what appeared to be minor problems led to the tragedy. It would be a long time before everything was "back to normal" at NASA.

When you read the reports associated with the crisis, it is clear that O-rings were not the only things eroding. One poor decision after another placed the entire mission in jeopardy. Badly designed processes and strategies, lack of courageous leadership, and ineffective communication strategies ultimately led to the loss of precious lives.

The parallels to building a church of groups are inescapable. A few changes in the account above, and we could easily be writing about a church disaster, one of the many we see in our interactions with leaders. **215** The same factors that led to the *Challenger* failure usually contribute to the breakdown of effective ministry. We hear these comments too often:

> We'll consider the apprentice idea later; right now we just want to get some groups started.

> Actually, we don't have a point leader yet because the elders want to allocate funds to more important projects; but we'll get by without one.

> If we just become a friendlier church, we won't have to worry about developing a complex assimilation process.

> Sure we need coaches, but we just don't have the time to develop them. And right now our staff has their hands full just caring for leaders, let alone adding coaches to the mix.

These issues can appear insignificant and easy to ignore—for the moment. After all, we have a successful ministry launch and everyone is excited. Groups are popping up everywhere! We'll worry about these things later. You're right. You will worry about them later, often losing lots of sleep in the process. But it does not have to be this way.

We hope we share something in common with you—a deep sense of urgency that demands we give our full attention to the seven areas outlined in this book. If so, you will tap into resources like those we have provided here. Once your church uses the troubleshooting guides contained in this book, carefully assesses each of the seven deadly sins, and implements the right strategies (like those we have outlined and others you will discover as God guides *your* adventure), we are confident your future will be bright. And since small group ministries tend to break often, you will need to reassess each area. When you feel something is stuck, we hope you'll return to these pages for fresh insights and answers.

Remember the story of the fictional First Community Church in this book's introduction? Many of our churches resemble First Community in some form. Imagine that the church had assessed current reality using the seven deadly sins, recognized inherent weaknesses, and addressed them with new strategies and designs. Imagine a different story:

> Four years ago, First Community Church launched three ministry initiatives designed to revive a dormant small group ministry. They asked their Christian education director to hand off the adult and children's Sunday schools and the AWANA program to key volunteers, so she could become the church's dedicated director of small groups. She began working with a handful of discipleship small groups and women's ministry small groups. The effort yielded eleven new small groups that year, but the small group effort has begun to plateau. Leaders are emerging, but it will take effort to move the church to the next level of small group ministry.
>
> Everyone—leadership, staff, and volunteers—is particularly concerned that the small group strategy is in jeopardy. Although the church has become more departmentalized as it has grown, each ministry sees how groups will take them to the next level. Each ministry, including the small groups department, is no longer satisfied to just keep its audience happy and avoid trouble. Small groups are no longer an option; they are becoming an essential component for transformation. The church believes that small groups are on track theologically, because each uses one of two curricula, both written by the associate pastor. But the staff is ready to experiment with new approaches to expand the array of groups so the church can meet people where they are ready for community.
>
> Last year, the church finished its new facility, doubling the usable space, and attendance grew 60 percent in six months. Newcomers who seek quick connection hope the clear assimilation strategy will meet their needs. They have reason to be confident, because they regularly hear from someone who is "holding their hands" and owns their process. And although the existing small groups average seventeen people each, apprentices have been identified to birth new groups, which will be open to newcomers seeking a small community. The

small groups director was in danger of burnout, trying to keep up with sixteen leaders. But now new coaches are starting to support those leaders, and the other ministries—including a new singles' ministry—are being built on a sound small group leadership structure.

First Community's elders are hopeful yet still have concerns. They wonder, "Will the small group approach really work here?" They've asked the senior pastor to work with staff to keep implementing solutions as they move ahead, and they remain unified on the small groups initiative. They have honestly faced doubts about small group strategies working at First Community, and are eager to find out how small groups can be made available for everyone. The senior pastor and two inexperienced staff members are learning the differences between program-based ministry and relationship-focused group approaches.

First Community continues to strategize a new future for their small group ministry. They continue to analyze their current tactics, study small groups throughout Scripture and church history, and try to assess first things first so they can prioritize key problems, given the church's limited time, money, and people. They are not sure all the new strategies will work, but they are making headway, thanks to unified effort and a clearly defined plan to solve problems. The future is not certain, but they are determined to move toward it *together.* Excitement grows each month. God is doing something amazing in their church through the ever-expanding network of spiritually transforming relationships.

The distinctions between the First Community Church here and in the introduction are the result of a handful of key decisions about each deadly sin. The decisions are never simple, just clear. They made a world of difference in First Community, and they will in yours too. Careful troubleshooting and honest evaluation set the stage for wise leadership decisions.

Someone said that it took only seventy-three seconds for the *Challenger* explosion to occur, that it was amazing so much could happen in so little time. But in reality, several years of poor decision making and neglect set the stage for the *Challenger* disaster; it took only seventy-three seconds to reveal the full impact of those decisions.

Small group ministry has its share of "O-rings." We have just given you seven. Don't neglect them. Evaluate them honestly and thoroughly. Make the right decisions and build the ministry with integrity. You want this launch to be successful and the mission to be accomplished. Precious life is at stake, and so is the future of the church. Great opportunities await those who are willing to do the work that needs to be done—now. We are confident you can and you will. We are pulling for you.

# Appendix 1

## Ministry Plans

| Ministry | Couples |
|---|---|
| Date | September 1997 |

| Strategic Goal | Desired Outcomes | Key Activities Next 4 Months |
|---|---|---|
| Fully utilize our campus to reach as many seekers as possible. We believe that would represent 20,000 attending weekend seeker services by the year 2000. | Weekend Service (May–Dec 1997) Three target weekends with baptism as one <br><br> Promiseland Summer Serve (1998) • Two weekends with 260 volunteers per weekend <br><br> Contagious Christian Course (1997) • 100% Staff • 50% Small Group Leadership • 25% Small Group Members | • Beginning December 1 launch 5-month evangelistic campaign (see Appendix A) • Complete evangelistic survey by December 1 • Design a rally November 8/9 that will increase the average weekend attendance and add 100 people to our assimilation report • Create a "Weekend Service Invitation" that is offered at all weddings and dedications by December 31 • Couples staff meetings integrates personal evangelistic initiatives by November 1 |
| Provide all people who call Willow their church a place in community. We believe that would represent 20,000 in small groups by the year 2000. | Total in Small Group Structure Dec 1997: 1,700 Dec 1998: 2,125 Dec 1999: 2,656 Dec 2000: 3,320 <br><br> Shepherding Plan (1997) • 100% Division Leaders • 75% Coaches | • Implement four month emphasis: Shepherding Plan • Hire additional staff to support growth • Challenge every small group with less than six per group to add one member by December 31 • Launch pilot parenting huddle by December 31 • Transition marriage mentor team to small group structure by December 31 • Launch Marriage Connection by December 31 |
| Have all Christ-followers gathered weekly for teaching and worship. We believe that would represent 8,000 weekly attending New Community by the year 2000. | Leadership Community/Communion % Leadership (avg.): 90% <br><br> SG Members/Voln (avg.): 80% | • Require each division leader to create "How to Increase New Community Commitment" plan by November 1 • Request S.G.S. team to provide an effective feedback system by November 1 • Offer free pizza and pop to all coaches who sponsor a pre-Leadership Community huddle |

# Ministry Plans
Page 2

| Ministry | Couples |
|---|---|
| Date | September 1997 |

| Strategic Goal | Desired Outcomes | Key Activities Next 4 Months |
|---|---|---|
| See core attenders maturing in their understanding of the "Five Gs.". We believe that would represent 8,000 participating members by the year 2000. | Total Participating Members<br>Dec 1997: 950<br>Dec 1998: 1,200<br>Dec 1999: 1,500<br>Dec 2000: 1,900 | • Require division leaders to be accountable for a measurable number of new participating members<br>• Send an invitation to every profiled non-participating member for January Participating Membership Class by December 15<br>• Complete renewal plan by November 15 by having Paul Krause meet with staff<br>• Send all participating members a Couples Ministry Christmas card by December 20 |
| Demonstrate Christ's compassion for the broken and lost around the world. We believe that would represent 4,000 people involved in extension opportunities by the year 2000. | Total Involved in Extension<br>1997: 350<br>1998: 700<br>1999: 1,100<br>2000: 1,600 | • Host ten extension projects by December 31<br>• Rent and fill bus for November 8 urban plunge<br>• Promote urban plunge and food drive via Couples newsletter<br>• Ensure every division leader has identified an extension partner by December 31 |
| Encourage innovative churches to bring about God-directed transformation worldwide. We believe that would represent 6,000 members of the WCA by the year 2000. | Volunteers for WCA Events<br>October 97 CLC: 300<br>May 98 CLC: 300<br>August 98 Summit: 300<br>October 98 CLC: 300 | • Provide 300+ volunteers for October CLC<br>• Have every staff person personally invite one volunteer leader to October CLC<br>• Staff will continue to be part of Small Group Seminar at October CLC |

# Ministry Plans

| Ministry | Women's / Mom's |
|---|---|
| Date | September 1997 |

| Strategic Goal | Desired Outcomes | Key Activities Next 4 Months |
|---|---|---|
| Fully utilize our campus to reach as many seekers as possible. We believe that would represent 20,000 attending weekend seeker services by the year 2000. | Weekend Service<br>• Rally weekend Nov 1/2 (1997)<br>• Five rally weekends (1998)<br><br>Promiseland Summer Serve (1998)<br>• Two weekends with 130 volunteers per weekend<br><br>Contagious Christian Course (1998)<br>• 100% Small Group Leadership<br>• 80% Small Group Members | • Kick-off of prayer triplet idea where each small group member brings name of seeker friend to small group for next 2 months; prayer in group for each name/ invite to target weekend/ celebrate stories in small group/ invite to group<br>• Women's Ministries staff following the prayer triplet idea<br>• 3 community open house events in preparation for November 1/2 and small group involvement<br>• Request: Highlight Women's, Men's and SAM by video and/or drama on target weekend<br>• Newsletter changing to be ministry and church update<br>• Verse Calendar to continue with verses related to message series<br>• September 25 = Special Contagious Christian training for leaders of Women's Ministries and Men's Ministry<br>• Friday morning CC course offered this ministry year |
| Provide all people who call Willow their church a place in community. We believe that would represent 20,000 in small groups by the year 2000. | Total in Small Group Structure<br>Dec 1997: 1,350<br>Dec 1998: 1,550<br>Dec 1999: 1,800<br>Dec 2000: 2,000<br><br>Shepherding Plan (1998)<br>• 100% Division Leaders<br>• 90% Coaches | • Transition executive women into small groups (Jan 98)<br>• Starting serving groups in the office (phone teams; project team)<br>• Evaluate why women are going elsewhere for growth and determine a strategy to recapture them (meetings with WCCC attenders of Precept, BSF, Moms in Touch)<br>• October 28 training for women investigating leadership in Women's Ministries<br>• Increase group size as fall-out from target weekend prayer-invite activity<br>• DL train/model the use of Shepherding Plan with their coaches |

# Ministry Plans
Page 2

| Ministry | Women's / Mom's |
|---|---|
| Date | September 1997 |

| Strategic Goal | Desired Outcomes | Key Activities Next 4 Months |
|---|---|---|
| Have all Christ-followers gathered weekly for teaching and worship. We believe that would represent 8,000 weekly attending New Community by the year 2000. | Leadership Community/Communion<br>% Leadership (avg.): 75%<br><br>SG Members/Voln (avg.): | • Encourage groups to meet before New Community (career groups, women with unbelieving husband groups, new believer/seeker groups)<br>• Highlight upcoming New Community in small groups, classes and newsletter |
| See care attenders maturing in their understanding of the "Five Gs.". We believe that would represent 8,000 participating members by the year 2000. | Total Participating Members<br>Dec 1997:  500<br>Dec 1998:  650<br>Dec 1999:  825<br>Dec 2000:  1,000 | • DL's working through organization charts to target groups with low participating members<br>• Join with Willow Creek Community Church membership classes<br>• Visit groups to answer questions concerning membership<br>• Note from coaches to non-members concerning the opportunity for significant spiritual growth between now and Christmas<br>• Small groups using membership, renewal and spiritual formation curricula.<br>• DL's and coaches will participate in training on renewal materials and process |
| Demonstrate Christ's compassion for the broken and lost around the world. We believe that would represent 4,000 people involved in extension opportunities by the year 2000. | Total Involved in Extension<br>1997:  200<br>1998:  350<br>1999:  500<br>2000:  600 | • Homeless shelter twice a month<br>• Organize two foreign country trips a year (DR and orphanage)<br>• Chicago Plunge = November 8 and 20<br>• Local Plunge = February 1998<br>• Project Angel Tree<br>• Adopt-a-Family for Christmas |

# Ministry Plans
Page 3

| Ministry | **Women's / Mom's** |
|---|---|
| Date | September 1997 |

| Strategic Goal | Desired Outcomes | Key Activities Next 4 Months |
|---|---|---|
| Encourage innovative churches to bring about God-directed transformation worldwide. We believe that would represent 6,000 members of the WCA by the year 2000. | <u>WCA Workshops Conducted</u><br>1997: 2<br>1998: 2<br><br><u>Volunteers for WCA Events</u><br>October 97 CLC: 150<br>May 98 CLC: 150<br>August 98 Summit: 150<br>October 98 CLC: 150 | • Pre-conference workshop in October 1997<br>• Continue providing 60% of conference volunteers<br>• Provide 25 women to relieve Harvest staff so they can attend Friday morning worship time<br>• Provide 50 homes for CLC guests<br>• Continuation of information and materials through phone calls and mail requests<br>• Resolve outside sales of Women's Ministries curricula |

# Ministry Plans

| Ministry | Promiseland |
| --- | --- |
| Date | September 1997 |

| Strategic Goal | Desired Outcomes | Key Activities Next 4 Months |
| --- | --- | --- |
| Fully utilize our campus to reach as many seekers as possible. We believe that would represent 20,000 attending weekend seeker services by the year 2000. | **Weekend Service**<br>No room closings | • Begin planning for Summer Serve in November<br>• Encourage all volunteer to attend the service, making tapes available for those who cannot attend<br>• Research creative solutions for what goes on for the Family Service during the Small Group Retreat 1998<br>• Further development of the "Lenny" program<br>• Continue to identify new children with verbal connect, Rainbow Team leaders, and oracle tracking |
| Provide all people who call Willow their church a place in community. We believe that would represent 20,000 in small groups by the year 2000. | **Total in Small Group Structure**<br>Dec 1997:  400  (Adults)<br>            3,000  (Children)<br>Dec 1998:  500  (Adults)<br>            3,600  (Children)<br>Dec 1999:  600  (Adults)<br>            4,000  (Children)<br>Dec 2000:  700  (Adults)<br>            4,300  (Children)<br><br>**Shepherding Plan (1997)**<br>• 100% Division Leaders<br>• 50% Coaches | • Identify and develop 35 new coaches<br>• Move parent helpers to substitutes to become small group leaders<br>• Recruit 300 new parent helpers<br>• Pursue space changes with Scott Troeger<br>• Each age/grade level will have one open house per ministry year<br>• Align our curriculum and training of our volunteers on how to teach and implement the 5 Gs to children<br>• Develop a strategy and tracking system for inactive children |
| Have all Christ-followers gathered weekly for teaching and worship. We believe that would represent 8,000 weekly attending New Community by the year 2000. | **Leadership Community/Communion**<br>% Leadership (avg.): 90%<br><br>SG Members/Voln (avg.): 150 adults | • Hold huddles, quarterly divisional huddles and rehearsals before service |

## Ministry Plans
Page 2

| Ministry | Promiseland |
|---|---|
| Date | September 1997 |

| Strategic Goal | Desired Outcomes | Key Activities Next 4 Months |
|---|---|---|
| See core attenders maturing in their understanding of the "Five Gs.". We believe that would represent 8,000 participating members by the year 2000. | Total Participating Members<br>Dec 1997: 400<br>Dec 1998: 500<br>Dec 1999: 600<br>Dec 2000: 700<br><br>• Full understanding and utilization of the Shepherding Plan by all coaches, small group leaders and apprentices | • Membership is a requirement to be a small group leader<br>• Piloting a membership class for our volunteers and parent helpers three times a year<br>• Membership information and class dates are provided to all who are being interviewed to serve in Promiseland<br>• Curriculum will have a 5 Gs focus/emphasis<br>• Continue vision-casting, developing and challenging our Shepherding Plan strategy |
| Demonstrate Christ's compassion for the broken and lost around the world. We believe that would represent 4,000 people involved in extension opportunities by the year 2000. | (Appropriate desired outcome yet to be determined) | • Incorporate into curriculum the children's participation with the Food Drive<br>• Include one project per grade level where serving opportunities are taught |
| Encourage innovative churches to bring about God-directed transformation worldwide. We believe that would represent 6,000 members of the WCA by the year 2000. | WCA Workshops Conducted<br>1998: One conference<br>1999: n/a<br><br>Volunteers for WCA Events<br>October 97 CLC: 50<br>May 98 CLC: 50<br>August 98 Summit: 50<br>October 98 CLC: 50 | • Teach workshops and prepare for 1998 Promiseland Conference<br>• Curriculum pilot due in January 1998 |

# Appendix 2

## WCCC Director of Small Groups Job Profile
## As of October 23, 2001

### How to Do the Job—Tone/Flavor

*Champion the movement of small groups at Willow Creek Community Church.*

The role is to listen—listen and listen well. I must ask great questions—and work to find the right questions—to permit and foster challenges to our thinking. When focused inside WCCC, I need to understand issues and people, build ownership of initiatives, and do great customer service (me going versus them coming). By focusing outside WCCC—through conferences, resources, learning and consulting relationships—I will import others' breakthrough thinking by finding the best small group ministry practices, synthesizing what is working elsewhere, and bridging useful concepts back to WCCC.

Effectiveness will require variable focus on several different aspects of Willow Creek Community Church's small group ministry and leadership, as follows.

### Focus on WCCC Overall: Problem-Solving

- Figure out precisely what each of the positions (area leader, division leader, coach, small group leader) must do
- Maintain and communicate small group definition (for example, sports, task, 101–401 bandwidth, etc.)
- Create coaches' conferences, small group leadership conferences, volunteer celebrations, ministry year kickoffs
- Refine nomenclature—change area leader, division leader, coach, small group leader titles?
- Formulate "Small Group Systems Influence" diagrams and charts

- Correct "leadership" language; change talk about leadership as gift versus roles versus skills
- Help reinvent assimilation strategies
- Lead policy making for small groups among employees
- Recast vision continuously (founded in Exodus 18, John 17, and Ephesians 4)
- Answer how the goal of being a church of small groups continues to be pursued
- Reconcile platform messages with actual practice
- Initiate seekers in open chairs as a systemic mind-set
- Capture "renegade" groups

## Focus on Area Leaders: Bridging

- Communicate small group initiatives
- Collaborate to set quantitative goals for each area (rolled up to WCCC goal)
- Meet one-on-one with each division leader (DL), then give performance feedback to area leader (AL)
- Avoid split loyalty (area leader versus director of small groups)
- Pull area leaders together as a group for small group decisions
- Teach area leaders how to more effectively lead division leaders

## Focus on Division Leaders: Improving

- Define DL focus, time management (versus AL reallocation to non–small group needs)
- Assist ALs in analysis of performance
- Identify the "DL gurus" that can lift the level of the rest of the group
- Standardize training
- Allow for DLs and coach differences in approach and needs
- Include sacerdotal functions
- Consider DL retreat, new DL orientation

- Train to the expectations (core competencies) of the DL job
- Transfer best current practices
- Draw out new discoveries from DLs
- Motivate by encouraging, envisioning, and endowing with value
- Improve productivity and sustainability of DLs
- Redefine span of care and responsibility (How do we handle a division of 700+ without burnout)
- Create administrative support strategies: assimilation, mailings, scheduling, and logistics
- Assist diffusion of the senior coach role
- Attend huddles and superhuddles
- Network DLs to talk to each other
- Enforce consequences for nonperformance
- "Pastor" the DLs by keeping an open door
- Write encouraging notes when DLs do something right

### Focus on Coaches: Raise the Tide

- Control quality of coaches and apprentices by personal interview (existing and future)
- Differentiate performance
- Standardize training (see DL outline, applied to coaching)

## Focus on Small Group Leaders: Apprentices

- Help with apprentice percentage, definition, and developmental path
- Standardize training (see DL outline, applied to coaching)

## Focus on Ministries: Advising

- Clarify and monitor the role of medium-sized groups
- Consult—sniff out problems and opportunities
- Help with common definitions (for example, apprentice, connection, etc.)
- Drive initiatives in (intentional shepherding, shepherding plan guide)
- Gatekeep strategy variations
- Validate strategic direction so as to enhance risk taking
- Update latest churchwide challenges
- Monitor for blind spots in the ministries
- Prompt new changes (fresh ideas versus set it up and let it run)
- Recruit new leaders and apprentices (especially in ministries chronically short)
- Assist with a developmental track to accelerate short-run leaders (two-to-four year runs)
- Foster leader retention

## Focus on Outside: Infuse Learning

- Attend events and visit key churches on small groups
- Read and stay on top of published materials
- Consult with key WCA churches
- Lean into the WCA small groups movement area (Donahue)

## Priorities and Battle Plan

### Priorities

1. Division leader performance and focus
2. Systems issues (lingo, standard practice, training, etc.)
3. Execution on fundamentals at all levels
4. Preparation for growth needs

### Battle Plan

1. Create weekly staff VHS meetings to train, problem solve, and build execution effectiveness
2. Initiate a new DL orientation retreat
3. Attend each area's staff/DL meetings—monthly
4. Conduct AL/DL triads—quarterly
5. Conduct DL one-on-ones—rotating
6. Regularly present/work through management team and area leaders on issues for resolution
7. Create and lead work teams to attack issues and create proposals
8. Collaborate with Human Resources Director and training leadership to reinvent leadership training system
9. Produce terrific events
10. Study the top ten small group ministries and experts for breakthrough ideas

# Appendix 3

## The Role of the Coach

| CATEGORIES | HUDDLES | VISITING GROUPS | ONE-ON-ONE MEETINGS |
|---|---|---|---|
| **LEADERSHIP DEVELOPMENT**<br><br>• *Vision Casting*<br>• *Skills*<br>• *Apprentices* | • Remind Leaders of the "mission" of small groups.<br><br>• Use each other's successes and struggles to show how God raises up and develops Leaders.<br><br>• Teach leadership skills - use the Leader's Handbook.<br><br>• Have your Apprentice lead parts of the huddle.<br><br>• Challenge Leaders to develop their Apprentices | • Build character and relational skills.<br><br>• Identify areas to be developed.<br><br>• Help them solve problems.<br><br>• Encourage development of the Apprentice in the group setting. | • Confirm the Leader's vision for ministry.<br><br>• Discuss character and skills that need attention and devise a plan to develop them.<br><br>• Help the Leader identify and train an Apprentice. |
| **PASTORAL CARE**<br><br>• *Spiritual*<br>• *Relational*<br>• *Personal* | • Model caregiving.<br><br>• Encourage Leaders to care for each other.<br><br>• Challenge leaders to grow spiritually.<br><br>• Help Leaders and Apprentices to build healthy relationships. | • Affirm Leaders during the meeting.<br><br>• Observe the Leader's relationships within the group.<br><br>• Determine if Leaders share ministry with members and Apprentices.<br><br>• Assist in conflict resolution and encourage the group to work through the stages of group life. | • Get to know Leaders personally. Concentrate on real needs.<br><br>• Be open and transparent with your life. Build an authentic relationship with each other.<br><br>• In specific ways, encourage a deep relationship with Christ.<br><br>• Conduct membership interviews and affirm participating members. |
| **MINISTRY SUPPORT & EXPANSION**<br><br>• *Prayer*<br>• *Affirmation*<br>• *Resources* | • Celebrate what God is doing in groups and personal lives.<br><br>• Pray for each other as a team.<br><br>• Problem-solve together.<br><br>• Exchange ideas and provide information.<br><br>• Have fun and be creative with your huddle.<br><br>• Help them to identify potential Leaders. | • Determine how you can pray for this group, its Leader and Apprentice.<br><br>• Talk about the strengths of their Leader and Apprentice.<br><br>• Identify helpful resources for study and for ministry.<br><br>• Let them know that you are available.<br><br>• Discuss expanding the ministry with the Open Chair and birthing and the value of Apprentices. | • Pray specifically for the Open Chair.<br><br>• Problem-solve.<br><br>• Celebrate all that God has done in their groups.<br><br>• Challenge them to use the participating membership process as a vehicle for launching a discipling relationship with group members. |

# T O O L S

## The Centralized Training Components

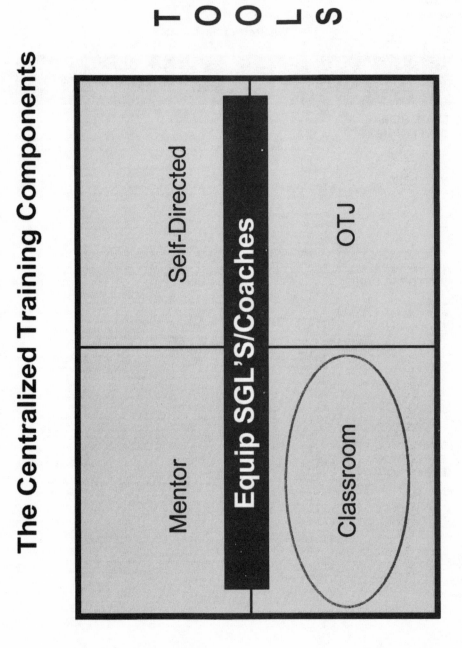

Mentor | Self-Directed

Equip SGL'S/Coaches

Classroom | OTJ

# The Classroom Training Path

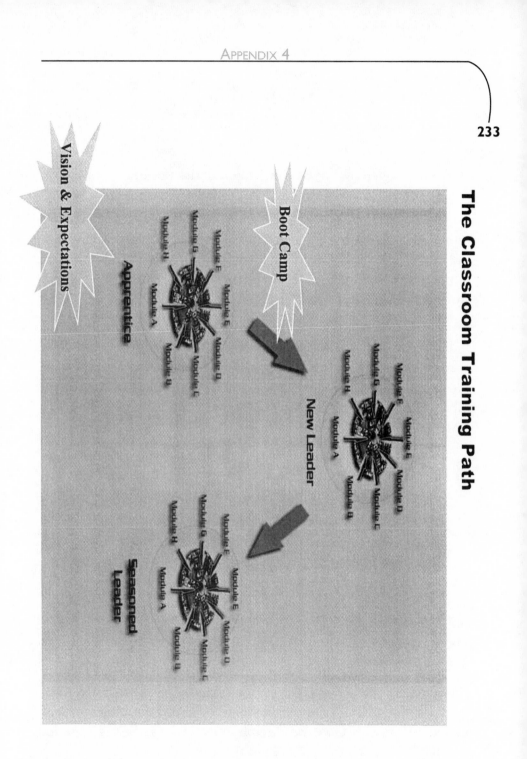

Vision & Expectations

Boot Camp

Apprentice

Module A
Module B
Module C
Module D
Module E
Module F
Module G
Module H

New Leader

Module A
Module B
Module C
Module D
Module E
Module F
Module G
Module H

Seasoned Leader

Module A
Module B
Module C
Module D
Module E
Module F
Module G
Module H

# Appendix 5

## Willow Creek Curriculum Series Profiles

*Interactions,* by Bill Hybels. Developed at Willow Creek, this dynamic small group study series encourages life-changing ministry within small groups as participants share lifestyles, interests, experiences, and values. Interactions builds on this common ground to foster honest communication, effective problem solving, deeper friendships, and growing intimacy with God.

*New Community Series,* by Bill Hybels, John Ortberg, with Kevin and Sherry Harney. This high-impact series teaches small groups how to study life-changing topics from a biblical perspective in the context of community. Every volume contains six sessions filled with in-depth Bible study, thought-provoking questions, and community-building exercises.

*Pursuing Spiritual Transformation,* by John Ortberg, Laurie Pederson, and Judson Poling. Explore fresh, biblically based ways to think about and experience life with God through Willow Creek's five G's: grace, growth, groups, gifts, and giving. You'll learn about the life-giving practices, experiences, and relationships God uses to change us from the inside out.

*Bible 101,* by Bill Donahue, Kathy Dice, Judson Poling, Michael Redding, and Gerry Mathisen. Bible 101 provides a solid foundational understanding of God's Word in a format uniquely designed for a small group setting.

*Walking with God,* by Don Cousins and Judson Poling. Practical, interactive, and biblically based, this dynamic series follows a two-track approach. Series 1 plugs new believers into the transforming power of a relationship with God and discipleship to Christ. Series 2 guides mature Christians into a closer look at the church.

*Tough Questions,* by Garry Poole and Judson Poling. This hard-hitting series creates unprecedented opportunities for your church to examine major questions and objections about the Christian faith. **235** Each volume leads to a fascinating exploration of vital truths, whether a participant is an atheist, a skeptic, a seeker, or a believer looking for a stronger faith.

# Appendix 6

## Modified Definition of a Small Group

*Small Group: A group of people who come together on a regular basis for a common purpose and are led by an identified leader who is assisting them in their progress toward full devotion to Christ by intentionally providing an environment for connection, community, and spiritual formation.*

### Nature of the Group

Group of People: Should be four to ten people, including the leader and an identified apprentice leader, plus an open chair to welcome new people (group members should be at least three years of age. If a group has more than ten people, it should be preparing to birth).

Come Together on a Regular Basis: Should gather in a face-to-face setting at least two times per month.

Common Purpose: The primary reason or affinity for which the group exists (reasons might include serving together to accomplish a task, providing support in a time of need, building and investing into the next generation, studying God's Word).

### Role of the Leader

Identified Leader: Must be someone who has been approved or who is in the leader identification and development process with a process completion and approval date established.

Assisting Group Members' Progress toward Full Devotion to Christ: Providing care and having concern for the group members' souls and spiritual progress toward a goal of spiritual maturity as defined by the five G's (grace, growth, groups, gifts, good stewardship).

Intentionally Providing an Environment: Guiding the group into relationships, experiences, and practices in which spiritual challenge and progress can be made.

### Environment Provided

Connection and Community: A place where each individual experiences a sense of identity and belonging and where people are being **237** Christ to each other by knowing and being known, loving and being loved, serving and being served, celebrating and being celebrated.

# Appendix 7

**Willow Creek Community Church Assimilation Process
Based on Flowchart Model**

Stage 1: Open

- **Opportunity** is mobilized and individual is moved to connect
- **Interest** is generated by:
  1. Bulletin tear-off card (from weekend services, from Axis)
  2. Event (open house, seminar, class, support group, target weekend, special event, ministry fair, etc.)
  3. Telephone call (from an ad in the weekly, ministry hotline, general call); e-mail, web site, mail, fax, or walk-in to a particular ministry area; staff referral or volunteer referral
  4. Information booth/welcome center (general, lobby, and atrium booths)
  5. Other (rare, random, nonrecurring situations)
  6. Transfer lead (lead came from another ministry)
- **Gather** name, address, phone number, e-mail of interested person
- **Input** information into the database
  - Check database for individual—update if necessary
  - If not found in database, enter individual's information
  - Forward individual to ministry assimilator for action

Stage 2: Assessment

- **Phone call** is made by staff or volunteer assimilation phone team
  - Call individual for brief assessment
    - First call—made within three days

Make notes about results of call and date for next call
Wait at least 24 hours

- Second call

Make notes about results of call and date for next call
Wait at least 24 hours

- Third call

Make notes about results of call
ALL THREE CALLS NEED TO BE MADE WITHIN 30 DAYS
- If no response after 30 days, send ATTEMPT TO REACH letter or e-mail

Close lead in database as NO RESPONSE

- **When Personal Contact is successful,** there are three possible responses—NO, MAYBE, YES
  - If NO, not interested in your ministry
    - Use qualifying questions to determine a fit in another ministry
    - If still no interest, close lead as INFO ONLY or LOST INTEREST
    - If interested in other ministry

      Transfer lead to assimilator in other ministry—TRANSFER
      ASSIMILATION
      Close lead in database as TRANSFER

  - If MAYBE, might be interested in your ministry
    - Information only requested?

      Mail requested information
      Close lead in database as INFO ONLY

    - Future event or follow-up requested?

      Close lead in database as FOLLOW-UP, with date
      indicating next personal contact to be made

  - If YES, person is now IN PROCESS stage
    - Update lead in database to IN PROCESS

**Stage 3: In Process**

- **Handoff**—Assimilator hands off information to appropriate ministry leader

- Assimilation tracking reports assist the assimilator to manage the leads and follow-up ministry leader
- **Training** and/or prerequisites required for placement?
  - If YES
    - Leader explains prerequisites and schedules training
    - Leader reports progress to assimilator
    - Update lead in database to In Process, Prerequisite Pending
  - If ALREADY MET
    - Leader reports progress to assimilator
  - If NO
    - Leader reports progress to assimilator
- **The big question: Is this person actively participating?** (Serving and/or participating on a regularly scheduled basis, generally once a month)
  - If YES
    - Go to stage 4—CONNECTED stage
    - Close lead in database as CONNECTED
  - If NO, ask questions
    - Is this person waiting for something? Note follow-up date
    - Have they lost interest? Back to Assessment stage
    - Use qualifying questions to determine other ministry interests. Transfer assimilation

## Stage 4: Connected

- Person is **Actively Participating** in a small group or serving opportunity
  - Individual profile is created from lead in database
  - Follow-up communication may be sent to check satisfaction
- Person is pursuing **Full Participation** through participating membership at Willow Creek

# Notes

### Chapter 3. Sin Two: Lack of Point Leadership

1. Brent Curtis and John Eldredge, *The Sacred Romance* (Nashville: Thomas Nelson, 1997), 155.

### Chapter 4. Strategies and Tools for Choosing Effective Point Leaders

1. Bruce Bugbee, Bill Hybels, and Don Cousins, *Network* (Grand Rapids, Mich.: Zondervan, 1994), 43.

2. Ibid., 38.

3. Ibid., 39.

### Chapter 8. Strategies and Tools for Developing Leaders

1. See Donahue, *Leading Life-Changing Small Groups*, 146.

2. A good source for lesson content in each of the suggested topics is Donahue, *Leading Life-Changing Small Groups*.

3. A curriculum plan of similar scope and duration should be created for the turbo huddle using Willow Creek's *Coaches Handbook* as a reference.

### Chapter 14. Strategies and Tools for Improving Assimilation

1. Henry Cloud and John Townsend, *How People Grow* (Grand Rapids, Mich.: Zondervan, 2001), 121. Emphasis in original.

# WILLOW
### Willow Creek Association

## Willow Creek Association
*Vision, Training, Resources for Prevailing Churches*

This resource was created to serve you and to help you build a local church that prevails. It is just one of many ministry tools that are part of the Willow Creek Resources® line, published by the Willow Creek Association together with Zondervan.

The Willow Creek Association (WCA) was created in 1992 to serve a rapidly growing number of churches from across the denominational spectrum that are committed to helping unchurched people become fully devoted followers of Christ. Membership in the WCA now numbers over 10,500 Member Churches worldwide from more than ninety denominations.

The Willow Creek Association links like-minded Christian leaders with each other and with strategic vision, training, and resources in order to help them build prevailing churches designed to reach their redemptive potential. Here are some of the ways the WCA does that.

- **A2: Building Prevailing Acts 2 Churches—Today**—an annual two-and-a-half day event, held at Willow Creek Community Church in South Barrington, Illinois, to explore strategies for building churches that reach out to seekers and build believers, and to discover new innovations and breakthroughs from Acts 2 churches around the country.

- **The Leadership Summit**—a once a year, two-and-a-half-day conference to envision and equip Christians with leadership gifts and responsibilities. Presented live at Willow Creek as well as via satellite broadcast to over one hundred locations across North America, this event is designed to increase the leadership effectiveness of pastors, ministry staff, volunteer church leaders, and Christians in the marketplace.

- **Ministry-Specific Conferences**—throughout each year the WCA hosts a variety of conferences and training events—both at Willow Creek's main campus and offsite, across the U.S., and around the world—targeting church leaders and volunteers in ministry-specific areas such as: evangelism, small groups, preaching and teaching, the arts, children, students, women, volunteers, stewardship, raising up resources, etc.

- **Willow Creek Resources®**—provides churches with trusted and field-tested ministry resources in such areas as leadership, evangelism, spiritual formation, spiritual gifts, small groups, stewardship, student ministry, children's ministry, the use of the arts-drama, media, contemporary music —and more.

- **WCA Member Benefits**—includes substantial discounts to WCA training events, a 20 percent discount on all Willow Creek Resources®, *Defining Moments* monthly audio journal for leaders, quarterly *Willow* magazine, access to a Members-Only section on WillowNet, monthly communications, and more. Member Churches also receive special discounts and premier services through WCA's growing number of ministry partners—Select Service Providers—and save an average of $500 annually depending on the level of engagement.

For specific information about WCA conferences, resources, membership, and other ministry services contact:

**Willow Creek Association**
P.O. Box 3188
Barrington, IL 60011-3188
Phone: 847-570-9812
Fax: 847-765-5046
www.willowcreek.com

# More life-changing small group discussion guides from Willow Creek

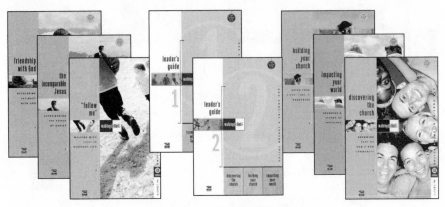

## Walking with God Series
## Don Cousins and Judson Poling

This series of six guides (and two leader's guides) provides a solid, biblical program of study for all of the small groups in your church. The Walking with God Series is designed to help lead new and young believers into a deeper personal intimacy with God, while at the same time building a strong foundation in the faith for all believers, regardless of their level of maturity. These guides are also appropriate for individual study.

| | |
|---|---|
| *Friendship with God: Developing Intimacy with God* | 0-310-59143-0 |
| *The Incomparable Jesus: Experiencing the Power of Christ* | 0-310-59153-8 |
| *"Follow Me!": Walking with Jesus in Everyday Life* | 0-310-59163-5 |
| *Leader's Guide 1* | 0-310-59203-8 |
| *Discovering the Church: Becoming Part of God's New Community* | 0-310-59173-2 |
| *Building Your Church: Using Your Gifts, Time, and Resources* | 0-310-59183-X |
| *Impacting Your World: Becoming a Person of Influence* | 0-310-59193-7 |
| *Leader's Guide 2* | 0-310-59213-5 |

*Look for Walking with God at your local Christian bookstore.*

**ZONDERVAN**™

**GRAND RAPIDS, MICHIGAN 49530 USA**

WWW.ZONDERVAN.COM

**WILLOW**
Willow Creek Resources

www.willowcreek.com

# Bring your group to a deeper level of InterAction!

## InterActions Series
### Bill Hybels

Help your small-group members develop into fully devoted followers of Christ. Inter-Actions discussion guides ask for a deeper level of sharing, creating lines of accountability between individuals and moving your group into action. Each book presents six thought-provoking sessions specifically designed to build on the dynamics and interplay of small groups.

| | |
|---|---|
| *Authenticity: Being Honest with God and Others* | 0-310-26588-6 |
| *Character: Reclaiming Six Endangered Qualities* | 0-310-26602-5 |
| *Commitment: Developing Deeper Devotion to Christ* | 0-310-26595-9 |
| *Community: Building Relationships within God's Family* | 0-310-26591-6 |
| *Essential Christianity: Practical Steps for Spiritual Growth* | 0-310-26604-1 |
| *Fruit of the Spirit: Living the Supernatural Life* | 0-310-26596-7 |
| *Getting a Grip: Finding Balance in Your Daily Life* | 0-310-26605-x |
| *Jesus: Seeing Him More Clearly* | 0-310-26597-5 |
| *Lessons on Love: Building Deeper Relationships* | 0-310-26593-2 |
| *Living in God's Power: Finding God's Strength for Life's Challenges* | 0-310-26606-8 |
| *Love in Action: Experiencing the Joy of Serving* | 0-310-26607-6 |
| *Marriage: Building Real Intimacy* | 0-310-26589-4 |
| *Meeting God: Psalms for the Highs and Lows of Life* | 0-310-26599-1 |
| *New Identity: Discovering Who You Are in Christ* | 0-310-26594-0 |
| *Parenting: How to Raise Spiritually Healthy Kids* | 0-310-26590-8 |
| *Prayer: Opening Your Heart to God* | 0-310-26600-9 |
| *Reaching Out: Sharing God's Love Naturally* | 0-310-26592-4 |
| *The Real Deal: Discover the Rewards of Authentic Relationships* | 0-310-26601-7 |
| *Significance: Understanding God's Purpose for Your Life* | 0-310-26603-3 |
| *Transformation: Letting God Change You from the Inside Out* | 0-310-26598-3 |

### Look for Interactions at your local Christian bookstore

**ZONDERVAN™**

GRAND RAPIDS, MICHIGAN 49530 USA

WWW.ZONDERVAN.COM

**WILLOW**
Willow Creek Resources

www.willowcreek.com

*Leading Life-Changing Small Groups*

Bill Donahue
and the Willow Creek
Small Group Team

The bestselling small group
guidebook—over 100,000 sold.
NOW UPDATED.

Like nothing else, small groups have the power to change lives. They're the ideal route to discipleship—a place where the rubber of biblical truth meets the road of human relationships.

For six years Bill Donahue provided training and resources for small group leaders so that Willow Creek could build a church of small groups. Now he is committed to creating tools that will help church leaders pursue the same goal—to provide a place in community for everyone in their congregation. In *Leading Life-Changing Small Groups*, Donahue and his team share in depth the practical insights that have made Willow Creek's small group ministry so effective.

### *The Comprehensive, Ready-Reference Guide for Small Group Leaders*

The unique, ready-reference format of this book gives small group leaders, pastors, church leaders, educators, and counselors a commanding grasp of:

- Group formation and values

- Leadership requirements and responsibilities

- The philosophy and structure of small groups

- Meeting preparation and participation

- Discipleship within the group

- Leadership training ... and much more

From an individual group to an entire small group ministry, *Leading Life-Changing Small Groups* gives you the comprehensive guidance you need to cultivate life-changing small groups ... and growing, fruitful followers of Christ.

Softcover    0-310-24750-0

**ZONDERVAN**™

GRAND RAPIDS, MICHIGAN 49530 USA
WWW.ZONDERVAN.COM

**WILLOW**
Willow Creek Resources

www.willowcreek.com

# TOUGH QUESTIONS

## Garry Poole and Judson Poling

"The profound insights and candor captured in these guides will sharpen your mind, soften your heart, and inspire you and the members of your group to find vital answers together."
— Bill Hybels

This second edition of Tough Questions, designed for use in any small group setting, is ideal for use in seeker small groups. Based on more than five years of field-tested feedback, extensive revisions make this best-selling series easier to use and more appealing than ever for both participants and group leaders.

Softcover

| | |
|---|---|
| *How Does Anyone Know God Exists?* | ISBN 0-310-24502-8 |
| *What Difference Does Jesus Make?* | ISBN 0-310-24503-6 |
| *How Reliable Is the Bible?* | ISBN 0-310-24504-4 |
| *How Could God Allow Suffering and Evil?* | ISBN 0-310-24505-2 |
| *Don't All Religions Lead to God?* | ISBN 0-310-24506-0 |
| *Do Science and the Bible Conflict?* | ISBN 0-310-24507-9 |
| *Why Become a Christian?* | ISBN 0-310-24508-7 |
| *Leader's Guide* | ISBN 0-310-24509-5 |

*Pick up a copy today at your favorite bookstore!*

# Building a Church of Small Groups
## A Place Where Nobody Stands Alone

Bill Donahue and Russ Robinson

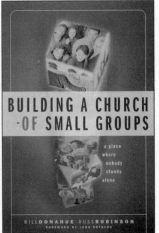

How can church become a place where nobody stands alone? Through small groups! Like nothing else, they provide the kind of life-giving community that builds and empowers the body of Christ and impacts the world. At Willow Creek Community Church, small groups are so important that they define the core organizational strategy. Bill Donahue and Russ Robinson write, "We have gone from a church with small groups ... to being a church of small groups."

*Building a Church of Small Groups* unpacks the:

- vision
- values
- strategies

required to integrate small groups into your entire ministry

Part one presents the theological, sociological, and organizational underpinnings of small groups. You'll discover why small groups, as reflections of God's communal nature, are so vital to church health.

Part two moves you from vision to practice. Here is how to develop thriving small groups based on authentic relationships, where truth and life intersect, conflict leads to growth, and skilled leaders help group members mature into fully devoted followers of Christ.

Part three shows you how to identify, recruit, and train group leaders and provide them with long-term coaching and support.

Finally, in part four, you'll learn how to deal with the critical process of change as your church develops its small group ministry.

Softcover ISBN: 0-310-26710-2

*Pick up a copy today at your favorite bookstore!*

ZONDERVAN™

GRAND RAPIDS, MICHIGAN 49530 USA

WWW.ZONDERVAN.COM

WILLOW

Willow Creek Resources

www.willowcreek.com

# Continue the Transformation

## Pursuing Spiritual Transformation Series
### John Ortberg, Laurie Pederson, and Judson Poling

Experience a radical change in how you think and how you live. Forget about trying hard to be a better person. Welcome instead to the richly rewarding process of discovering and growing into the person God made you to be! Developed by Willow Creek Community Church as its core curriculum, this planned, progressive small group approach to spiritual maturity will help you:

• Become more like Jesus • Recapture the image of God in your life • Cultivate intimacy with God • Live your faith everywhere, all the time • Renew your zest for life
*Leader's guide included!*

| | |
|---|---|
| *Fully Devoted: Living Each Day in Jesus' Name* | 0-310-22073-4 |
| *Grace: An Invitation to a Way of Life* | 0-310-22074-2 |
| *Growth: Training vs. Trying* | 0-310-22075-0 |
| *Groups: The Life-Giving Power of Community* | 0-310-22076-9 |
| *Gifts: The Joy of Serving God* | 0-310-22077-7 |
| *Giving: Unlocking the Heart of Good Stewardship* | 0-310-22078-5 |

Look for Pursuing Spiritual Transformation at your local Christian bookstore.

**ZONDERVAN**™

GRAND RAPIDS, MICHIGAN 49530 USA
WWW.ZONDERVAN.COM

**WILLOW**
Willow Creek Resources

www.willowcreek.com

# Continue building your new community!

## New Community Series
### Bill Hybels and John Ortberg
#### With Kevin and Sherry Harney

If you appreciate not having to choose between Bible study and building community, then you'll want to explore all eight New Community Bible study guides. Delve deeply into Scripture in a way that strengthens relationships. Challenging questions will encourage your group members to reflect not only on Scripture but also on the old idea of community done in a new, culturally relevant way.

Each guide contains six transforming sessions—filled with prayer, insight, intimacy, and action—to help your small group members line up their lives and relationships more closely with the Bible's model for the church.

| | |
|---|---|
| *Exodus: Journey Toward God* | 0-310-22771-2 |
| *Parables: Imagine Life God's Way* | 0-310-22881-6 |
| *Sermon on the Mount1: Connect with God* | 0-310-22883-2 |
| *Sermon on the Mount2: Connect with Others* | 0-310-22884-0 |
| *Acts: Rediscover Church* | 0-310-22770-4 |
| *Romans: Find Freedom* | 0-310-22765-8 |
| *Philippians: Run the Race* | 0-310-23314-3 |
| *Colossians: A Whole New You* | 0-310-22769-0 |
| *James: Live Wisely* | 0-310-22767-4 |
| *1 Peter: Stand Strong* | 0-310-22773-9 |
| *1 John: Love Each Other* | 0-310-22768-2 |
| *Revelation: Experience God's Power* | 0-310-22882-4 |

Look for New Community at your local Christian bookstore.

**ZONDERVAN**™

GRAND RAPIDS, MICHIGAN 49530 USA
WWW.ZONDERVAN.COM

**WILLOW**
Willow Creek Resources
www.willowcreek.com

# Reality Check Series
## by Mark Ashton

*Winning at Life:* Learn the secrets Jesus taught his disciples about winning at life through the stories he told.

*Jesus' Greatest Moments:* Uncover the facts and meaning of the provocative events of the final week of Jesus.

*Leadership Jesus Style:* Learn the leadership principles taught and lived by Jesus.

*Hot Issues:* Find out how Jesus addressed the challenges of racism, feminism, sexuality, materialism, poverty, and intolerance.

*When Tragedy Strikes:* Discover Jesus' perspective on the problem of suffering and evil in the world.

*Future Shock:* Uncover Jesus' perspective on the mysteries of the future as revealed in the Bible.

*Sudden Impact:* Discover the life-changing power of Jesus as he interacted with his contemporaries.

*Clear Evidence:* Weigh the arguments for and against the Jesus of the Bible.

| | |
|---|---|
| *Winning at Life* | 0-310-24525-7 |
| *Jesus' Greatest Moments* | 0-310-24528-1 |
| *Leadership Jesus Style* | 0-310-24526-5 |
| *Hot Issues* | 0-310-24523-0 |
| *When Tragedy Strikes* | 0-310-24524-9 |
| *Future Shock* | 0-310-24527-3 |
| *Sudden Impact* | 0-310-24522-2 |
| *Clear Evidence* | 0-310-24746-2 |

**ZONDERVAN**™

GRAND RAPIDS, MICHIGAN 49530 USA

WWW.ZONDERVAN.COM

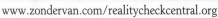

**WILLOW**
Willow Creek Resources

www.willowcreek.com

www.zondervan.com/realitycheckcentral.org

We want to hear from you. Please send your comments about this
book to us in care of zreview@zondervan.com. Thank you.

GRAND RAPIDS, MICHIGAN 49530 USA

WWW.ZONDERVAN.COM